THERAPIST GUIDE
TO THE
MMPI & MMPI-2:
Providing Feedback
and Treatment

Richard W. Lewak, Ph.D.
Clinical Psychologist
Del Mar Psychiatric Clinic
Del Mar, California

Philip A. Marks, Ph.D.
Professor Emeritus
Ohio State University

Gerald E. Nelson, M.D.
Psychiatrist
Del Mar Psychiatric Clinic
Del Mar, California

 ACCELERATED DEVELOPMENT INC.
Publishers
Muncie   Indiana

Therapist Guide to the MMPI & MMPI-2: Providing Feedback and Treatment

Technical Development: Virginia Cooper
Tanya Dalton
Delores Kellogg
Marguerite Mader
Sheila Sheward

Library of Congress Cataloging-in-Publication Data

Lewak, Richard W.
Therapist guide to MMPI & MMPI-2 : providing feedback and treatment / Richard W. Lewak, Philip A. Marks, Gerald E. Nelson.
p.   cm.
Includes bibliographical references.
ISBN 1-55959-006-8
1. Minnesota Multiphasic Personality Inventory. 2. Mental illness--Diagnosis. 3. Mental illness--Treatment. I. Marks, Philip A., 1928-   . II. Nelson, Gerald E. 1933-   . III. Title. IV. Title: Therapist guide to MMPI and MMPI-2.
RC473.M5L49   1990
155.2'8--dc20   89-81012
                                                 CIP

LCN: 89-81012

 ACCELERATED DEVELOPMENT INC., PUBLISHERS
3400 Kilgore Avenue, Muncie, Indiana 47304
Toll Free Order Number 1-800-222-1166

DEDICATION

To Linda, Caroline, and Gertrud

FOREWORD

This book presents one of the most creative, innovative approaches to the use of the MMPI in personality assessment that I have seen. It emphasizes a client-centered, interactive method of interpretation by means of which the test taker becomes the primary beneficiary of the MMPI assessment rather than the clinician who is administering the test. The clinician, however, also benefits from using this book because of the unique blend of research findings and clinical expertise these authors bring to the MMPI interpretation process. The authors have stated the purpose of their book well when they say "(This is) an advanced level reference source of empirical and experiential test meanings and hypotheses, plus (it shows) a way of sharing, validating, and integrating these (hypotheses) into the process of treatment (p. 3)."

The book has many unique features in keeping with its creative, innovative approach. The authors cover the usual interpretive material for the four validity and ten clinical scales and 21 of the most common two point codetypes but they do this in a unique way. Each MMPI validity scale, clinical scale, and codetype has the following:

1. *Notes to the therapist* is a section intended to orient the therapist to the nature of that scale or codetype. In many cases, this section also includes information on appropriate medication for that scale or codetype.

2. *Issues* is an experiential formluation of one or more correlates that have been empirically derived for each scale or codetype. These correlates are formulated in terms that are understandable to clients and presented in a manner so that the client as well as the therapist can validate their accuracy.

3. *Background and early learning experiences* that may have led to an evaluation of the scale(s) or codetype.

4. *Suggestions for self-help.*

The most creative feature of this book, however, is the authors' use of feedback about the MMPI test results to enhance the client's mental health. In order to do this, the authors assume that the client is capable of understanding test results through either written or verbal feedback, an assumption that is especially likely given the authors' ability to express test elevations in non-threatening and empathetic phrases which are used in the feedback sessions. The authors advocate that the client evaluate each of the feedback statements by assigning a number indicating agreement/disagreement to each statement in a written report, or, in the case of verbal feedback, telling the test interpreter the agreement/disagreement that he or she has for the interpretive statement just made. In either case "the client is the criterion for the veridicality of the MMPI feedback statements that have been made" truly a rare belief in most clinical circles. Thus, the test taker becomes an active and powerful participant in the assessment process.

This book is also useful for clinicians who decide to use the MMPI in the more traditional manner of doing a blind analysis of the test and writing a report to the referring clinician. It brings together a unique synthesis of the empirical research for the test, and Dr. Alex Caldwell's conditioned fears approach to the interpretation of the MMPI scales (Caldwell, 1985). In addition, the authors have added information about the test derived from their many years of experience using the MMPI in their clinical practices. This blending of three different approaches to MMPI interpretation, viz. empirical research, the conditioned fears approach to the test, and the authors' clinical experience, gives the reader the best of all worlds interpretively. The successful blending of all three is truly a gargantuan task which has been beautifully executed by the authors of this book.

As you can see, I believe this book occupies a most unusual place in the field of MMPI literature. Its richness and blend of empirical data and clinical expertise makes it a prized addition to the body of knowledge regarding the MMPI. I especially encourage you to try the authors' feedback approach with the test. I believe you will find the use of it will enhance the MMPI results for your clients, for you, and for the therapeutic relationship itself, thereby tripling the effectiveness of the assessment process.

Jane Duckworth, Ph.D.
October 1989

ACKNOWLEDGEMENTS

We would like to express our thanks to the many individuals who in various ways contributed to making this book possible. A number of years ago the senior author, while then a graduate student, began attending Alex Caldwell's seminars at the Neuropsychiatric Institute at the University of California in Los Angeles. He was excited with the way that Alex was thinking about the MMPI, and for a number of years thereafter took many opportunities to talk with him about his ideas, some of which form the basis of this book. RWL is also grateful to Lowell Storms for having initiated his love affair with the MMPI after he took his first abnormal psychology course from him at the University of California in San Diego. He is also grateful to Lowell for having become "MMPI friends."

None of the authors has had the opportunity to connect with Alex for a number of years but if this book contributes in some meaningful and unique way to the MMPI literature, Alex Caldwell's initial impetus was very significant.

Others also helped in thinking through some of the ideas on which this book is based. To Peter Briggs, Robert Carson, Phil Erdberg, Alan Friedman, Dave Nichols, and David Ralph we are especially appreciative.

Judy Emes, our secretary, was skillful in juggling our schedule to give us time to think and write and tolerate our "mishegas." We thank Lee Crumpton for the hours of typing and editing that she devoted to the manuscript. Marcy Hill, with her keen intelligence and sheer energy was also extremely helpful.

Others contributed in a number of other meaningful, though more subtle, ways. Margaret Peshel of Mesta Vista Hospital was particularly important to RWL at a crucial point in his professional development. Gertrud Nelson contributed the benefit of her writing ability by her careful editing. Caroline Marks helped PAM with her support. And Linda Rock allowed RWL numerous Sundays for dictating instead of frolicking in the California sun.

We each offer a special thanks to Jane Duckworth for taking time to read the manuscript and for her kind, generous words in the Foreword. To our publishers, Joe Hollis and Maggie Mader, we owe a special debt for their endless patience and understanding in working with authors so easily distracted by surfing, sailing, and gardening.

Finally, thanks are also extended to the clients with whom we have worked. Their willingness to trust us has allowed us a richer understanding of their emotional experiences.

Richard Lewak

Phil Marks

Jerry Nelson

October 25, 1989

CONTENTS

CHAPTER I

INTRODUCTION

The MMPI, originally published in 1943, is currently the most widely used and studied objective personality test in the world. It has become the most frequently administered psychological test (Lubin, Larsen, & Matarazzo, 1984), with approximately 10,000 books and articles written documenting its use (Butcher, 1987). The test is published by the University of Minnesota Press and is available through NCS to qualified professional users. (National Computer Systems, 1985, 1989)

In the early 1980s, a major restandardization project was begun by NCS and the University of Minnesota Press. The overall purposes were to (1) modernize the items without changing the scales, (2) restandardize the test with a broader and more nationally representative sample, and (3) maintain sufficient continuity with the original MMPI (hereafter MMPI or MMPI-1) so as not to compromise the research on which the tests empirical correlates are based. For a description of the restandardization project and characteristics of the new samples, the reader should consult the *Manual* of MMPI-2 (Hathaway & McKinley, 1989). MMPI-2 has many of the traditional features of MMPI-1, including the original test format, essentially the same number of items, the standard validity and clinical scales providing for the same K—corrections, and separate norms for men and women. However, unlike MMPI-1, the converted scores for scales 1, 2, 3, 4, 6, 7, 8, and 9 are now uniform T-scores, while those for L, F, K, 5, and 0 remain as before linear T-transformations. One result of the new norms is a "ceiling" effect where, for most scales, fewer scores now will occur at the higher elevations. For some scales the drop in elevation is marked. On scale 5 for men, for example, as much or more than a 10 T-score difference may occur, where for other scales like 0, the difference is much less. The reason for such a change in scores with the new norms is uncertain, but may relate to the average educational level of the new sample where approximately three-fourths of the men and over two-thirds of the women have considerably more than a high-school education and are of a consideraly higher socio-economic group than the general population. Thus, neither the T-scores nor the codetypes of the original MMPI are necessarily equivalent to MMPI-2. The *Manual* reports one study of psychiatric patients in which only about two-thirds of the code pairs remained the same when the two T-normative tables were used. And, at this early stage in the development of MMPI-2, no rules are available to adjust for these changes. The implication for this work is that when using MMPI-2, the person preparing the report either should base their feedback and treatment on the material given for our single scales, or apply the raw scores of MMPI-2 to the original norms before using the codetype information. **We strongly recommend that the codetype correlates and corresponding feedback be restricted for use only with the original norms.** We do report for MMPI-2 adjusted T-scores for the single scales and recommend the use of the appropriate associated data for MMPI and MMPI-2.

PURPOSE, ASSUMPTIONS, AND ORIENTATION

This *Guide* is written for therapists of any school of thought, for clinicians, physicians, counselors—pastoral, edu-cational, etc.—and mental health professionals who have a solid understanding of the construction, development, uses, and limitations of the MMPI, and who are ready to learn a new way of employing the MMPI directly in their work with clients. We will describe a step-by-step procedure wherein MMPI results are interpreted, interpretations are individualized, individualized interpretations are shared with the client in feedback, and validated feedback can be integrated into the therapeutic process. By combining the MMPI with treatment, we attempt both to individualize assessment (Fischer, 1985) and provide a means for evaluating the pragmatic utility of the MMPI as an assessment device (Dana, 1985; Hayes, Nelson, & Jarrett, 1987; Meehl, 1959; McReynolds, 1985).

We assume that the reader has some background knowledge from course work or readings in areas of personality (e.g., Singer, 1984), psychopathology (e.g., Carson, Butcher, & Coleman, 1988), psychotherapy (e.g., London, 1985), and personality assessment (e.g., Goldstein & Hersen, 1984). The reader must have a thorough working knowledge of the construction, administration, and scoring of the MMPI perhaps through attendance at one or more professional workshops (e.g., Advanced Psychological Studies Institute, 1987; University of Minnesota, 1987), or through reading the original and revised Manual (Hathaway & McKinley 1983, 1989) and one or another of the general sources (Duckworth & Anderson, 1986; Friedman, Webb, & Lewak, 1989; Graham, 1987; Greene, 1980; Marks, Seeman, & Haller, 1974).

Our approach evolves from over ten years of clinical trials with various interpretive, feedback, and treatment techniques developed and used at the Del Mar Psychiatric Clinic in California (Lewak, 1985, 1987; Lewak & Marks, 1987). This clinic is a private, fee-for-service group practice of psychologists, psychiatrists, clinical social workers, and marriage and family therapists. Most members work with individuals, couples, families, and groups and routinely use the MMPI as an integral part of their diagnostic and treatment activities. The concept is based in part on the MMPI theoretical conditioning model of Caldwell (1976, 1977, 1985) and in part on the adaptive behavioral conceptions of Kunce (1979) and Kunce and Anderson (1976). The approach is in ways similar to the joint-feedback technique of Erdberg (1979) as influenced by suggestions of Berg (1985) and the humanistic and individualized assessment proposals advanced by a number of others (e.g., Craddick, 1975; Dana, 1982; Fischer, 1979, 1985; Sugarman, 1978; Urban, 1983). This is not, however, a book about psychological assessment, writing psychological reports, or even a text on the MMPI. Rather, it is an advanced level reference source of empirical and experiential test meanings and hypotheses plus a way of sharing, validating, and integrating these into the process of treatment.

OVERVIEW OF WAYS
TO INTERPRET THE MMPI

While different types of information are available from an MMPI protocol for interpreting the test (e.g., content, scale and subscale, index), most interpretations will traditionally derive from the validity scales and from inter-relations of the clinical scales. Historically at least two ways have been utilized of extracting information from MMPI test profiles. The original validity and interpretive meaning were conveyed in the clinical *Atlas* of Hathaway and Meehl (1951) which summarized case history, symptom and diagnostic information compiled from patients independently of the test and linked to the test by classifications based on the MMPI scale codes (Hathaway & McKinley, 1983). By examining this information for all patients with similar or identical scale codes, the interpreter could identify common case characteristics which would then be assumed to apply to all patients generating the same MMPI code. Later, as more information became empirically available, the interpreter would examine scores on the validity and clinical scales, evaluate profile elevation, shape, and scatter, perhaps take into account the patient's adaptational style (Carson, 1969) along with other moderators and then arrive via the ***clinical method*** with a profile interpretation.

The second way of interpreting MMPI profiles is by the ***actuarial method*** which, inspired by Meehl (1956), developed from the early research of Drake and Oetting (1959), Marks and Seeman (1963), and Gilberstadt and Duker (1965). Following this procedure the interpreter would first classify the patient's profile code, and then interpret the test using information derived, again independently of the MMPI, but from empirical-statistical research on groups of patients with similar MMPI codes (Marks & Sines, 1969). In actual practice, however, probably few interpreters will strictly follow an actuarial approach. Frequently interpretative data are not available or what is available may not completely apply to every specified profile. Most MMPI interpretations, therefore, will involve a combination of methods and some blending of interpretive information, as illustrated by the Marks MMPI Adolescent and MMPI Adult computer-based interpretations, which supplement acturial code type data with clinical interscale, diagnostic and treatment information (Marks, 1987; Strassberg, Cooper, & Marks, 1987). Other workers, following the lineage of Diamond (1957), Carson (1969, 1986), and Caldwell (1972, 1978, 1984), will conceptualize and interpret the scales from one or another theoretical viewpoints (cf. also Kunce, 1979; Trimboli & Killgore,

1983). Finally, regardless of method, most workers who regularly use the MMPI in clinical practice recognize, as stated by Dahlstrom, Welsh, and Dahlstrom, (1972) that "substantial knowledge about general personality concepts is needed over and above a basic understanding of the MMPI and its *research literature* before meaningful and useful interpretations can be drawn from the test" (p. 292, italics added).

COMMENTS OF CUSTOMARY MMPI USE

Contemporary MMPI usage usually will depend upon the purpose of referral, the population served, and the practices of each particular setting. However, most interpreters will employ the test in order to gain an understanding of the client—although not necessarily for themselves (or even the client)—but for the purpose of completing an assessment which is then conveyed to another professional in some form of oral or written report. Usually these reports will comment on the client's approach to the test, estimate consistency and accuracy, describe the client's general personality (in terms of symptoms, traits, behaviors), elucidate conflicts and defenses, assess (although rarely) assets and positive personality attributes; consider factors of risk, control, and overall level of adjustment; and then typically (re-)classify the client by yet another system of diagnostic constructs (e.g., the DSM-IIIR—a procedure widely held to be the *sine qua non* for providing effective treatment (Marks, 1961). Our purpose is not to discuss traditional forms of MMPI clinical interpretations or traditional MMPI clinical reports. However, to examine briefly that body of the "research literature" on which virtually all MMPI interpretations and reports are based is instructive. The majority of the empirical correlates which underlie the test, and which are listed immediately after each scale and codetype, originate from check lists, Q-sorts, case summary forms, personal history forms, therapy notes, hospital charts, archival files and the like of (1) students from a university counseling center (Drake & Oetting, 1959); (2) emotionally disturbed children, adolescents and their parents (Marks, 1961); (3) women in a university psychiatric inpatient and outpatient setting (Marks & Seeman, 1963); and (4) men in a Veteran Administration GM & S psychiatric hospital (Gilberstadt & Duker, 1965). Although later other correlates came to comprise the empirical data base for MMPI interpretations (Butcher, 1987), they too were compiled mainly from work with "abnormal" or clinical cases (See e.g., Boerger, Graham, & Lilly, 1974; Hedlund, 1977; Lachar, 1968; Lewandowski & Graham, 1972; Gynther, Altman, & Sletten, 1973), with some recent notable exceptions (Graham, & McCord, 1985; Marks, 1982; Nelson & Marks, 1986). Thus, the core personality descriptive terms and statements (i.e, the "correlates") which are typically used to interpret the MMPI derive from similar sources as the structural dimensions of the instrument itself, and, as was evident from a subset empirically developed by Marks (1961), that upward of three-fourths of these terms may be pathological or "maladaptive" in content. This would not be surprising for a test primarily devised to obtain clinical-diagnostic information from psychiatric and medical patients were it not for the fact that the language itself also may be negatively encoded. Preliminary to a larger study of all words in contemporary American English describing aspects of personality, Norman (1967) empirically compiled a pool of trait terms (some nouns but mostly adjectives) of which as many as two-thirds were rated more undesirable than desirable in content. In summarizing this work, Goldberg (1982) noted that far more personality adjectives than personality nouns were used in the "English lexicon, and that a higher proportion of nouns than adjectives carry negative implications" (p.230).

To summarize, the MMPI was conceived as a *clinical* instrument. Most of the basic *clinical* scales were constructed with *clinical* groups, to diagnose *clinical* problems characterized in *clinical* terms. The basic scales were developed originally not as measures of personality but as measures of psychopathology, and while these scales can now be applied to a wide variety of *clinical* and *non-clinical* problems (cf. Dahlstrom, Welsh, & Dahlstrom, 1972; 1975), their mainstream use remains still for evaluating abnormal, maladaptive, or "undesirable" aspects of personality rather than normal, adaptive, or "desirable" ones. The interpretations of these scales require considerable knowledge and skill, and, unlike counseling reports, are traditionally designed not for the person who is taking the test but for communication to another professional. Terms such as "hostile," "dependent," "secondary gain," "demanding," "manipulative," "acting out," etc. are common, although a number of clinicians have voiced concern that they are antithetical to building a relationship (Fischer, 1972; Dana & Graham, 1976; Sugarman, 1978). However, not only are such terms *negative* and *pejorative*, but some are *evaluative* and often *irrelevant*. They cannot readily be shared with clients because their judgemental content could interfere with the development of a therapeutic alliance and may even be harmful to the client's self-concept. Our thesis is that a therapeutic alliance is more likely forged when clients feel that the therapist has an understanding of their personality, and most importantly, their central thoughts, feelings, and concerns. This is precisely the kind of understanding that could develop in an open non-judgemental discussion of findings in which the client is part of the evaluation *process*, rather than simply part of the evaluation product.

Another problem with traditional MMPI interpretations and reports is that they rarely include suggestions for treatment that flow directly from the findings, which is of little help to the therapist. Often their treatment implications are vague, even in reports which may otherwise provide a conceptual understanding of the client. Moreover no way is provided for knowing if the results are possibly negatively intrusive in therapy (Blatt, 1975) or if they at all contribute to beneficial treatment outcome (Hayes, Nelson, & Jarrett, 1987).

ORIGIN AND RATIONALE OF
THE FEEDBACK APPROACH

Most clients are particularly vulnerable and fearful when they seek the assistance of a mental health professional or when they experience physical symptoms causing them to seek medical help. They want relief from their symptoms and distress but they ask for even more from their primary care provider; they want respect, caring, and understanding from another human being who also knows of their fears, weaknesses, and mistakes. The therapeutic process invariably engages fears that probably developed in childhood when they were most dependent and vulnerable. If they were treated with dignity and respect as children they will expect similar treatment as adults. If they were mistreated as children they will most likely have difficulty developing a trusting relationship even with their therapist. If the therapist has an empathic understanding of the client's personality and can communicate this empathy, the client will more quickly come to trust and maintain vulnerability and will be more open to help, support, and change.

Our own approach is an *empirical-phenomenological approach* which is based on the formulations of Caldwell (1976, 1977). Unquestionably, we are all products of genetic and environmental factors. From our perspective, maladaptive (or abnormal) behavior is a product of stress (fear) operating within an individual who has a diathesis (predisposition, or set of vulnerabilities) for the type of disorder that occurs. We assume that each person inherits a repertoire of available psychological defenses (antibodies) against stress. Under in- creased stress those defenses which effectively serve to reduce it become fixed and maintained in accordance with their rein- forcing value. What seems to follow is that any particular defense could best be understood in the context of the stress that initially induced it. Take for example **Scale 1** of the MMPI (Hypochondriasis). People with elevated **Scale 1** scores are typically described as " . . . immature," "dependent," "psycho- logically naive." and "preoccupied with somatic concerns" (Marks, Seeman, & Haller, 1974). The terms immature, psycho- logically naive, etc., make sense when seen from the perspective of a frustrated therapist whose task may be to rid the client of the habit of switching attention to physical health when other psychologically painful conflicts arise. However, from the client's perspective a concern about physical health may at one stage have been an adaptive response to a perceived, overwhelming threat to the client's physical integrity. Staying in bed, worrying about deteriorating, and being preoccupied with the availability of medical help makes sense if one is terrified of bodily damage or death. Therefore it is reasonable to assume that someone like Howard Hughes, imprisoned in his own germ-free environment was terrified of physical illness. Caldwell's view was that eight of the ten MMPI clinical scales *each* reflect different patterns of fear-conditioned (defensive) avoidant behaviors as indicated in Table 1.

In Table 1 are listed each of the eight clinical scales with the associated fear and it's conditioned or defensive response.

Table 1

MMPI Clinical Scales and Associated Fear-Conditioned Defensive Responses

Scale	Fear	Response
1	Physical pain, illness or death	Overprotecting the body
2	Significant and irretrievable loss	Stopping of wanting or needing
3	Emotional pain, anger or sadness	Denying or positivizing feelings
4	Being unwanted, rejected or abandoned	"Numbing out" emotional involvements
6	Being criticized, devalued or humiliated	Maintaining hypersensitivity and vigilance
7	Unexpected and unpleasant events	Thinking ahead and worrying
8	Hostility, being disliked or despised by those upon whom one depends	"Shutting down" cognitive processing
9	Failing significant others	Increasing activity and expectations

For example, clients who score high on **Scale 2** have probably experienced a painful and irretrievable loss and they respond by avoiding feelings of need or want in order to avoid further loss. Similarly, clients with elevated **Scale 9** fear deprivation or failure and respond with increased activity in the hope of achieving reward and approval. They constantly plan ahead to avoid the onset of being let down and depressed. Generally, the more elevated the scale, and the more the scales are elevated, the more those clients protect themselves through defensive behaviors. Individual temperament will usually determine the kind of fears to which a person is most vulnerable. Furthermore, early childhood experiences condition the person to be afraid and defensive whenever he or she feels caught in a similar experience. A person humiliated and teased as a child (**Scales 6** and **8**) will be sensitive and afraid of hostility and criticism as an adult and will respond with defensive behaviors such as withdrawal and avoidance. **Scales 5** and **0** are not hypothesized to represent conditioned fear-avoidance responses.

The therapist is seen by us as a guide who uses a range of techniques from many theoretical persuasions to help the client resolve those fears that obstruct a life full of enjoyment. The MMPI is like a roadmap, the feedback statements or issues are the directions, and the background and early learning experiences are points for the therapist to engage the client. The client provides the motivation to travel, determines the destination and speed, and participates in the treatment adventure as an integral part of the discovery process.

A number of important reasons exist for providing feedback and for incorporating the information into the therapy itself. Our experience and the experience of many others is that simply feeling understood by someone is a relief to many clients and can in itself be of substantial value (Erdberg, 1979). We assume that most clients would like to know why they are taking the MMPI and would appreciate having some explanation of the results, although the latter may be less expected of clinical than non-clinical clients (Snyder, Ingram, Handelman, Wells, & Heiwieler, 1982). Also considerable agreement exists that most clients want feedback (Dana & Graham, 1976; Snyder et al., 1982)—that it reduces communication barriers (Craddick, 1975; Fischer, 1985), increases client involvement (Heller, 1972;

Blatt, 1975), can be self-affirming (Swann & Read, 1981), and validate their understanding of themselves (Bernard & Huckins, 1975; Halperin & Snyder, 1979). Furthermore, feedback that is relevant and specific (Harris & Greene, 1984) does not necessarily have to be accurate or favorable (Layne, 1979; Layne, & Ally, 1980) in order to be accepted by the client. Generally, feedback is viewed as a critical component of therapy (Aronson, 1980; Sundberg, 1977), and the client's receptivity of the information plays a central role in the therapeutic process (Silberschatz, Fretter, & Curtis, 1986; Snyder, Ingram, & Newburg, 1982; Urban & Ford, 1971). The feedback process encourages the client to participate actively in assessing the need for treatment and the therapy approach that is eventually taken. Client involvement in decisions that affect them has received considerable attention (Fischer & Brodsky, 1978; Pope, 1988; Pope, Tabachnick, & Keith-Speigel, 1987). With the passage of the Buckley Amendment and other "right to access" legislation, clients have the right to know the content of their records and psychological reports.

ORGANIZATION OF THE GUIDE

The phenomenological and empirical correlates of the thirteen basic scales of the MMPI and of twenty-three commonly occuring two-point codetypes are described in this Guide at different T-score levels. The T-ranges are typically over 80, between 70 and 80, 55 and 70, and 40 and 49. Where descriptions for T-scores over 80 are the same as for T-scores over 70, the descriptions for those over 80 have been omitted. Where there is an empirical basis for correlates of T-scores below 40, these also are included. For example, for **Scale 1** the suggestion has been (Duckworth & Anderson, 1986) that elevations below 40 reflect a cavalier attitude towards one's physical health sometimes to the point of disregard for physical symptoms. For the codetypes, however, no descriptors are given for elevations below a T-score of 55. The same correlates are recommended for use with the basic scales of MMPI-2, but *not* with the two-point codes, which at this stage are of doubtful equivalence to MMPI-1. For MMPI-2, the adjusted T-score ranges are 76 and over, between 66 and 75, 56 and 65, 41 and 55, and less than 41. For both the original MMPI and the revision, feedback is provided throughout the T-ranges for **Scale 5** (separately for men and women) and for **Scale 0.**

CHAPTER 2

DEVELOPMENT OF THE GUIDE

In this chapter is described how the Guide was developed and how it is organized. It begins with the selection of MMPI scales and codetypes and describes the nature, origin, and purpose of each section of the feedback information. We, as authors, assume that the reader is familiar with the construction, administration, scoring, and clinical interpretation of the MMPI and recommend a thorough knowledge of the *Manual* (Hathaway & McKinley, 1983) and of one of the basic source books (Friedman, Webb, & Lewak, 1989; Graham, 1987; Green, 1980) as a minimal qualification for using this approach. Users of MMPI-2 should also be familiar with the *Manual* for the restandardized version (Hathaway & McKinley, 1989).

SELECTION OF SCALES, CODES, AND DESCRIPTORS

The *Guide* was conceived to help the therapist use the MMPI to achieve a better understanding of the client and to help the client become an informed participant sharing in the treatment process. Specifically, the *Guide* was developed to provide feedback on T-scores of the basic **validity** and **clinical scales** including, **L, F, K, Hs, D, Hy, Pd, Mf, Pa, Pt, Sc, Ma,** and **Si.** While hundreds of scales have been developed from the MMPI that could have been used, the basic scales are the ones that have generated the most research and are the only ones universally scored whenever the test is administered. For these reasons the basic scales were the ones selected on which to base our approach.

A similar decision involved the selection of two-point codes or code types, where for the clinical scales alone 90 possible pairs or 45 possible paired-scale interchangeable combinations exist. In this instance we selected 21 interchangeable pairs as among those most frequently encountered, most widely studied, and best known to the authors (see Marks, 1984; see also Dahlstrom, Welsh, & Dahlstrom, 1972: Swenson, Pearson, & Osborne, 1973; and Webb, 1970). The doubtful equivalence of the two-point codes, and the absence of empirical correlates for these codes precluded a selection of similar codetypes for MMPI-2. We, again, strongly recommend that workers wishing to use our codetype material with MMPI-2, first transform the raw scores to the original T-scores and only then proceed to try and classify the results. The following are the 21 codetypes selected for feedback and based on the norms of MMPI-1:

1-2/2-1	2-3/3-2	3-4/4-3	4-6/6-4	6-8/8-6	7-8/8-7	8-9/9-8
1-3/3-1	2-4/4-2	3-6/6-3	4-7/7-4	6-9/9-6		
	2-6/6-2	3-7/7-3	4-8/8-4			
	2-7/7-2	3-9/9-3	4-9/9-4			
	2-8/8-2					
	2-9/9-2					
	2-0/0-2					

The basic ingredients of which most MMPI clinical interpretations are made consist of the correlates of scales (mainly of high points) and scale combinations (primarily of two points, referred also as codetypes) which were empirically derived independent of the test in studies of different subject groups. Therefore the overall interpretive meaning of the MMPI—in contrast to the "Validity Scale" scores (on L, F, and K) from each particular administration of the test—are embodied in the correlates derived from previous research. (For a discussion of the empirical approach, see Dahlstrom, Welsh, & Dahlstrom, 1972; Graham, 1987; Greene, 1980; Marks & Sines, 1969). Listed in each code and codetype and discussed later in this chapter are the correlates on which most of the interpretations in Chapter 5 are based. While the information contains only the most common correlates for each scale and code described in this *Guide*, it does provide a rich source of clinical interpretive data. As a convenience to the reader, each correlate has been classified by content into one of four categories:

Concerns/Complaints: Includes common concerns, expressed or implied, and major complaints at the time of taking the test. May also include reason(s) for referral or seeking professional help (e.g., physical health, pain, unhappiness, stress).

Thoughts: Includes ways of thinking, contents of thoughts and cognitive responses to fear situations (e.g., self-blaming, worrisome, indecisive, critical).

Emotions: Includes prominent moods, feelings, and emotional responses to fear situations (e.g., anxious, depressed, restless, irritable).

Traits/Behaviors: Contains terms that describe personality patterns, social roles, and characteristic modes of behavior (e.g., passive, dependent, unassertive, manipulative).

NOTES TO THE THERAPIST

Preceeding the interpretative material for each clinical scale high-point and two-point code is a section entitled *Notes to the Therapist.* This section is written in traditional clinical, professional-to-professional language and is intended to orient the therapist to the nature of that scale or code irrespective of any particular score elevation. Generally, however, the more elevated the score(s) the more likely the information associated with that scale or code should apply. Conversely, low scores (those below 40T) should be interpreted cautiously and may reflect behavioral tendencies under stress rather than enduring personality characteristics.

Summarized next are probable salient personality characteristics for the scale or code. The section also highlights important psychodynamic and descriptive features, and offers interpretative hypotheses of predisposing conditions and possible early childhood experiences.

A discussion follows with the treatment approaches and techniques that we and others have found especially useful in working with clients (Caldwell, 1977, 1978; Carson, 1986; Erdberg, 1985; Lewak, 1985, 1987; Lewak & Duckworth, 1986;

Lewak & Marks, 1987). Included are comments on some indications for medication and on the side effects and addiction potential of using various drugs.

For the reader interested in a more extensive discussion of the clinical applications of MMPI scales and codes, we recommend consulting one of the following sources (Dahlstrom, Welsh, & Dahlstrom, 1972; Duckworth & Anderson, 1986; Friedman, Webb, & Lewak, 1989; Graham, 1987; Greene, 1980). For a discussion of the MMPI and use of psychotropic drugs see Nichols (1986), Ritz (1965), and Siddall and Keogh (1980).

ISSUES

Our orientation for interpreting the MMPI is most clearly illustrated in the section on *Issues*, which lists the experiential formulations that represent the essence of our feedback approach. As we have already indicated, we began with the purpose of developing a language for interpreting the MMPI that would communicate empathy and be easily understood and meaningful to clients. We have seen where most of the data base already available for interpreting the test is comprised of many terms which are technical (e.g., "introjecting," "dissociating," "ideas of reference"), strongly negative or pejorative ("obnoxious", "incompetent," "hostile"), highly evaluative ("ingenius", "psychotic", "has a poor prognosis"), or are otherwise imprecise ("balanced," "insecure," "immature") or obscure ("calculated," "refractory," "neurasthenic"). These are terms that in our experience often threaten and confuse clients or are far removed from their everyday thoughts, feelings, and experiences. Many of the correlates are simply ill-suited to explaining a person's MMPI scores and are repugnant to many therapists. However, these correlates do form the basis of our system. In the same tradition of the founders of the MMPI we accepted them as the most useful and psychometrically defensible starting point to construct a different way of characterizing a person rather than as some criteria of "truth"—in the sense of what a person is like—in and of themselves.

To us for the purpose of feedback and for the MMPI to become of value in the process of therapy, the correlates would seem to have to be formulated in terms that were understandable to clients and presented in a manner so that the client as well as the therapist could validate the feedback experience. Thus we approached the correlates from a phenomenological perspective and in talking with clients came to conceptualize the correlates in terms of issues dealing with inner thoughts, feelings, and concerns. Each issue became an experiential formulation of one or more correlates empirically derived and associated with a MMPI scale and code. We would ask clients and those closest to them just how they felt, what they thought, and how they experienced themselves and the descriptors associated with their MMPI scales and codes. In this manner, for example, the *panic* and *terror* correlates of **Scale 8** suggested to us the issue "Right now the world is a very frightening place for you," the *alienation* and *distrust* suggested the issue "You are probably feeling very apart from others and it's hard for you to know how others are feeling about you", and the *confusion* and *feeling different* correlates the issue "You are probably confused about your own thoughts and moods, and wondering if there is something really wrong with you."

Some issues appeared relatively simple (i.e., noncausal) and straightforward like "You are probably very open to other people's points of view and their ideas about how you should behave" for the correlate *suggestable* (and perhaps also for *naive, dependent,* or *responsive*) of **Scale 3**; whereas others were more complex, causal, and inferential like "You may be going through a particularly stressful time right now and dealing with it by trying to be brave, by trying to look at the bright side of things, and by not letting yourself feel too much anguish for fear it will overwhelm you," representing a number of correlates (such as *lack of insight, Pollyanna defense, optimism, denial*) of **Scale 3** as well.

Some scales and codes have a number of similar correlates while others will share the same correlate or have several that are similar, but each reflecting a slightly different motivational focus. *Shy, timid, introverted, seclusive, aloof, distant,* and *prefers being alone* all characterize **Scale 0** but are formulated in issues of different concerns for clients with **Scale 0** elevations. For examples;

"You are shy, sensitive and uncomfortable around strangers and large groups of people that you do not know."

"It is difficult for you to meet new people and make 'small talk'."

"People with your profile rarely need much social stimulation and spend most of their time on their own."

"Other's may misperceive you as indifferent because you guard your privacy rather jealously."

Both anxiety and worry are common characteristics of **Scale 2** and **7,** but we learned from our clients that the origin of their anxiety and worry is definitely not the same. The origin associated with elevated **Scale 2** lies in the past, as in the issue "You are probably spending most of your time worrying about the past; feeling guilty about things you have said or done and feeling hopeless about things ever changing." For elevated **Scale 7** the focus, as revealed in the following issue, is toward the future: "It is as if you are worrying about what might happen next; as if one unforseeable event could occur and 'upset the applecart' leading to a disaster."

The correlates **hostile, angry,** and **resentful** are common across a number of scales and codes. However, in talking to clients with elevated scores on these scales we learned that their experiences respectively were not always quite the same. Clients with elevated **Scale 4** "Often will view the world as a 'dog-eat-dog' place where should they become vulnerable and 'off guard,' others will use them and take advantage of them." However, when **Scale 4** is a two-point code the experience of **hostile, angry** and **resentful** has a different meaning depending on the second highest scale of the code, as in the following examples.

2-4/4-2 "You may feel that the world has let you down and that the odds of ever getting what you want in life are overwhelming."

3/4-4/3 "You generally want to please people and see the best in people. Perhaps for this reason you tend to deny anger and probably not even know when you are angry with others until at some point you explode."

4-6/6-4 "You may find yourself constantly resentful of people who have power over you, and afraid of attack by anyone who has control over you."

4-8/8-4 "You may be experiencing periods of 'black moods' where you feel alone, empty and disconnected from everything and everyone around you."

4-9/9-4 "Generally, you are easy going and even charming until someone frustrates you, confronts you or crosses you. Then you can become extremely angry and your anger can be expressed in ways that sometimes have severe repercussions."

Separate issues for different T-score ranges of each scale and of each code also are listed depending upon the correlates available and our experiences with the scale and code. In cases where correlates have a specific range or scale elevation, the issues are formulated to correspond to that range or elevation. For example, the following are among the correlates, associated issues, and corresponding T-score ranges for **Scale 2:**

Unhappiness "There seems to be little in life right now that gives you pleasure" (80 T and above, MMPI-1; 76 T and above, MMPI-2).

Loss of energy "Perhaps you are able to do your basic chores but once you have finished these it is very difficult for you to generate energy for other activities" (70-79 T, MMPI-1; 66-75 T, MMPI-2).

Lacking self-confidence "You are probably being a little more circumspect than usual and a little less likely to take risks" (55-69 T, MMPI-1; 56-65 T, MMPI-2).

In other instances correlates are formulated in modified intensity appropriate to their range or elevation. Thus, the **energy** correlate of **Scale 9** is formulated to vary with T-scores as follows:

"You are a person with a very high level of energy" (80 T and above, MMPI-1; 76 T and above MMPI-2)
"You probably have a very high level of energy" (70-79 T, MMPI-1; 66-75 T, MMPI-2)
"You have a moderately high level of energy" (55-69 T, MMPI-1; 56-65 T, MMPI-2))
"Your energy right now is very low" (45 T, MMPI-1; < 50 T, MMPI-2)

The number of issues available for feedback will differ from scale to scale and code to code (see the Table of Interpretations in Chapter 4). The Listings of Scale and Code Characteristics of Chapter 4 are organized and presented in the same manner as they are recommended for use (see section on Providing Feedback). *Scales L, F,* and *K* appear first, only the correlates of these scales are not formulated as issues, but rather as interpretations of the client's approach to the test. However, similar to the issues, separate statements are for each scale depending upon the scale's T-score range or level of elevation.

BACKGROUND AND EARLY LEARNING EXPERIENCES

This section is based upon the assumption that unresolved painful childhood experiences will sensitize a person to similar situations throughout life. From this perspective, any present situation which elicits emotional memories of past painful events is likely to lead to anxiety or defensive behavior. The expressions "once bitten twice shy" or "the burnt child fears fire" aptly reflect this clinical perspective. The section includes a description of early learning and conditioning experiences hypothetically associated with each scale and code and presumably common among persons with the same MMPI results. This section is not elevation specific but general for the code type.

SUGGESTIONS FOR SELF HELP

Some evidence exists from the use of bibliotherapy and cognitive behavioral therapy that self-help may benefit clients at least as much as traditional therapies and can be cost effective in terms of professional time and expense (Franks et al., 1982, 1984; Mahalik & Kivlighan, 1988; Mahoney & Thoresen, 1974;

Thoresen & Mahoney, 1974). This section provides some learning-based, Gestalt, and common-sense suggestions for self-help which can serve as "homework" for practice assignments following feedback or between therapy sessions. In all instances, separate suggestions are listed for each scale and code but are general and not elevation specific. There are no suggestions provided for the *validity scales* or for *Scale 5* and *0.*

CHAPTER 3

USING
THE GUIDE

The *Guide* was developed from our experience with clients ages 18 and older, having ten or more years of schooling, residing in urban and suburban southern California communities, earning at least lower-middle level incomes, and who were seeking outpatient help for a wide range of personal, marital, family, work-related, or other relationship problems. For the most part our clients were well educated, psychologically sophisticated and were willing to take the MMPI and directly took part in validating the feedback about their results. They were given the Group or R (booklet) form of the test either just before or immediately following their first clinic contact. We mention this because our procedures may not be suitable for other types of clients or for clients tested under markedly different circumstances. This approach may not be applicable, for example, for psychiatric hospital patients, in correctional settings, or for individuals from more limited social or cultural backgrounds. It would not be appropriate for adolescents since it is based on K-corrected adult norms.

PREPARING THE CLIENT FOR TESTING

At the time of first contact clients are informed of the nature and purpose of taking the MMPI and are given a clear indication of how the results are going to be used. They are told that after completing the test they will participate in a joint-feedback session of evaluating the findings and may bring a recorder to tape the session. This helps fulfill the client's right to give or withold informed consent to complete the MMPI (and to participate in treatment) and, with the expectation of feedback, encourages open and candid compliance with the testing request.

The client is then given a pamphlet with the following introductory information.

MMPI: QUESTIONS & ANSWERS

You have been asked to take the MMPI. Here are some questions that are commonly asked about the test. Please read over these before you take the test. If you have other questions please feel free to ask.

1. **What is it?** MMPI is short for the Minnesota Multiphasic Personality Inventory. Currently it is the most often used personality test in the world.

2. **How do I answer the questions?** Answer the questions as you think and feel right now. Work quickly because no one question is "vital." It is the pattern of answers that makes a difference and is most useful.

3. **Do I have to answer all the questions even if I don't know the right answers?** Try to answer all the questions. If you can't answer them, leave no more than a few unanswered. If you are unsure about an answer then use the following rule: If the answer to the question is more true than false, answer it true. If it is more false than true, answer it false. For example, the question "I get headaches often?" could be answered as follows. I get headaches sometimes but not "often" and therefore the answer is false.

4. **Why am I taking this test? Does it mean something is wrong with me?** We have asked you to take the test because it will help us to get

to know you better in less time. Many who come to the clinic are asked to take it for this reason. Also, it is cost effective.

5. **Why does the test ask so many questions that clearly don't apply to me?** The test was constructed to identify people who were well within normal limits in terms of their personality and also to identify people who were much more disturbed. If a questions does not apply to you, simply answer false, or true, whichever is correct. The test is versatile in the sense that it can usually detect when a person is healthy as well as when a person has some serious problems.

6. **How can you tell anything about me from all those questions anyway?** After your answer sheet is finished it is scored on a number of scales to see how you score on different dimensions of personality. There are also scales which tell us how you approach the test. Did you do so cautiously, candidly, or were you minimizing problems or perhaps even overstating them.

7. **Will I get feedback from my test?** Yes. The actual test protocol will not be given to you. But, a full explanation of the results will be provided.

8. **What if I disagree with the results?** That is something you are encouraged to discuss. You may want to bring a tape recorder and tape the feedback session so that you can listen on your own and formulate questions that you might have for your therapist. Remember, the test is for your own benefit.

9. **Can I take the test just to learn about myself even if I'm quite satisfied with my present situation?** Absolutely. We have found that individuals and couples often get a clearer sense of

themselves and their relationship after a feed-back session. It can help put things in perspective.

10. **What is the cost of the test?** See the clinic fee schedule. The fee covers administration, scoring, and processing. Feedback will come in a regular session for which you will pay your usual fee to your therapist.

After reading over the pamphlet clients are asked if they have any other questions which, if so, are answered as briefly and directly as possible. Once clients fully understand why they are taking the MMPI, are assured that their results will remain confidential, and agree to participate, they are given the test booklet and answer sheet and asked to read and follow the standard test instructions.

An important aspect to assure is that the person actually responsible for administering and scoring the test maintains sound professional practice and is thoroughly familiar with the standardized procedures described in both *Manuals* (Hathaway & McKinley, 1983, 1989). Moreover, although the test administrator and/or therapist might not be a psychologist, an advisable procedure is for both to be aware of the responsibilities outlined in the *Ethical Principles of Psychologists* (APA, 1981) and in the *General Guidelines for Providers of Psychological Services* (APA, 1987). The therapist providing the report should be a licensed health-care professional qualified to purchase and use the text (see National Computer Systems, 1985, 1989).

PREPARING TEST RESULTS

The interpretative material contained in this *Guide* is accessed through T-scores for the four **validity scales** (**?, L, F,** and **K**) and the 10 **clinical scales,** with the appropriate **K** additions. The procedures for calculating these can be found in each of the MMPI source books already mentioned, and they also appear in both *Manuals* (Hathaway & McKinley, 1983, 1989). In addition to T-scores, the 10 clinical scales also must be coded which can be done in a simple three-step procedure. First, substitute the numerals 1 to 0 for the scales Hs to Si as is already done in the Hathaway (1947) and Welsh (1948) standard coding arrangement. Thus **Scales 1 = Hs, 2 = D, 3 = Hy, 4 = Pd, 5 = Mf, 6 = Pa, 7 = Pt, 8 = Sc, 9 = Ma,** and **0 = Si.** The second step is to rank the numbers assigned to these scales in order of their descending T-score values. The final step is to underline all adjacent scales with the same T-score values. No other symbols or designations are necessary.

For example, Arnold's scores listed in the following illustration would be coded 2745613809, where **Scale 2** has the highest score (T=86), **Scale 7** the next highest (T=84), **Scale 4** next (T=79), . . . and **Scale 9** is the lowest score (T=46). And, since no scores are equal no scales are underlined.

ARNOLD'S MMPI-1 RESULTS

T Sc	<50	50	55	48	65	86	62	79	74	70	84	61	46	55
Number					1	2	3	4	5	6	7	8	9	0
Scale	?	L	F	K	Hs	D	Hy	Pd	Mf	Pa	Pt	Sc	Ma	Si

A somewhat different situation occurs in the example of Bob. Here **Scale 4** is the highest scale (T=80). **Scales 2** and **8** are next and equal (T=77), **Scale 5** is next (T=76), followed by **Scales 7** and **9.** Therefore, whenever two or more scales are equal not only are they underlined but the ordinal position of the scales will always determine their order of coding. Thus, the scales for Bob are coded 4285796310, indicating **4** as the highest scale, **2** and **8** second and equal, **5** next highest, followed by **7** and **9** which are also equal, etc. And, since scales **2** and **8**, and **7** and **9** both are equals, both pair of scales are underlined.

BOB'S MMPI-1 RESULTS

T Sc	50	53	70	50	59	77	61	80	76	64	75	77	75	56
Number					1	2	3	4	5	6	7	8	9	0
Scale	?	L	F	K	Hs	D	Hy	Pd	Mf	Pa	Pt	Sc	Ma	Si

A correctly prepared set of test results will always include two kinds of information: (1) The ten digit clinical code, with the scales ranked in descending order of magnitude and underlined if equal; and (2) The T-scores for **Scales ?, L, F, K, 1, 2, 3, 4, 5, 6, 7, 8, 9,** and **0,** with the appropriate **K** additions for **Scales 1, 4, 7, 8,** and **9.**

EVALUATING VALIDITY AND
SCALES ?, L, F, AND K

Typically the first and at times most difficult step after administering, scoring, and coding the MMPI is determining whether scores are "valid" and useable. Validity in a practical sense deals with the adequacy of a test for making the kinds of decisions or generating the kinds of interpretations the test user wishes to make. We have already seen, for example, where in traditional applications of the MMPI (such as in professional to professional consultations) most of the correlates listed have met the validation standards recommended for clinical test use (APA, 1985). Validity as measured by **Scales ?, L, F,** and **K,** however, deals more with the utility of scores generated from each particular MMPI test administration. Thus, where the former addresses the substantive and technical characteristics of the test, the latter pertains more to the attitudes or test-taking orientation of the client. This is in an effort to evaluate each client's response to the test that the question is raised of whether the results are valid and useful. Unfortunately, after over forty years of exploring different strategies for answering this question, as yet no uniform procedure for detecting valid from invalid MMPI results (see e.g., Buechley & Ball, 1952; Evans, 1984; Gallucci, 1984; Gough, 1950; Greene, 1978, 1979; Hathaway & McKinley, 1983, 1989; Meehl, 1945; Meehl & Hathaway, 1946; Nichols, Greene, & Schmolck, 1989) exists.

While validity is an important consideration in providing and evaluating feedback as it is in traditional consulting with the MMPI, the process and criteria for determining it are as different as the two applications themselves. First, the feedback approach requires no a priori assumptions about the "truth" value of the issues or correlates on which the issues are based. It does not assume that the issue formulations are distinct, or all inclusive, or that any one issue is more important, or is formulated more precisely than any other. Nor does it require any assumptions about the accuracy of hypothetical or causal background events. It views these simply as propositions to be validated by the client from the client's own experiential perspective and then secondarily verified by the client's therapist. Ideally, the criterion for validity would be complimentary perspectives through which client and therapist share similar views. However, the client is ultimately the criterion of the veridicality of feedback. The therapist helps indicate the context in which particular understandings or misunderstandings arise and encourages the client to expand on additional individual issues beyond those of the feedback. The "proof of the pudding" is in the client experiencing and confirming each element of the feedback report. The end product of traditional MMPI consultations only can be as valid as the correlates or the interpretations themselves. The open-end product of feedback, however, requires individualized confirmations and empirical validity beyond that of the correlates or the interpretations on which they are based.

INTERPRETING DISCORDANT (INVALID) RESULTS

With proper preparation and instruction we see very few clients whose validity scores exceed those for which the interpretative materials of Chapter 4 would not be appropriate or recommended. Rarely does a client answer all questions as true, false, randomly, or who leaves a large number of questions unanswered. Occasionally we do see unusually elevated *?, L, F,* and *K* scores and quite depressed *K* scores, and have developed some procedures for identifying and dealing with them. Thus, we have chosen the term "discordant results" in preference to "invalid results" as a more appropriate way to reference such findings.

In almost all cases involving discordant results the therapist can say something about the way the client may have been feeling while answering the test, given that the client answered the questions in the first place. An obvious, but important point is to be aware of what could have motivated the client *not* to comply or to respond with a particular type of discordant result. We are reminded of the case of an extremely distraught woman who took the MMPI with the expectation of receiving feedback. The person who administered, scored, and coded the test returned the results with the word "INVALID" written across the protocol. The therapist then told the client that her results were invalid. This devastated the woman who believed she had somehow "failed" the test when in fact she had tried hard to answer it accurately although she was very confused at the time. Thus, whenever giving clients feedback on discordant results be aware that offering them some explanation for the results is always appropriate even if the results are otherwise of limited value.

The following validity scale scores are considered sufficiently discordant with the purpose and instructions of feedback to warrant the corresponding interpretations and recommendations.

? Scale: MMPI-1, and MMPI-2, T-score = to or > 50

Indicates that the client either omitted or double-answered a large number of questions. This rarely occurs, but can when the client is overly cautious, indecisive, uncooperative, or has difficulty understanding the questions. In any instance the test should be returned and the client encouraged to "try again to finish the unanswered (or double-answered) questions."

L Scale: MMPI-1, T-score > 70; MMPI-2, > 80

Indicates that the client answered a large number of *L Scale* items. This can occur if the client has below average intelligence, less than a high school education, or is socially or culturally deprived. It also can occur if the client wants desperately to create a favorable impression, or has an idealistic and perhaps unrealistic view of self as being beyond social or moral reproach. In any event, if possible the test should be retaken.

K Scale: MMPI-1, T-score > 75; MMPI-2, > 71

Indicates that the client answered a large number of *K Scale* items. This can occur if a person is extremely guarded and perhaps unable or unwilling to explore personal problems or fears. Suggestions to the client that the test is invalid, however, could lead to confusion, anger, and further denial and resistance. We recommend that the client's feelings about their vulnerabilities be explored and that the test be retaken with specific instructions: "to answer the questions again, only this time as if you were feeling at your 'lowest' or 'worst'."

K Scale: MMPI-1, T-score < 35; MMPI-2, < 40

Indicates that the client answered very few *K Scale* items. This may indicate an exaggeration of the client's fears and vulnerabilities, or it may indicate confusion, malingering, or panic about the severity of current symptoms or problems. In any event we recommend that the client be retested with specific instructions "to answer the questions again, only this time as if feeling at your 'peak' or 'very best'."

All elevations on *Scale F*, and all over elevations on *Scales L* and *K*, are considered accordant with the testing instructions and are interpreted in Chapter 4 under the heading of "Approach to the Test."

COMPOSING THE FEEDBACK REPORT

As previously stated, when properly prepared and instructed the majority of clients will complete the MMPI with usable results for feedback. That is, their validity scale scores will not exceed the limits: *?* greater than 50 T, and *L* less than 70 T, and *K* ranging from 35 T to 75 T. The corresponding limits for MMPI-2 are *?* less than 50 T, *L* less than 80 T, and *K* ranging between 40 and 70 T. In the event the validity scores exceed their limits, the reader should consult the preceding discussion on interpreting discordant results.

A number of ways exist of preparing and conducting MMPI feedback, but for the therapist first learning the procedure the recommended way will always require the composition of a written report. Also a software version is available which prints out a condensed feedback report currently available from Applied Innovations, Inc. (See Lewak, Marks, & Nelson, 1988).

What, then, are the steps in composing an appropriate and individualized feedback report? We have discussed the importance of preparing the client for testing; of properly administering, scoring, and coding the test, and of determining if the results are discordant or usable. We will now illustrate the succeeding steps with the coded scores of the client Charles:

STEPS IN PROCEDURE

CHARLES' MMPI-1 RESULTS

T Sc	<50	46	73	46	60	76	62	81	66	70	68	72	55	73
Scale	?	L	F	K	1	2	3	4	5	6	7	8	9	0
Code	4208675319													

1. Verify the Results

Review the scores for **Scales ?, L, F,** and **K** and confirm that they are within the limits prescribed.

2. Format the Report

Begin with the following heading and instructions on the first page of the report.

MMPI-1 Adult Feedback Report

Client's Name: *Gender:*
Test Date: *Report Date:*

(Client's name)...your MMPI results suggest that you have completed the test in the following manner and that the following issues and experiences are important to you. Please read each and then circle on the scale following, the number corresponding to your feelings about it right now.

5	4	3	2	1	0
Very True	*Mostly True*	*Partially True*	*Mostly False*	*Very False*	*Uncertain*

3. Enter the Approach

Note the validity scales scores, which for Charles are L=46 T, F=73 T, and K=46 T. Locate in Chapter 4 the corresponding statements that indicate Charles' approach to the test and write these accordingly. Since no statement is provided for an L score below a T-score of 50, the report would begin with the F statement for the T-score range of 65 to 74 and conclude with the K statement for the T-score range of 36 to 46. The individualized report would thus begin.

Approach to the Test

Charles, your profile suggests that you may be experiencing a good deal of stress right now that troubles you and makes you feel it may be difficult to manage. 5 4 3 2 1 0

You answered the questions in a very frank and open way admitting to how you feel and what troubles you without trying to put up a positive front. 5 4 3 2 1 0

4. Classify the Code

Using only the original norms compare the two highest scales of the client's code with each of the two-point codes listed in the Table of Contents or in Table 2. If the scales match, then compare their scores in Table 2 with the code-type scale elevation and difference criteria. The two highest scales of Charles' code are 4 and 2 which match the 2-4/4-2 two-point code. Reference to Table 2 indicates that in order to classify Charles' scales with the 2-4/4-2 code, scales 2 or 4 must be greater than a T-score of 60. The difference between scales 4 and 2 must be within 10 T-points when either scale 4 or 2 is greater than 70 T. Since Charles' scale 4 equals 81 T and scale 2 equals 76 T, the criteria are met and the results can be classified by the 2-4/4-2 code. The issues appropriate for those elevations should be written under the appropriate heading in the next section of the report. If the two highest scales do not match one of the two-point codes and do not correspond to the classification criteria, or if the client has been administered MMPI-2, skip to Step 9 on *The Single Scale Approach*, or alternatively, replot the raw scores of MMPI-2 with norms of MMPI-1 and proceed to classify the code as above.

TABLE 2

TABLE 2
T-Score Elevation and Difference Criteria
for Classifying Scales by Two-Point Codes

Two-Point Code	Scale Elevations and Differences**
1-2/2-1	1 or 2 $\geq$ 60T* **and** 1 - 2 **or** 2 - 1 $\leq$ 5T (55-69T range) **or** 1 -2 **or** 2 - 1 $\leq$ 8T ($\geq$70T range)
1-3/3-1	1 or 3 $\geq$ 60T* **and** 1 - 3 **or** 3 - 1 $\leq$ 5T (55-69T range) **or** 1 - 3 **or** 3 - 1 $\leq$ 8T ($\geq$ 70T range)
2-3/3-2	2 or 3 $\geq$ 60T* **and** 2 - 3 **or** 3 - 2 $\leq$ 5T (55-79T range) **or** 2 - 3 **or** 3 - 2 $\leq$ 10T ($\geq$80T range)
2-4/4-2	2 or 4 $\geq$ 60T* **and** 2 - 4 **or** 4 - 2 $\leq$ 5T (55-69T range) **or** 2 - 4 **or** 4 - 2 $\leq$ 10T ($\geq$70T range)
2-6/6-2	2 or 6 $\geq$ 60T* **and** 2 - 6 **or** 6 - 2 $\leq$ 5T (55-69T range) **or** 2 - 6 **or** 6 - 2 $\leq$ 8T ($\geq$70T range)
2-7/7-2	2 or 7 $\geq$ 60T* **and** 2 - 7 **or** 7 - 2 $\leq$ 5T (55-69T range) **or** 2 - 7 **or** 7 - 2 $\leq$ 10T ($\geq$ 70T range)
2-8/8-2	2 or 8 $\geq$ 60T* **and** 2 - 8 **or** 8 - 2 $\leq$ 5T (55-69T range) **or** 2 - 8 **or** 8 - 2 $\leq$ 12T (70-89T range) **or** 2 - 8 **or** 8 - 2 $\leq$ 15T ($\geq$90T range)
2-9/9-2	2 or 9 $\geq$ 60T* **and** 2 - 9 **or** 9 - 2 $\leq$ 3T (55-59T range) **or** 2 - 9 **or** 9 - 2 $\leq$ 8T ($\geq$60T range)
2-0/0-2	2 or 0 $\geq$ 60T* **and** 2 - 0 **or** 0 - 2 $\leq$ 5T (55-59T range) **or** 2 - 0 **or** 0 - 2 $\leq$ 15T ($\geq$ 60T range)
3-4/4-3	3 or 4 $\geq$ 60T* **and** 3 - 4 **or** 4 - 3 $\leq$ 5T (55-69T range) **or** 3 - 4 **or** 4 - 3 $\leq$ 10T ($\geq$ 70T range)
3-6/6-3	3 or 6 $\geq$ 60T* **and** 3 - 6 **or** 6 - 3 $\leq$ 5T (55-69T range) **or** 3 - 6 **or** 6 - 3 $\leq$ 8T ($\geq$ 70T range)
3-7/7-3	3 or 7 $\geq$ 60T* **and** 3 - 7 **or** 7 - 3 $\leq$ 5T (55-69T range) **or** 3 - 7 **or** 7 - 3 $\leq$ 8T ($\geq$ 70T range)
3-9/9-3	3 or 9 $\geq$ 60T* **and** 3 - 9 **or** 9 - 3 $\leq$ 5T (55-69T range) **or** 3 - 9 **or** 9 - 3 $\leq$ 10T ($\geq$70T range)

*One scale must $\geq$ 55T.

**Read the highest scale minus the second highest scale must $\leq$ x within the associated T score range.

Table 2 (Continued)

Two-Point Code	Scale Elevations and Differences**
4-6/6-4	4 or 6 ≥ 60T* **and** 4 - 6 **or** 6 - 4 ≤ 5T (55-69T range) **or** 4 - 6 **or** 6 - 4 ≤ 10T (≥ 70T range)
4-7/7-4	4 or 7 ≥ 60T* **and** 4 - 7 **or** 7 - 4 ≤ 5T (55-69T range) **or** 4 - 7 **or** 7 - 4 ≤ 10T (≥ 70T range)
4-8/8-4	4 or 8 ≥ 60T* **and** 4 - 8 **or** 8 - 4 ≤ 5T (55-69T range) **or** 4 - 8 **or** 8 - 4 ≤ 10T (≥ 70T range)
4-9/9-4	4 or 9 ≥ 60T* **and** 4 - 9 **or** 9 - 4 ≤ 5T (55-69T range) **or** 4 - 9 ≤ 15T (≥ 70T range) **or** 9 - 4 ≤ 5T (≥ 55T range)
6-8/8-6	6 or 8 ≥ 60T* **and** 6 - 8 **or** 8 - 6 ≤ 5T (55-69T range) **or** 6 - 8 **or** 8 - 6 ≤ 10T (≥ 70T range)
6-9/9-6	6 or 9 ≥ 60T* **and** 6 - 9 ≤ 5T (≥ 55T range) **or** 9 - 6 ≤ 5T (55-69T range) **or** 9 - 6 ≤ 10T (≥ 70T range)
7-8/8-7	7 or 8 ≥ 60T* **and** 7 - 8 **or** 8 - 7 ≤ 5T (55-69T range) **or** 7 - 8 **or** 8 - 7 ≤ 8T (70-89T range) **or** 7 - 8 **or** 8 - 7 ≤ 10T (≥ 90T range)
8-9/9-8	8 or 9 ≥ 60T* **and** 8 - 9 **or** 9 - 8 ≤ 5T (55-69T range) **or** 8 - 9 **or** 9 - 8 ≤ 10T (≥70T range)

NOTE: MMPI-2 T-scores are used by permission. Acknowledgement is given to Minnesota Multiphasic Personality Inventory-2. Copyrighted by the Regents of the University of Minnesota, 1989, U of M Press.

5. List Code-Type Issues

Begin with the issues unique to the two-point code at it's appropriate scale elevation. Thus, for Charles the report would include issues 1 through 12 (from the 70-80 T range), each followed by the 5 4 3 2 1 0 scale validating the issue, as in the sample below:

Issues (Present thoughts, feelings and concerns)

1. *Right now you are feeling somewhat defeated, hopeless and trapped like the world has let you down and the odds of your ever getting what you want are not good.*   5   4   3   2   1   0

2. *You probably also are feeling worthless, defective and unlovable.*   5   4   3   2   1   0

6. Consider Other Issues

We always supplement two-point issues with issues from the third highest scale and with issues from the fourth highest scale as well if these scales are greater than 60 T and less than 5 T-scores apart from the next highest scale. We also always include issues for **Scales 5** and **0,** regardless of T-score, but normally in the order they are coded. No fixed rules exist for the number or particular content of issues to add. The issues are listed roughly in order of importance or in order of frequency with which they are likely to occur. Usually we will include about five issues from each additional scale, but each therapist should decide what issues and how many issues to add based upon his or her own interest and experience.

Returning to Charles' results we note that **0** is the third highest scale (T equals 73), **8** is the fourth (T equals 72), and that both scales are greater than 60T and less than 5T apart. We would then add issues corresponding to T equals 73 for **Scale 0,** followed by issues for T equals 72 for **Scale 8.** In so doing we should note that the issues are no longer associated with the two-point code, but are for **Scales 0** and **8** respectively. Scale reference can be made simply by including it's number with the issue and extending the numbers in their original sequence, or by adding the scale to the issue and starting the numbers in a new sequence. For example, in the former; **Scale 0** is added to issues 13 and 14, etc, as follows:

> *0/13. You are shy, somewhat sensitive and extremely uncomfortable with strangers and in large groups of people.* 5 4 3 2 1 0
>
> *0/14. Around new people you probably feel self-conscious and insecure.* 5 4 3 2 1 0
>
> *0/15 etc . . .*

...and, adding **Scale 8** issues successively:

> *8/18. Right now the world is a rather confusing and frightening place for you.* 5 4 3 2 1 0

8/19. It is hard for you to understand other people's reactions to you. 5 4 3 2 1 0

8/20 etc . . .

We would then complete the issues by listing those for **Scale 5** where the T-score is 66, as follows:

5/23. Men with your profile usually have a good balance between their masculine and feminine sides.
5 4 3 2 1 0

5/24. You have some cultural and aesthetic interests but you also enjoy some traditionally masculine interests. *5 4 3 2 1 0*

7. Include the Background Experiences

Locate the background information associated with the code and write this in the next section of the report. When using the single scale approach, we often include background information from the second highest scale but always in the order of scale elevations. However, for Charles this would include only the material for the code, as follows:

Background Experiences

People with your profile often had a painful and difficult childhood. Perhaps your parents were cold, angry and unpredictably rejecting. One or both may have been authoritarian and unable to relate to you except when they punished you. Perhaps from an early age you had to rely on your own resources, numbing out your feelings in order to survive. 5 4 3 2 1 0

Throughout your life it has probably been hard for you to get close to people and express your feelings for fear that if you let down your guard people would take advantage of you or disappoint you. Perhaps something recently happened and you feel the same old feelings that you had as a child. You feel that you are not worth loving and that you are destined to be rejected. Nothing you do will make things better. If this is so, you may be protecting yourself by being emotionally distant from someone you actually care about. You may be reluctant to repair the rift for fear of being disappointed again.   5   4   3   2   1   0

8. List the Suggestions for Self-help

This is the final section of the report, which the therapist may or may not wish to include, modify, or expand. We usually will list the suggestions for the second highest scale as well as the first when resorting to the single scale approach. The statements as designed require no validation or verification. The suggestions in the case of Charles are as follows.

Self-help Suggestions

a. *Whenever you feel in a black mood or hopeless, try to find one small thing that you could do to make yourself feel better. No matter how small it may be, do it and do not give up.*

b. *Observe how small set-backs have a tendency to leave you feeling defeated and negative. When something starts to go well, watch that you don't expect it to go wrong and then give up before you really have given it a chance. Work on staying positive even though it may be hard for you.*

c. *Observe how often you focus on what is "wrong" at any given time rather than also noticing the things that go right. When something does go right, allow yourself to enjoy it.*

d. *Reduce your drug and alcohol intake. Whenever you feel tense, rather than using drugs or alcohol, find new ways of relieving the stress. Try to recognize stress before you do something impulsive.*

e. *People with your profile often benefit a great deal when they exercise regularly.*

9. The Single Scale Approach

For a number of clients their highest two scales will fail to match one of the 21 two-point codes; or, they will not have at least two scales with scores greater or equal to 55 T of which one is at least equal to 60 T; or, whose T-score difference between scales exceeds the range for the elevations given in Table 2. These results are not interpretable by the two-point approach and require use of the single scale material. In this instance, the therapist should skip steps 4 and 5 and proceed alternately to step 9 a, b, and c.

a. Identify the highest clinical scale and list in order all issues associated with that scales T-score elevation as given for MMPI-1 or MMPI-2. It will be helpful to indicate the scale number to which each issue belongs, which can be done by writing it before the issue in the numbering sequence. For example, the highest scale for the client below is 2, and so the issues associated with scale 2 would be listed 2/1., 2/2., 2/3., 2/etc., each followed by its own corresponding statement. It is also essential after each issue to include the scale (from 5 to 0) for validating the issue as indicated in the instructions at the beginning of the report.

b. Identify the second highest clinical scale and list in order a minimum of the first five (up to all) issues associated with that scales T-score elevation. There is no set rule for the number of second (third, fourth, or even fifth) scale issues to include in a report and we have used as many as 40 in the time of several separate feedback sessions. As with the highest scale above, it is always desirable to designate the scale to which each issue belongs, and it is always essential to include the six point scale (5 4 3 2 1 0) for validating each separate issue.

c. Return to Step 7 and continue.

Generally, the single scale approach will parallel the two-point or code-type approach in preparing the report but, as we have indicated above, with some variations. Take for example Dorothy's results, which are as follows:

DOROTHY'S MMPI-1 RESULTS

T Sc	<50 50 53 45 53 69 57 55 42 65 48 61 40 52
Scale	? L F K 1 2 3 4 5 6 7 8 9 0
Code	2673410759

The results from Step 1 are in accord with our stated purpose and instructions and are usable for feedback (i.e., **?** is less than 50T, **L** is less than 70T, and **K** is between 35 and 75T). Following Step 2, the report is formatted:

MMPI-1 Adult Feedback Report

> Client's Name: Dorothy   Gender: F
> Test Date: 8/15/88   Report Date: 8/17/88

> *Dorothy, your MMPI results suggest that you've completed the test in the following manner and that the following issues and experiences are important to you. Please read each and then* **circle** *on the scale following, the number corresponding to your feelings about it right now.*

5	4	3	2	1	0
Very True	*Mostly True*	*Partially True*	*Mostly False*	*Very False*	*Uncertain*

Taking Step 3 we next select the appropriate validity scale statements (for L = 50 and K = 45) and list them as follows:

Approach to the Test

> *Dorothy, the way you approached the test suggests that you try to avoid criticism for saying the "wrong" things.* 5 4 3 2 1 0

> *You answered the questions in a very frank and open way, admitting to how you feel and what troubles you without trying to put up a positive front.*
> 5 4 3 2 1 0

*Skipping to Step 9 we list all issues for the highest scale (**Scale 2**) within the T-range of 55-69, as for example:*

Issues (Current Thoughts, Feelings and Concerns)

2/1. Right now you are feeling a little more sad and dejected than you normally feel. 5 4 3 2 1 0

2/2. Perhaps you are feeling uncertain and less optimistic now because of a recent set-back or per- ceived loss. Or perhaps you are being somewhat cautious and circumspect by nature. 5 4 3 2 1 0

2/3. etc, . . . 2/11.

Next we list a minimum of the first five issues of the second highest scale, **Scale 6,** by designating the scale and numbering the issues in their listed order (i.e., 6/1., 6/2., . . . 6/11.) or in a continuous numerical sequence (i.e., 6/12., 6/13., . . . 6/16.). The therapist is encouraged in composing the report to eliminate statements that are redundant. Since, for example, **Scale 2** issue 11. (55-69 T) reads "Generally, however, your profile is that of a normal and healthy individual," it would not be necessary to repeat for **Scale 6** issue 1. (55-69 T) the sentence "your profile is essentially normal and it reveals a number of strengths." Thus the **Scale 6** issues, as numbered consecu- tively, would begin:

6/12. "You value being alert, rational and analyt- ical and you are generally an inquisitive person." 5 4 3 2 1 0

6/13, etc. . . . 6/16

At this point we typically look to the third highest scale which in this case is **Scale 8.** When the third scale appears as a peak (i.e., is higher than the scales on either side by greater than 5 T-scores) or is within 10 T-scores of the first and second scale, we will include the first five issues for it as well. In this instance **Scale 8** is greater than **Scale 7** by 13, and **Scale 9** by 21 T-scores respectively. Since it is also within 10 T-scores of

Scales 2 and *6,* we would continue to list the issues correspondingly. For example:

> *8/17. "You are a bright and creative person who enjoys your own fantasies and idiosyncracies."*
> *5   4   3   2   1   0*

> *8/18, etc. . . . 8/21*

Following this, the therapist should return to step 6 and proceed as indicated for *Scales 5* and *0.*

ILLUSTRATIVE FEEDBACK REPORT

The following summarizes the information essential to using this Guide and provides an example of a complete and properly prepared feedback report. It begins with the test results. The report itself first gives identifying data and the standard instructions for reading and validating the feedback material. It is then comprised of an approach statement for *Scales F* (65-74 T) and *K* (35-46 T) and listings of issues 1 to 17 for codetype (6-8/8-6 greater than 70 T), of five issues (0/18 to 0/22) for *Scale 0* (70-80 T), and five issues (5/23 to 5/27) for *Scale 5.* These are followed by codetype background experiences and, at the discretion of the therapist but on a separate page, the suggestions for self-help. In this instance where *0* is the third highest scale, no additional issues beyond *Scale 5* are included in the report.

ELLEN'S MMPI-1 RESULTS

T Sc	<50	40	70	36	48	57	40	69	34	73	63	78	68	71
Scale	?	L	F	K	1	2	3	4	5	6	7	8	9	0
Code	8604972135													

MMPI-1 Adult Feedback Report

Client's Name: Ellen   *Gender: F*
Test Date: 8/20/88   *Report Date: 8/22/88*

Ellen, your MMPI results suggest that you have completed the test in the following manner and that the following issues and experiences are important to you. Please read each and then circle on the scale following, the number corresponding to your feelings about it right now.

5	4	3	2	1	0
Very	*Mostly*	*Partially*	*Mostly*	*Very*	*Uncertain*
True	*True*	*True*	*False*	*False*	

Approach to the Test

Your profile suggests that you are experiencing a good deal of stress right now that is troubling you and you feel may be hard to manage. 5 4 3 2 1 0

You answered the questions in a very frank and open way admitting to how you feel and what troubles you without trying to put on a positive front. 5 4 3 2 1 0

Issues (Current thoughts, feelings and concerns)

1. Generally you are a person who has a number of strengths. For example, you are a creative and sensitive person. Your profile suggests, however, that you are going through a very difficult time right now. 5 4 3 2 1 0

2. It has always been easier for you to escape painful situations by turning to your inner-world of fantasy rather than to confront either people or the stressful situation. 5 4 3 2 1 0

3. Right now your sensitivity, creativity, and imagination may be working against you. 5 4 3 2 1 0

4. Presently, little in life seems to give you pleasure. Most of the time you feel alone, empty, and unhappy.
5 4 3 2 1 0

5. Perhaps the world is confusing to you right now and it is hard to connect or communicate with others in a meaningful way. 5 4 3 2 1 0

6. Other people seem to be wearing masks which makes it difficult to see or understand what is going on with them or what they are really thinking or feeling.
5 4 3 2 1 0

7. Most of the time you may live with a good deal of fear and confusion because the way people respond to you seems peculiar and hard to understand. 5 4 3 2 1 0

8. Perhaps you are feeling that other's are hostile, that they are harboring hostile intentions and feelings towards you.
5 4 3 2 1 0

9. Sometimes you may feel an empty numbness and other times a deep rage boils inside you. 5 4 3 2 1 0

10. It is hard to express that anger because you do not want to expose yourself and be attacked by others in return.
5 4 3 2 1 0

11. Occasionally when you feel that the hostility and anger from others is reaching dangerous proportions, you will lash out to defend yourself. 5 4 3 2 1 0

12. At these times you may think of violent ways to defend yourself, and you may lay elaborate plans that will pay back your enemies or eliminate them forever.
5 4 3 2 1 0

13. It may be hard for you to figure out what is real and what is imaginary which makes it hard to open up and let people know your thoughts and feelings.
5 4 3 2 1 0

14. Much of the time you probably blame yourself. You feel that you are defective, that there is something wrong with you, or that you are seriously broken or damaged inside.
5 4 3 2 1 0

15. The thoughts inside your head are so loud that you can almost hear them as voices talking to you.
5 4 3 2 1 0

16. Sometimes these voices may be telling you to protect yourself and get rid of your enemies and at other times the voices may be telling you to destroy yourself.
5 4 3 2 1 0

17. In either case, the world seems bleak, confusing, and frightening right now. 5 4 3 2 1 0

0/18 You are shy, somewhat sensitive and extremely uncomfortable with strangers and in large groups of people.
5 4 3 2 1 0

0/19. Around new people you probably feel self-conscious and insecure. 5 4 3 2 1 0

0/20. In new situations you may find yourself unable to converse comfortably. 5 4 3 2 1 0

0/21. Right now it may be hard for you to know who to trust or with whom to share your very sensitive feelings. You are often so easily hurt. 5 4 3 2 1 0

0/22. You are a person who rarely needs social stimulation and would often rather spend time by yourself.
5 4 3 2 1 0

5/23. Women with your profile tend to be both practical and idealistic. You have a good balance between your masculine and feminine sides. 5 4 3 2 1 0

5/24. They enjoy beauty and attractiveness but also can have some interests in how things work. 5 4 3 2 1 0

5/25. You are a person who likes gentle and sensitive companions who can understand your feelings and ideas. But you can also enjoy companions who like to get things done. *5 4 3 2 1 0*

5/26. In fact, talking about feelings, accomplishments and relationships with family and friends is important to you and may occupy a significant part of your time. *5 4 3 2 1 0*

5/27. Generally you enjoy a balance between romantic ideas and practical things. *5 4 3 2 1 0*

Background and Early Learning Experiences

"People with your profile were often extremely sensitive as children. They were sensitive to uncaring, to anger and to put-downs. They grew up in an environment where they experienced a good deal of hostility. Perhaps one of your parents was particularly harsh or even cruel at times, especially when you did something which displeased them. Perhaps you were subjected to the harshness of siblings or friends as well. If so, you very likely learned then to avoid situations where you felt vulnerable to the people who have control over you or who might evaluate or criticize you. You may have escaped into daydreams as a way of numbing yourself to the pain of humiliation. *5 4 3 2 1 0*

Perhaps right now you are feeling vulnerable, alone, and sensitive to being criticized, harmed or emotionally abandoned. Perhaps someone who was previously supportive has withdrawn their support and you feel angry, hurt or frightened. This may remind you of your childhood when you felt frightened but couldn't count on support from others for fear of humiliation. *5 4 3 2 1 0*

Self-help Suggestions

1. Often medication can help to take away that sense of dread and anxiety. Should your thoughts become so loud that you hear them as voices, perhaps medication will help you feel calmer and think clearly. There are types of

medicines available that can help you to think more clearly without interfering with your ability to see clearly what is going on around you. You should discuss this with your therapist.

2. At first it may be very hard for you to trust your therapist because it is hard for you to trust anyone. It will be important to discuss this with your therapist as well.

3. If your therapist makes you angry, it is important to tell him or her and you will discover that you will not be attacked or humiliated for expressing those feelings. People with your profile have often swallowed their anger in order to avoid being picked on or degraded. Perhaps you and your therapist can work on ways for you to express anger when you feel it so that it won't back up and accumulate. Those bottled up feelings cause you to become tense and confused.

4. Although you are probably feeling terrible right now, it is important that you do not blame yourself and see yourself as defective or impared. The feelings you are experiencing now are normal for someone who has been through the kind of pain and stress that you have been through and with help you can feel better.

CHAPTER 4

LISTING OF SCALE AND CODE CHARACTERISTICS

This chapter provides single-scale and paired-scale or two-point (*viz.* codetype) characteristics. Each scale or codetype information begins with some empirical correlates associated with the scale or code and grouped into categories classified by content. First appear the validity scales which separate statements for various T levels indicating the client's "approach to the test." The T-scores given for MMPI-2 are adjusted and based on the new norms and on the content of the corresponding feedback. It is important to note that all of the *codetype* material is based on the original norms of MMPI-1. Only for the single scales are separate T-score values given for MMPI-2. As we have already indicated, the person using MMPI-2 who wishes to employ the codetype material must first convert the raw scores of MMPI-2 to the original norms, which can be done by reference to the T-tables published in various sources (e.g., Dahlstrom, Welsh, & Dahlstrom, 1972; Friedman, Webb, & Levak, 1989; Graham, 1987; Greene, 1980; Hathaway & McKinley, 1983).

Next appear the clinical scales beginning with scale 1, which is followed by the selected codetypes associated with the scale in ascending numerical order (e.g., 1-2/2-1, 1-3/3-1). The remaining scales follow consecutively from **Scale 2** through **Scale 0.** Characteristics of the scales and codes are organized into introductory and medication notes for the therapist, and issues, background experiences, and suggestions for self-help for the client.

VALIDITY SCALES

L SCALE

Descriptors

Concerns: Honesty, morality, social propriety, desire to make favorable impressions, fear of being criticized and judged.

Thoughts: Conventional, rigid, inflexible, naive, insightless, unoriginal, virtuous, moralistic.

Emotions: Self-controlled, denying, repressing.

Traits: Conforming, conscientious, perfectionistic, scrupulous, self-righteous.

Approach to the Test

T-score: MMPI-1, 60-69; MMPI-2, 60-79

(Client's name), the way you approached the test suggests that you were feeling vulnerable to being criticized and judged. You have very high standards and so it is easy for you to feel vulnerable to some kind of moral review. Perhaps you felt that the test would 'expose' you in some way and you approached it very cautiously.

T-score: MMPI-1, 50-59; MMPI-2, 50-59

(Client's name), the way you approached the test suggests that you try to avoid criticism for saying the 'wrong' things.

NOTE: MMPI-2 T-scores are used by permission. Acknowledgement is given to Minnesota Multiphasic Personality Inventory-2 copyrighted by the Regents of the University of Minnesota, 1989, University of Minnesota Press.

F SCALE

Descriptors

Concerns: Contact with reality, question of identity, not being taken seriously, special life experiences (i.e., personal, health, family, work, religious), fear of mental and emotional distress.

Thoughts: Deviant, unusual, confused, retarded, opinionated, curious, delusional, hallucinatory; deficits in attention, concentration, judgement.

Emotions: Complex, withdrawn, alien, feeling anxious, moody, dissatisfied, confused, restless.

Traits: Unconventional, nonconforming.

Approach to Test

T-score: MMPI-1, > 80; MMPI-2, > 85

Your profile suggests that you may be panicked about how much stress you are under right now. You may be so frightened that you are confused about what is happening to you and you want guidance as to what you can do about it.

T-score: MMPI-1, 75-80; MMPI-2, 75-85

Your profile suggests that you may be experiencing a great deal of stress right now. It is troubling you and causes you to fear it may be unmanageable.

T-score: MMPI-1, 65-74; MMPI-2, 65-74

Your profile suggests that you may be experiencing a good deal of stress right now that troubles you and makes you feel it may be difficult to manage.

T-score: MMPI-1, 55-64; MMPI-2, 55-64

Your profile suggests that you may be experiencing some stress right now that is troubling you but does not feel unmanageable.

K SCALE

Descriptors: High Scores

Concerns: Problems in everyday living, maintaining self-focus and a balance between self-approval and self-criticism.

Thoughts: Defensive, non-disclosing, cautions about revealing self, lacking insight and understanding, intolerant.

Emotions: Inhibited, constricted.

Traits: Shy, independent, self-reliant, self-controlled, positive self-concept, high ego strength.

Descriptors: Medium Scores

Concerns: Problems in everyday living, maintaining self-focus and a balance between self-approval and self-criticism.

Thoughts: Clear thinking, wide interests, capacity for dealing with daily problems, balance between self-protection and self-disclosure.

Emotions: Adequate resources, good coping skills, few signs of emotional disturbance.

Traits: Enthusiastic, verbal, self-reliant, independent, enterprising.

Descriptors: Low Scores

Concerns: Inability to cope, loss of control, not being taken seriously, being socially awkward and uncomfortable, experiencing acute and severe distress.

Thoughts: Confused, self-dissatisfied, lacking insight, self-critical, self-disclosing, excessively open and revealing.

Emotions: Inhibited, cynical, inadequate coping mechanisms.

Traits: Sarcastic, fault-finding, self-depreciating, negative self-concept, low ego-strength, suspicious, retiring, compliant.

Approach to Test

T-score: MMPI-1, 67-75; MMPI-2, 62-70

Your test results suggest that you are a person who is 'hard to read' emotionally. Normally you are not openly nor strongly expressive so that people will have to multiply the intensity of your words to appreciate a sense of empathy for you. For example, if you say you are 'somewhat upset' you may in fact be very upset. Sometimes people may mistake your emotional reserve for coldness or indifference.

T-score: MMPI-1, 59-66; MMPI-2, 54-61

You answered the questions in a way suggesting that you deal with your thoughts and feelings well enough so that you are rarely unbalanced by them.

T-score: MMPI-1, 47-58; MMPI-2, 45-53

You answered the questions openly without trying to be too self-critical. You tried to be honest and accurate about how you feel and what troubles you at this time.

T-score: MMPI-1, 36-46; MMPI-2, 40-44

You answered the questions in a very frank and open way admitting to how you feel and what troubles you without trying to put up a positive front.

CLINICAL SCALES

SCALE 1

Descriptors

Concerns/Complaints: Physical health, disease, fatigue, weakness, fear of body damage, pain, and death.

Thoughts: Rigid, selfish, self-defeating, lacking insight, critical, cynical, dull.

Emotions: Unhappy, dissatisfied, pessimistic, unenthusiastic, physically ill and/or handicapped; lacking anxiety, drive, ambition; expressing anger and hostility indirectly, perhaps through bodily symptoms.

Traits/Behaviors: Egocentric, self-centered, narcissistic, demanding, stubborn, whiney, complaining, controlling, manipulative, dependent, irritable; also conscientious, careful, considerate, sincere.

Therapist's Notes

Scale 1 elevations are associated with a fear of bodily harm, physical illness, pain, and death. The assumption is that clients with elevated *Scale 1* scores are constantly afraid of body damage and illness. Intense physical sensations, especially unusual ones, are frightening because they fear that the symptom will lead to increasing pain, serious illness, and eventually death.

Additionally the hypothesis is that a childhood illness in these patients or in their families, or physical abuse in childhood during which they feared for their life conditioned a variety of self-protective behaviors that shielded them from further injury. This self-protective response reduced psychomotor activity. Their focus of attention is on maintaining physical integrity and the availability of medical help. Attempts to reassure them and then change their focus of attention to their psychological problems only increases their fear that no one understands their physical illness, and that they will be overwhelmed by pain and have no one to whom to turn. A more effective approach would be through desensitization: The patient repeatedly retells the painful, frightening earlier experiences, verbally and with physical expression, discharging the feelings that taught the client to overprotect against bodily harm, illness, or loss of body function.

Medication Notes

Patients with an elevated *Scale 1* are very focused on medication. The placebo effect can be powerful with such patients but rarely of lasting effect. Side-effects are distressing to these patients because they are sensitive to their body responses. Drowsiness or even relaxation can be distressing to patients with an elevated *Scale 1* because they experience all physical sensations as potentially dangerous.

Anxiolytic medications in low doses can be useful for these patients but beware of dependency. Tricyclic antidepressants, while potentially useful, cause "intolerable" side-effects. Trazadone, a new antidepressant which appears to be free from most annoying side-effects, and buspirone, a new anxiolytic, may decrease fear for these patients without disabling side-effects.

FEEDBACK STATEMENTS

Issues—T-score: MMPI-1, $\geq$ 80; MMPI-2, > 75

1. *Your body is a constant source of anxiety and fear for you, so right now your worries about health take up most of your time and energy.*

2. *This constant fear and worry about your physical health may be taking its toll and leaving you feeling extremely defeated, pessimistic and bitter. You may even find yourself resigned to living the rest of your life chronically ill and in pain.*

3. *So much of your time is spent worrying about your physical well-being that it is hard for you to accomplish anything, to find outside interests or things you can do that won't incur additional pain.*

4. Symptoms such as headache, stomachache, weakness, fatigue, and shakiness are probably common right now.

5. You also may consult a number of physicians for your symptoms without any benefit or relief.

6. You are a person who tries to conserve your energy; unexpected demands on you can make you angry and upset.

7. When people try to force you not to focus on your physical problems you tend to resist them. You feel they don't understand what you are going through. They do not know how frightened you are.

8. Financial worries, family problems, confrontations, or heavy responsibilities tend to aggravate your physical problems.

9. You probably have to rely on others to help you in your daily living; this is usually very frustrating for you.

10. If so, you may have developed a number of ways to get people to help you. At the same time, however, you resent not being able to do things for yourself.

Issues—T-score: MMPI-1, 70-79; MMPI-2, 66-75

1. At this time your health takes up a lot of your time and energy, and your body is a continued source of worry for you.

2. Your apprehension and concern about your physical health may leave you feeling somewhat defeated, pessimistic and bitter. You wonder if you will have to spend the rest of your life in this kind of pain and anguish.

3. You may spend so much time worrying about your physical well-being that it is difficult for you to attempt to accomplish anything; you fear incurring additional pain.

4. Symptoms such as headaches, stomachache, weakness, fatigue, and shakiness may be frequent and recurring.

5. You may consult a number of physicians for your symptoms without getting benefit or relief and without feeling understood.

6. You try very hard to conserve your energy, so when unexpected demands are made on you, you get angry.

7. If people try to force you to do things, you may find yourself resisting them. You feel that they don't really understand what you are going through.

8. Financial worries, family problems, responsibilities, or anticipating a confrontation with some one can aggravate your physical symptoms.

9. Occasionally you may have to rely on others to help you take care of things because of your physical problems; this may be frustrating for you and for them.

10. If so, then you may have developed ways of getting people to help you, even though you resent not being able to do everything for yourself.

Issues—T-score: MMPI-1, 55-69; MMPI-2, 56-65

1. Your concerns over your physical well-being may be a source of worry for you.

2. You are more focused on your health than usual. You may have been ill recently or are afraid of becoming ill.

3. Your focus on health may be related to an illness of your own or someone else's illness which frightens you because of its unanticipated severity.

4. Periodically you may find yourself unable to do something because you don't feel well enough or have strength enough to try.

5. Periods of fatigue and shifting aches and pains may be related to stresses such as dealing with accumulated responsibilities or the possibility of a difficult confrontation.

6. *If people try to force you to do something when you are not feeling well, you may refuse to do it or you may even do the opposite because they don't understand how bad you feel.*

Issues—T-score: MMPI-1, 40-49; MMPI-2, 41-55

1. *Your profile shows that you have fewer bodily concerns and worries than is normal for people your age.*

2. *You are the type of person who pushes yourself physically.*

3. *If you are ever ill, you tend to avoid dealing with the illness until it is absolutely necessary.*

4. *Any illness or physical disability makes you angry and resentful about having to care for your body.*

Issues—T-score: MMPI-1 < 40; MMPI-2, < 41

1. *Your profile suggests that you can be somewhat cavalier in your approach to your body and to physical illness generally.*

2. *You tend to ignore physical symptoms until you have to take care of them and then you become reluctant and resentful—somehow blaming your body for letting you down.*

3. *Your tendency to ignore physical problems and to push yourself beyond reasonable limits may relate to a childhood in which one of your parents was ill and you felt they used their illness in some way that was upsetting to you.*

Background and Early Learning Experiences
(Applicable for profiles with elevations greater than 60 for MMPI-1 and MMPI-2.)

People with your profile often had periods during childhood when they were seriously ill or extremely frightened by the possibility of being physically harmed. Perhaps an explosive or abusive parent, or perhaps a serious accident or illness in the family predisposed you to this fear for your physical well-being. If you have been terrified in the past for your health and physical safety and/or suffered physical illness or injury, this may cause you to stay in bed right now or learn everything you can about various illnesses to protect yourself against the possibility of physical harm. Even minor physical upsets might frighten you for fear that they could lead to something worse.

Self-help Suggestions

1. When your physical problems and fears seem to get worse, see if in fact you're not angry or even afraid of something else. Keep a diary of times when your symptoms get worse and see if they are linked to stress.

2. Try to enjoy the times you do feel physically well. Give yourself permission to let go of your fears about your body whenever you feel well.

CODETYPE 1-2/2-1

Descriptors

Concerns/Complaints: Physical health, somatic symptoms, pain, weakness, insomnia, fatigue, unhappiness, tension, stress, weight, loss of interest, forgetfulness, excessive drinking, blackouts, alcoholism.

Thoughts: Physical health, lacking in insight, indecision, self-blaming, self-deprecating, avoiding responsibility, worrisome.

Emotions: Feeling weak, tired, fatigued, depressed, anxious, fearful, restless, irritable, worried, self-conscious, insecure, denying, somatizing, repressing.

Traits/Behaviors: Passive, dependent, unassertive, rigid, high-strung, over-reacting to minor stress.

Therapist's Notes

Clients with this profile conform to the stereotype of the disgruntled medical patient who is angry and complains about the unfairness of an illness or injury. The profile reflects a blocked mourning process. The hypothesis is that these clients discharge their anger and sadness about their losses through physical symptoms. These clients crave personal care and their needs for reassurance are met by their physician's attention to their physical ailments. Therapy should focus on helping them express their anger and their sadness about past losses without blaming themselves. Gestalt techniques in which their body "talks out" feelings may help them discharge the fear and anguish reflected in their physical symptoms.

Medication Notes

Patients with this profile generally do not like psychological explanations for their anxiety or depression. They complain more frequently of side-effects from psychotropic medications and need more "hand-holding" than other patients as far as medications are concerned. If the prescribing physician has little patience for constant reassurance, medical intervention will probably fail to provide symptom relief.

These patients can respond to antidepressants. A bed-time dose of trazadone or a tricyclic such as imiprimine can restore disturbed sleep patterns and ultimately relieve the depressed mood. Anxiolytic drugs may be indicated if anxiety is impairing daily function. If a benzodiazepine is used, it should be time-contingent, not anxiety-reducing contingent. Beware of patients becoming dependent on anti-anxiety medications. Non-habi-tuating buspirone or imiprimine may be more useful for long-term treatment of anxiety.

FEEDBACK STATEMENTS

Issues—T-score: MMPI-1, > 80; MMPI-2, NA (Not Applicable)

1. *At this time you probably feel overwhelmed by worry, anxiety and tension.*

2. *Very likely you spend a good deal of time worrying, feeling that your best years are over and the future looks hopeless and bleak for you.*

3. *You may even confuse symptoms of anxiety with symptoms of heart attacks or some other life threatening condition.*

4. *Your health is a major concern to you. You may have many physical worries, such as stomachaches, diarrhea, backaches and headaches. Perhaps there are some symptoms that increase during times of stress and die down when you feel less stressed.*

5. *You may spend a good deal of time seeing physicians, but rarely do your visits to the doctor bring you any real relief or satisfaction. Sometimes you feel downright frustrated and angry that your body gives you so much trouble or that the doctors seem so incapable of giving you good care.*

6. *Your physical symptoms may also increase whenever you have to confront a difficult situation with others, or whenever you are worried about financial or family responsibilities.*

7. *Confrontations of any kind are extremely upsetting to you, so you tend to avoid them.*

8. *Consequently you may often feel taken advantage of. For this reason you are apprehensive about dealing with people who you see as forceful and assertive.*

9. *People with your profile often feel fatigued—they have to push themselves to get things done. Sometimes, when you feel utterly exhausted, new and unexpected demands make you feel overwhelmed.*

10. *Your sexual activity is likely to be reduced; so also your alertness and general energy. This makes you feel that the best years of your life are being wasted.*

11. *You probably have serious bouts with the "blues": Times when you feel hopeless about the future and guilty about things that happened in the past.*

12. *You may feel stuck—unable to make decisions and unable to concentrate effectively on what you are doing.*

13. *At these times you may have trouble sleeping, either with getting to sleep or with being able to sleep through the night.*

14. *You may spend considerable time worrying about what might go wrong next. You want to be ready for this and don't want to be caught off guard.*

15. *It may be hard for you to relax and enjoy life because you expect bad things to crop up at any moment and spoil everything.*

Issues—T-score: MMPI-1, 70-79; MMPI-2, NA

1. *Right now you seem to feel worried, anxious and tense.*

2. *You worry about your health and feel that life is passing you by. You can't think of anything much to look forward to.*

3. *Sometimes people with this profile experience symptoms of anxiety and mistake them for a heart attack or some other serious illness.*

4. *You experience headaches, stomach upsets, backaches or dizziness from time to time.*

5. *You probably seek medical help, but too often treatment seems ineffectual and your symptoms come and go for no good reason.*

6. *Your physical symptoms may also intensify whenever you confront a difficult situation with others.*

7. *In fact, confrontations of any kind upset you a good deal, so you would rather avoid them.*

8. *You may often feel taken advantage of by others. This makes you feel apprehensive and cautious with people you see as forceful and assertive.*

9. *You are easily tired and fatigued. You find that you have to drive yourself in order to get ordinary things done and you feel you have little endurance.*

10. *Your sex drive may also be somewhat lower than before. This, together with your low energy level, contributes to periodic bouts of pessimism about ever being happy again.*

11. *You probably have blue moods when you feel despondent about the future and guilty about the past.*

12. *During these times decision-making becomes even more difficult than usual and concentration takes great effort.*

13. Your sleep may be fitful with difficulties getting to sleep or difficulties sleeping through the night.

14. You worry about what can go wrong next. You want to be ready for the next disaster so it doesn't catch you off guard.

15. It is difficult for you to enjoy anything for fear that it won't last—disaster lurks around the corner.

Issues—T-score: MMPI-1, 55-69; MMPI-2, NA

1. Your profile is within the normal range but it suggests that from time to time you are prone to worry and feeling blue. These feelings may center around health problems.

2. You may have some physical worries such as backache, headache, stomachaches, or chest pains.

3. Confrontations are difficult for you so you try to avoid them and then find yourself taken advantage of more often than you like.

4. Your tendency to avoid conflict and give in to forceful people may aggravate you and lead to episodes of guilt and self-recrimination.

5. You may complain of tiredness and a feeling that your strength and endurance have diminished.

6. Your mood may be less buoyant than you would like so that small setbacks depress you more easily than before.

7. During these times you may find that your sex drive is diminished as is your general alertness and energy.

8. Decisions may be more difficult to make at these times, and your sleep may be fitful and disturbed.

9. You are cautions about "counting your chickens before they hatch"—that is, you do not want to get excited about new possibilities that might only fall through in the end.

In your caution, you want to protect yourself against possible disappointment.

Background and Early Learning Experiences

During childhood, people with your profile often experienced periods of intense fear about the possibility of physical harm. It is possible that your own apprehension about health comes from the fact that you or someone close to you was seriously ill or injured when you were young. You may also have had an explosive or abusive parent who frightened you. If so, this may have instilled in you a fear of anger because angry outbursts may lead to violence or pain. All this worry and concern you suffer about the possibility of illness or disaster might best be understood as your way of being ready for anything. You don't ever want to be unprepared or caught off guard. You probably won't allow yourself to relax and trust that "all will be well"—that way you protect yourself from eventual disappointment. The trouble, however, is that right now this way of protecting yourself isn't working for you: so little in life seems bright or promising, and you won't let yourself look forward or hope in the future.

Self-help Suggestions

1. *Whenever you find yourself worrying about your health see if you could also be worrying about some other problems or responsibilities. Make a list of all your other worries besides your physical ones.*

2. *Whenever your physical symptoms are aggravated, see if you could be tense about someone being angry with you. Or perhaps you are angry with someone else? If so, try to face that person directly.*

3. *When you feel overwhelmed by worries, try to stop those thoughts. Think about something that you can do now. Make a list of past worries that never came true.*

4. *Force yourself to face easy confrontations whenever you can; you will learn, that way, to be more assertive. Then you can cope with more difficult confrontations in the future.*

5. *Start a program of regular, physical exercise.*

CODETYPE 1-3/3-1

Descriptors

Concerns/Complaints: Tension; aches and pains in the head, neck, chest, back, arms and legs; numbness, blurred vision, insomnia, weakness, fatigue, dizziness, eating problems, nausea, vomiting, forgetfulness; symptoms worsen when stressed; fear of physical and emotional pain.

Thoughts: Lacking in insight, heterosexual, and social skills; preferring only medical (organic) explanation of symptoms; resisting rational thinking.

Emotions: Feeling weak, tired, insecure, perplexed; harboring anger, hostility, resentment; overcontrolled, deriving secondary gain, needing attention, affection, sympathy; denying, projecting, repressing.

Traits/Behaviors: Immature, dependent, passive, docile, overly responsible, industrious, achievement oriented, competitive.

Therapist's Notes

Clients with this profile complain of fatigue and exhaustion, but rarely of depression. The hypothesis is that their ambivalence toward therapy reflects their fear that they will somehow be judged as "bad" and then rejected by others. The assumption is that seeing physicians for their physical symptoms acts as a source of comfort and reassurance, and that confronting them with nonorganic or psychological explanations is frightening so they therefore may resist it.

These clients typically block out angry and sad feelings associated with the mourning process which is considered by many as a major factor in depression. They often cry, but not about specific painful losses. On occasion they can express anger but usually in an indirect manner and not about the specific event or person responsible. This is because they are afraid to express anger or sadness. Their response to pain is to deny it. They prefer to look at the bright side of things and to develop physical symptoms as a response to the stress of denial.

The primary goal of therapy is to help the patient engage and finish mourning for any past losses. These patients are often afraid to feel intense emotions so therapy should proceed slowly. Training in assertiveness will help them deal with confrontations. Catharsis and systematic desensitization might help relieve the stored up feelings which prevent them from engaging *emotional and psychological* pain. Relaxation exercises are useful to help relieve some of their physical symptoms.

Gestalt techniques to help them express their anger can be useful though they may resist playing out a role for fear they will lose control and then be overwhelmed by their fears. They will need encouragement to be assertive for they fear that confrontation with others will repeat their childhood experience of loss. They make positive therapeutic gains when they can express anger toward their therapist and discover that they have not been emotionally abandoned by the therapist.

Medication Notes

Potentially addicting medications are best avoided for these patients. They tend to develop rapid habituation to drugs which lower anxiety, whether caused by physical or emotional pain. They tend to be distressed by any usual side-effects of psychotropic drugs, and they also tend to be placebo-responsive. If anxiety is disabling, imiprimine may help to lower anxiety and alleviate the underlying depression.

FEEDBACK STATEMENTS

Issues—T-score: MMPI-1, ≥ 70; MMPI-2, NA (Not Applicable)

1. *Your profile indicates that you have grown accustomed to accepting a great deal of pain and discomfort.*

2. *You are probably in pain and misery most of the time but you value being cheerful and positive about things so you try to live with the pain and endure it, and even be cheerful about it.*

3. You probably experience a variety of physical symptoms such as headaches, backaches, stomach upsets, tingling in your hands and feet, numbness, and nausea.

4. Your physical symptoms very likely get worse under stress, especially if you are in a situation where you have to confront somebody or if somebody confronts or is angry with you.

5. Seeing physicians to help you deal with your health concerns might be frightening because you anticipate that they will become impatient and angry with you and not attend to the full extent of your physical concerns.

6. Furthermore, you worry whether the doctor will discover some new and terrible illness. At the same time, if the doctor doesn't find ways to help you, it leaves you feeling hopeless and afraid.

7. You worry a good bit of the time about what might possibly go wrong with your body next. This constant concern about your health leaves little energy to think about pleasant, happy things that might spark your interest.

8. People with your profile often suffer from feelings of complete exhaustion, so even small demands on your energy can make you angry.

9. You probably find that you have to push yourself to accomplish even some basic chores.

10. You are a very sensitive person, so that being hurt or rejected is very painful for you and you dread having to perhaps hurt or reject someone else.

11. You will spend a lot of energy trying to avoid painful confrontations even to the point of wanting to deny what is unpleasant. You hope that if you just ignore the unpleasantness, it will just go away.

Issues—T-score: MMPI-1, 55-69; MMPI-2, NA

1. *Your profile, which is essentially normal, suggests that you are under some level of tension at this time. You are trying to be brave so you hold in your feelings, are polite, and try to keep everything running smoothly and quietly.*

2. *You try to look at the bright side of things and won't allow yourself to get down or depressed about some of the problems you are having.*

3. *However, trying to remain positive in the face of problems may stress you physically, you may suffer from occasional headaches, stomachaches, backaches, or nausea.*

4. *If so, these symptoms will tend to get worse when you have to deal with confrontations, when you anticipate that someone is going to become angry with you, or when you have to take on difficult responsibilities.*

5. *There are times when you may find yourself crying or feeling blue and you just don't know why you're feeling this way.*

6. *Sometimes people with your profile will cry and laugh at the same time. This is often because they have experienced some sad things in life which they couldn't let themselves mourn over or even feel. They fear that those painful feelings might flood them and overwhelm them. If that is your experience, you may find that periodically this sadness just seeps out a little at a time and you might cry.*

7. *Your desire to stay positive then might be revealed by your trying to laugh through the tears.*

8. *You love to please others, so as a "pleaser," anger and conflict are difficult for you to express or confront.*

Background and Early Learning Experiences

Some people with this profile were reared by an angry or explosive parent who frightened or even terrified them. Others experienced some extreme loss or losses and had no one to whom to turn who would help them cope with their fear and accompanying sadness. Their response was to try to numb out the feelings of emotional pain. They worked to avoid feeling hurt and overwhelmed. Their smiling attempts to be positive in the face of pain is their defense—being cheery when they really are afraid.

Sometimes they have difficulty remembering their child-hoods, especially periods that may have been painful. You probably have a tendency to deal with unpleasant things by trying to look on the happy or positive side. Being so positive may interfere in your relationships and make it difficult to explore problems because you don't like to deal with negativity and conflict.

Self-help Suggestions

1. When your physical symptoms seem to get worse, check to see if in fact you are anxious—afraid to face some conflict or afraid of being angry with somebody close to you.

2. When you feel strong enough to stand up for yourself, tell others when you feel angry towards them—practice confronting others honestly—so that the anger doesn't build up inside of you and cause you tension.

3. Work on giving yourself permission to do what you want to do. Be less concerned about what you "ought" to be doing for others, which is often only done at your own expense.

SCALE 2

Descriptors

Concerns/Complaints: Low self-confidence, poor self-esteem, security fears, low morale, unhappiness, depression, worries, anxiety, somatic symptoms, inability to concentrate; fear of irretrievable loss.

Thoughts: Worrisome, indecisive, self-critical, self-deprecating, self-defeating, distressed, slow, retarded, silent, dark, gloomy, retiring, guilt-ridden, narrow, self-blaming.

Emotions: Feeling sad, blue, unhappy, irritable, dissatisfied, discouraged, defeated, useless, worthless, inadequate, inhibited; tearful, crying, nonaggressive, intrapunitive, overcontrolled.

Traits/Behaviors: Shy, retiring, cautious, critical, anxious, depressed, slow moving, sluggish, pessimistic; also deliberate, objective, realistic, contemplative, conventional.

Therapist's Notes

The hypothesis is that **Scale 2** elevations are associated with the perceived or actual loss of some highly valued physical or emotional object. The assumption is that clients with elevated **Scale 2** scores respond to this loss by blocking out feelings of need or want in order to avoid the pain of possible further loss. They remain too paralyzed in the despair to enjoy the present. These clients may be willing to discuss their past losses and the feelings of dispair of ever being happy again but therapy must encourage the expression of anger and sadness about these losses. Furthermore, they need to be freed of blaming themselves for these unhappy feelings and losses.

Medication Notes

In high elevations (MMPI-1, $\geq$ 80; MMPI-2, > 75) medication is often essential. Trazadone and the tricyclic antidepressants are commonly used antidepressants. Lithium is used in those patients who have a clinical diagnosis of manic depressive illness, depressed type. The MAO inhibitors are used when the patient's depression fails to respond to the other antidepressants.

Patients with a high score on **Scale 2** only are not a homogeneous group in their response to medications. Some respond quickly to trazadone or another common antidepressant. Others, perhaps those whose depression is characterological, resist medication because it disturbs an equilibrium that they have established for themselves.

These patients, after intensive uncovering therapy, often develop other kinds of profiles (e.g., 2/7/8 or 2/4/7/8) which may explain why they did not initially respond to the medication. In some cases, where no history of depression exists and the present disturbance is due to a recent loss, medication may not be necessary. The presence of recent vegetative signs of depression is a good indicator that medication could be helpful.

FEEDBACK STATEMENTS

Issues—T-score: MMPI-1, > 80; MMPI-2, > 75

1. *You have a number of strengths. You are generally a thoughtful, circumspect, and analytical person who takes life and responsibilities very seriously.*

2. *However, right now some of your strengths may be working against you, for you are feeling very dejected, gloomy, and depressed.*

3. *There seems to be little in life right now that gives you much pleasure.*

4. *You are probably spending most of your time thinking about the past, feeling guilty about things you've done or said, and feeling hopeless about things ever changing.*

5. *You feel sad most of the time with periods when life feels absolutely unbearable.*

6. *There is little that you enjoy right now so it is hard to feel motivated to do ordinary tasks.*

7. *While you may be able to do some basic chores, you may find little motivation to pursue enjoyable activities.*

8. In fact low energy is probably a cause of concern to you.

9. Even the smallest effort leaves you feeling tired and depleted.

10. Life seems to pass you by and you feel as though you are missing out.

11. Unfortunately, you probably blame yourself for your loss of energy and lack of interest. This compounds your sense of hopelessness, helplessness, and despair.

12. Your sleep may also be constantly interrupted so you awaken feeling tired and without energy. Your appetite may be markedly diminished, or you may take comfort in eating.

13. Your interest in sex may be low. You find it difficult to concentrate, make decisions, and plan for the future.

14. Guilt is a constant companion. You blame yourself for every mistake or omission you made in the past.

Issues—T-score: MMPI-1, 70-79; MMPI-2, 66-75

1. You have a number of strengths. You are generally a thoughtful, circumspect and analytical person who takes life and its responsibilities seriously.

2. Right now, however, some of your strengths may be working against you. You are feeling dejected, down, and depressed.

3. Right now life is not as pleasant as it could be or has been for you in the past.

4. You are probably spending most of your time thinking about the past, feeling guilty about the things you've said or done, the mistakes you feel you have made, and feeling pessimistic about getting out of this rut.

5. Your mood is often dark with periods of painful sadness.

6. Right now it seems that it is hard for you to get moving and to accomplish all your usual chores and tasks.

7. Perhaps you are able to do your basic chores, but once you have finished these it is very difficult for you to generate energy for other activities.

8. Your level of energy may in fact be a source of some concern to you since the smallest effort exhausts you, leaving you tired and worn out.

9. This makes seeking out new interests or being involved in life very difficult.

10. Likely you blame yourself for your low energy and lack of interests. This adds to your sense of feeling hopeless and powerless.

11. Your sleep may be disturbed frequently, so you awaken feeling tired, and with little energy.

12. Your interest in sex may be low and also your ability to concentrate and make decisions.

Issues—T-score: MMPI-1, 55-69; MMPI-2, 56-65

1. Right now you are feeling a little more sad and dejected than you normally feel.

2. Perhaps you are feeling uncertain and less optimistic now because of a recent set-back or perceived loss. Or perhaps you are somewhat cautious and circumspect by nature.

3. You are feeling less optimistic and hopeful about the future than usual. You experience periods of guilt and anxiety about the mistakes you have made in the past.

4. Perhaps a recent loss or perceived loss has made you reluctant to invest hope or optimism in the future for fear you may suffer another loss or disappointment.

5. You also may be experiencing a little more guilt and anxiety than you normally do.

6. You are probably a little more circumspect than usual and less likely to take risks.

7. Perhaps you are analyzing mistakes that you made and blaming yourself for making them.

8. You may experience less energy and interest in life than you would like right now.

9. Daily activities may seem burdensome and tiring and so you guard against getting involved in new ones.

10. When your worries accumulate, your sleep suffers as does your interest in sex.

Issues—T-score: MMPI-1, 40-49; MMPI-2, 41-55

1. You are a person who generally stays positive and optimistic, with an even and available flow of energy.

2. Things rarely get you down for very long and when you do get down you easily bounce back.

3. You believe that people can solve their own problems if they only try.

Issues—T-score: MMPI-1, and MMPI-2, < 40

1. Your profile indicates that you are determined never to let anything get you down.

2. This may mean that even when real losses occur you refuse to succumb to bad feelings about them.

3. Other people's depressions or bad moods probably irritate you because you believe that we can all feel better if we just work on it.

Background and Early Learning Experiences for Elevated Profiles

People with your profile often had childhoods with little opportunity for play or carefree periods of pleasure. Perhaps a parental illness, divorce, or the early death of a parent or brother and sister left you with more responsibility than a child can reasonably be expected to handle. Or perhaps some more recent loss has left you feeling that happiness is hopelessly unattainable to you, and that life will only become more difficult and painful in the future. In any instance, you probably feel badly about yourself and blame yourself for the losses in your past. Your self-image is poor and it is hard right now to see how anything you do could make things better.

Self-help Suggestions for Elevated T-scores

1. *Try to find small rewards and pleasures that you can give yourself on a daily basis and keep a record of these.*

2. *When you are feeling pessimistic about the future, force yourself (if necessary) to write down some of the things that have gone well for you recently, so you can keep things in perspective.*

3. *Try to stop from constantly blaming yourself for things you think have gone wrong.*

4. *Begin a regular exercise program. Exercise will actually change your body-chemistry that underlies your depression.*

5. *Keep a record of your accomplishments and things that you have done well.*

CODETYPE 2-3/3-2

Descriptors

Concerns/Complaints: General unhappiness, loss of interests, being physically ill, lowering of ability and performance.

Thoughts: Lacking insight, serious, self-doubts, sexual dissatisfaction.

Emotions: Feeling weak, exhausted, fatigued, helpless, physically ill, tense, nervous, worried, agitated, insecure, inadequate, apathetic, depressed, easily hurt, "bottled up" inside; overcontrolled, difficulty expressing feelings, tolerating unhappiness, smiling while depressed.

Traits/Behaviors: Selfish, demanding, self-centered, egocenric, immature, outgoing, dependent, Pollyannish; developing shallow and superficial relationships.

Therapist's Notes

Clients with this profile tend to be oriented toward their responsibilities. They are "home-bodies" with few if any activities outside the home. Their physical symptoms are often related to stress. They tend to be self-sacrificing and take on a martyr's role. Often they have blocked the full feelings of sadness and anger that accompany mourning so their unhappiness leaks out as sad affect. They find it very difficult, however, to cry and fully engage and express anger about any specific events that may have occurred in the past. They spend considerable time blaming themselves for their losses. Gestalt techniques to help them unblock their anger can be useful. They need to discover that asserting themselves will not result in the emotional abandonment they experienced in their childhood. Once they can safely express anger toward the therapist and not feel they will be emotionally abandoned, further progress is possible.

Medication Notes

Patients with this profile often can benefit from antidepressant medications but they tend to be difficult to medicate because of their sensitivity to even minimal side-effects. They often deny their emotional and psychological discomfort so medication must be presented in a persistent yet cautious manner. Medication should be seriously considered if vegetative signs of depression occur such as sleep disruption, insomnia, loss of appetite and significant psychomotor retardation. Antidepressants with minimal side-effects such as trazadone are often the drug of first choice with low doses gradually increased to effective levels with much support and encouragement by the therapist. Anxiolytics may be necessary for short periods of time to lower anxiety precipitated by psychotherapy. Patients with this profile may deny habituation and dependency with convincing sincerity.

FEEDBACK STATEMENTS

Issues—T-score: MMPI-1, $\geq$ 80; MMPI-2, NA (Not Applicable)

1. *Your profile indicates that you are feeling very depressed, very sad, and at times very hopeless about things ever changing for you.*

2. *But you try to hold your feeling in. You want to be brave and look at the bright side of things.*

3. *At times you may even laugh and cry at the same time, reflecting your attempt to be brave despite your great sadness.*

4. *You also may feel quite tense a good deal of time, with tension becoming so severe that it affects your physical health.*

5. *You may then be afflicted with headaches, neckaches, stomach aches, lower back pain, numbness in your fingers and extremities, and perhaps even symptoms involving bowels or bladder.*

6. *You probably also are very sensitive to any form of anger or rejection by others, so you end up trying to please people—doing favors that you don't really want to do.*

7. You assume that everyone is as sensitive as you are, so it may be hard for you to confront others or tell them things that would make them feel rejected.

Issues—T-score: MMPI-1, 70-79; MMPI-2, NA

1. Your profile indicates that right now you are feeling depressed and sad and you worry that you may never be happy again.

2. You may experience some physical discomfort—symptoms such as headaches, neckaches, stomachaches, lower back pain, numbness in your fingers and extremities, and perhaps even symptoms involving bowels or bladder.

3. You probably also have times when you feel worried, guilty, and pessimistic but you try to be brave and look at the bright side of things.

4. You have a tendency to blame yourself when things go wrong. Then you feel despondent and down on yourself.

5. You also may find it hard to confront people so that you end up sacrificing yourself for your family and friends.

6. Your losses may have been so painful that there were times when you felt as though you could almost die of pain. Now when you are upset your whole body may ache all over.

7. You also may feel panic about your physical health and want to see a physician. If you visit your doctor, you may worry that either something important will be overlooked or that you will be diagnosed with some new and terrible illness.

Issues—T-score: MMPI-1, 55-69; MMPI-2, NA

1. Your profile is essentially normal. It does reveal that you are a person who tends to sacrifice your wants and needs for others.

2. Being assertive and standing up for yourself may be difficult for you, and face-to-face confrontations with others may be quite painful.

3. You may develop headaches, stomach upsets, or other physical symptoms when you have to deal with angry or sad situations.

4. You may have learned to put up with some physical symptoms that are long-standing in nature and which may become aggravated under stress.

Background and Early Learning Experiences

As a child you may have experienced some serious loss. You also may have been exposed to powerful negative experiences: a parent who was explosive or alcoholic. You may have suffered some basic neglect when your needs were inadequately cared for and you had no one to whom you could turn for help. You probably dealt with these experiences and losses by being brave. Showing your real feelings could have made things worse, so you learned to look cheerful and cover your worry. This may be why, even today, you try to avoid negative feelings and even manage to be positive about them. In the past you also may have been rewarded somehow for sacrificing yourself for others and overlooking your own needs. You may have learned not to allow yourself to know just how sad and angry you are. But sadness and anger over past losses and neglect may still be with you and it shows itself in periodic crying spells and feelings of sadness, hopelessness, and loneliness.

Self-help Suggestions

1. Try to remember some childhood experience in which you felt a sense of terrible loss but weren't allowed to feel your sadness and anger because no one was there to help you. See if you can re-experience some of those feelings now.

2. Observe how often you fail to pursue your wants because you feel hopeless about ever satisfying them. Watch how you want to give up long before you have even tried to engage that want.

3. Whenever your body aches with pain or your symptoms get worse, see if you are struggling to be brave and hold back some sad or angry feelings. Give yourself permission to confront people a little more.

4. An exercise program can be very useful, even though you may hate the idea or have tried one in the past and failed to carry it through.

5. Watch for how you may nurture yourself in ways that are self-destructive or self-defeating, such as by overeating or drinking.

6. It is probably hard for you to deny anyone a favor or request, but try to set some limits especially in areas where you feel particularly used.

CODETYPE 2-4/4-2

Descriptors

Concerns/Complaints: Difficulty with law and authority, socially alienated and angry with the "system," criminal arrests, alcohol and drug use, addiction, job loss, home, marital and familial discord, sexual difficulties, suicide threats and attempts fear of caring and intimacy in case of disappointment.

Thoughts: Insincere, self-defeating, self-destructive, unable to control actions adequately, suicidal. Thinking is dominated by a sense of hopelessness and defeat.

Emotions: Feeling unhappy, inadequate, worthless, depressed, dissatisfied, anxious, remorseful, hostile, resentful, self-conscious, easily frustrated; guilt-ridden and engendering, inability to delay gratification, self-punitive.

Traits/Behaviors: Impulsive, manipulative, passive, dependent, restless, egocentric, immature, energetic, introverted.

Therapist's Notes

Clients with this profile often feel hopelessly trapped in an intolerable situation. Their anger will oscillate between rage at the world for putting them in their present predicament and anger with themselves for having allowed it to happen. They tend to be self-defeating and self-destructive, especially with alcohol or drugs. Their propensity for impulsive suicide attempts is high. The hypotheses is that as children they never learned basic trust. They felt they could not turn to adults in their life for help because these adults were either unavailable or would make their situation worse. Consequently they turned to their own resources and developed a distrust of emotional closeness. The precipitating circumstance for their present referral is usually a perceived disappointment which leaves them feeling trapped, angry, and alienated.

Begin therapy by helping them develop a bond with someone they can trust. Next, help them to rage against their fate and express the angry feelings which will unblock the mourning process. An important procedure is for them to have a series of goals to work toward on a weekly, or perhaps even on a daily basis. Therapy then can concentrate on how these goals are or are not accomplished. They feel it is useless to engage in positive undertakings because they fear disappointment and failure. Help them to notice how often they engage in this self-defeating behavior. Progress is best made by their accomplishment of specific small goals within a specific period of time. Be aware that these clients can be frustrating to treat because they enter treatment with an attitude of defeat.

Medication Notes

This profile is the most addiction prone of any MMPI profile. Drugs with potential for abuse should be avoided. Also the therapist should be aware that these patients will be unreliable in the use of any medication and that they can be suicidal. Tricyclic antidepressants and trazadone can be useful when the patient has vegetative signs of depression, particularly a disturbed sleep pattern. Obviously, great care must be exercised in giving suicidal patients tricyclic antidepressants. Trazadone carries much less risk and fewer annoying side-effects.

FEEDBACK STATEMENTS

Issues—T-score: MMPI-1, $\geq$ 80; MMPI-2, NA (Not Applicable)

1. *Your profile indicates that right now you are feeling very defeated and hopeless about things ever working out for you.*

2. *You may feel that the world has let you down and that it is very unlikely that you will ever get what you want out of life.*

3. *There are times when you feel very angry and want to blame and punish yourself for the spot you are in. At these times you may give up on things, even when they are going well for you.*

4. You may find that you want to punish yourself in other ways that are self-defeating and which leave you feeling even worse. You may be using drugs and alcohol in ways that you know are harmful for you.

5. You feel so hopeless and so angry with yourself that you feel like giving up on life and you may even think about killing yourself.

6. At other times your anger about your present situation is turned outward and you blame the world for your predicament.

7. Your anger at these times may show as a coldness and aloofness towards others and you may find yourself being sarcastic and negative and pushing people away from you.

8. Your profile also shows that you feel separate from people, very alone and that you have nowhere to belong.

9. It is hard for you to trust others, to be vulnerable. This prevents others from understanding you or offering you support or care.

10. It may be hard for you to be vulnerable and expose your feelings because you think that if you do people will disappoint you or let you down.

11. You probably do not have many friends in whom you trust or confide.

12. Right now your motivation in general is very low, and it is hard for you to get excited or interested in any new activity.

13. Even small frustrations are reason for you to give up on what you are doing, regardless of consequence or price you will pay.

14. Right now you are feeling so low and so defeated that it is hard for you to mobilize energy, to get much accomplished or to think things through clearly or well.

15. Because you do not feel able to solve your problems, when tension does build, you will probably do things impulsively to relieve the tension.

16. Then you may find yourself drinking or using drugs or doing other impulsive things to make yourself feel better.

Issues—T-score: MMPI-1, 70-79; MMPI-2, NA

1. Right now you are feeling somewhat defeated, hopeless, and trapped, like the world has let you down and the odds of your ever getting what you want are not good.

2. You probably also are feeling worthless, defective and unlovable.

3. There are times when you feel angry with yourself and blame yourself for your present situation.

4. At these times you want to punish yourself and you may allow things to happen that are bad for you without attempting to do anything about it.

5. When you feel angry and blame yourself, you may do some self-defeating things, like giving up even when things might be going well for you.

6. At other times you feel angry with the world, blaming outside circumstances, other people, and unfortunate events for your predicament.

7. When you are angry, you may find yourself being negative towards people, pushing them away by being sarcastic and cold even as they are trying to get close to you.

8. It may be hard for you to trust people right now because if you become vulnerable and open, you may be painfully disappointed again.

9. It may be hard for you to tell people how you are feeling because you see the world as a "dog eat dog" place where people take advantage of you if you reveal yourself.

10. It is probably very hard for you to develop trusting and intimate relationships and you may be feeling particularly isolated right now.

11. When tension builds you are likely to do something impulsive to relieve the tension or the feelings of hopelessness and frustration.

12. Your impulsive behavior may include the use of drugs and alcohol, then you may lose control and do angry and self-defeating things.

Issues—T-score: MMPI-1, 55-69; MMPI-2, NA

1. Right now your profile shows that you are feeling somewhat defeated and trapped in an unpleasant predicament.

2. You are feeling let down, as though "the rug has been pulled out from under you." You are worried whether you will be able to resolve the difficulty.

3. You probably are feeling a lot more anger right now than you have previously felt.

4. From time to time you may blame yourself for your current predicament. You feel guilty and bad about yourself.

5. You may find yourself giving up on things, even as they go well for you, because you anticipate that somehow you are going to fail again.

6. At times you may be negative and angry towards others. You may want to keep people at a distance because you are afraid that you are going to let them down or be let down by them.

7. Right now it is probably harder than usual to let yourself trust others.

8. You may feel that if people get to know you they may not care for you or they may disappoint you.

9. Perhaps a recent disappointment in an intimate relationship leaves you feeling betrayed and alone.

10. Small frustrations may irritate you and easily cause you to give up on things.

11. It may be hard for you to motivate yourself and get going on new activities.

12. Right now you are probably more impulsive than you usually are, as though you need immediate relief from your frustration and sadness.

13. Sometimes people with your profile use drugs and alcohol as a way of relieving stress. When they do, it seriously increases the risk of behaving in an impulsive and self-defeating way.

Background and Early Learning Experiences

People with your profile often had a painful and difficult childhood. Perhaps your parents were cold, angry, and unpredictably rejecting. One or both may have ben authoritarian and unable to relate to you except when they punished you. Perhaps from an early age you had to rely on your own resources, numbing out your feelings in order to survive.

Throughout your life probably you have had difficulty getting close to people and expressing your feelings for fear that if you let down your guard people would take advantage of you or disappoint you. Perhaps something recently happened and you feel the same old feelings that you had as a child. You feel that you are not worth loving and that you are destined to be rejected. Nothing you do will make things better. If this is so, you may be protecting yourself by being emotionally distant from someone you actually care about. You may be reluctant to repair the rift for fear of being disappointed again.

Self-help Suggestions

1. Whenever you feel in a black mood or hopeless, try to find one small thing that you could do to make yourself feel better. No matter how small it may be, do it and do not give up.

2. Observe how small set-backs have a tendency to leave you feeling defeated and negative. When something starts to go well, watch that you don't expect it to go wrong and then give up before you really gave it a chance. Work on staying positive even though it may be hard for you.

3. Observe how often you focus on what is "wrong" at any given time rather than also noticing the things that go right. When something does go right, allow yourself to enjoy it.

4. Reduce your drug and alcohol intake. Whenever you feel tense, rather than using drugs or alcohol, find new ways of relieving the stress. Try to recognize stress before you do something impulsive.

5. People with your profile often benefit a great deal when they exercise regularly.

CODETYPE 2-6/6-2

Descriptors

Concerns/Complaints: Depressed, fatigued, physical complaints, suicidal ideas and attempts.

Thoughts: Critical, skeptical, resentful, angry, openly hostile, "chip-on-the-shoulder" attitude, looks for someone to blame, will induce rejection by others.

Emotions: Feels tearful, moody, overly sensitive, easily offended, distrustful, touchy, agitated, insecure, both intrapunitive and extrapunitive, rationalizing, projecting.

Traits/Behaviors: Demanding, self-centered, self-indulgent, self-dramatizing, dependent, blaming.

Therapist's Notes

Clients with this profile feel trapped, bitter and resentful. They feel they are in a hopeless situation which is not of their own doing. While they are resentful about it, whenever they focus on a possible solution they feel vulnerable to attack or criticism. Since they see their predicament as unfair and unreasonable they respond by withdrawing and feeling unfairly treated. The hypothesis is that they were reared by adults who were quick to reprimand and criticize them no matter how hard they tried to please. Their response was to block their anger and turn it inward on themselves. They learned to become passive whenever they were criticized or were faced with unreasonable demands. The hypothesis is that they avoided responding with anger or retaliation for fear of calling even more and greater attacks and reprimands upon themselves. As adults they sometimes have problems with chemical dependency which may be an attempt to self-medicate their depression.

Therapy should concentrate on helping the client discover and express the anger which blocks the completion of their mourning process. They need help to become more assertive, and to relinquish the martyr's role. These clients are uncomfortable with explorative therapy and view it as intrusive and humiliating. This is because they constantly anticipate judgment or criticism.

Medication Notes

As with all patients who have elevations on **Scale 2,** the **2-6/6-2** patient often benefits from the use of anti-depressants, particularly trazadone and tricyclic antidepressants such as imiprimine. These patients are cautious about any medication which interferes with their sense of vigilance.

Anxiolytics with habituation potential such as the banzodiazipines should be used with caution. Buspirone which thus far has not shown the tendency to be abused may be used for chronic distressing anxiety. Non-sedating phenothiazines with fewer annoying side-effects such as trifluoperazine or thioridazine may be used in low dosages when anxiety is severe or if there is paranoid ideation.

FEEDBACK STATEMENTS

Issues—T-score: MMPI-1, > 80; MMPI-2, NA (Not Applicable)

1. *Right now you are feeling very sad, down, tense, worried, and bitter.*

2. *You probably feel trapped in a current predicament and this makes you feel defeated and angry. Furthermore, you see no way of escaping the trap.*

3. *This drains your energy or initiative and makes it hard for you to think clearly and feel good about yourself.*

4. *You may feel hopeless about escaping your predicament without feeling criticized by others.*

5. *You may feel like a victim because this trap seems unfair and none of your own doing.*

6. *Because you are feeling so down and despondent, you also may be having some other signs of depression like*

waking up too early in the morning and not being able to get back to sleep.

7. *Your energy level may be low and you may need to push yourself to accomplish even minor activities.*

8. *Your sex drive is probably low and your appetite affected.*

9. *If someone frustrates you or hurts you, you are likely to become very quiet and not say anything for long periods of time.*

10. *You are a person who tends to feel hurt before you feel angry.*

11. *This is probably because you want to be a rational and reasonable person—when you feel hurt you would rather not express anger until you feel your anger is justified. Expressing anger may just lead to others "paying you back."*

12. *You are angry about what has happened to you, but you do not see much you can do about it right now.*

13. *You are a person who tries to be fair and you are sensitive to criticism. Criticism tends to wound you deeply and you get angry at any unfairness.*

14. *Right now you may feel so vulnerable to criticism that you can't tell who is an enemy and against you and who is a friend you can trust.*

Issues—T-score: MMPI-1, 70-79; MMPI-2, NA

1. *Right now you are going through a period of moderate to severe sadness and general unhappiness.*

2. *This may be characterized by periods of sad moods, worrying, loss of initiative, and feelings of inferiority.*

3. *You may even feel trapped, and be bitter and angry about your predicament and how things have worked out for you.*

4. Whenever you try to think of a solution you only see how the solution would lead to such criticism that you have to stay in the entrapping situation. There simply is no way out.

5. Very likely you feel like a victim, and that your situation is quite unfair and none of your fault.

6. Fairness has always been important for you. When you see unfairness it makes you angry, in fact it reminds you of the times when you were unfairly treated yourself.

7. You are extremely sensitive to criticism. Criticism hurts you a great deal and you work hard to avoid it.

8. If someone is dissatisfied with you or angry with you, that hurts you.

9. People with your profile often feel very wounded before they feel angry.

10. If someone frustrates you or upsets you, you may find yourself withdrawing and becoming quiet rather than expressing your anger.

11. In fact, you may treat people with long periods of silence whenever they upset you.

12. This probably relates to your wanting to be rational and reasonable. You don't want to express unreasonable feelings, lest others retaliate by humiliating and criticizing you.

13. You also have very high standards and are quick to blame yourself if you do not conform to these high standards. If you haven't done things in the best way possible, you tend to get angry and disappointed with yourself.

14. You also may find that you have to push yourself to get ordinary things accomplished.

15. Your sex drive may be diminished and your appetite also may be low.

16. You may be distrubed by periods of sleeplessness or early morning waking when you are unable to get back to sleep.

Issues—T-score: MMPI-1, 55-69; MMPI-2, NA

1. Right now you are going through a period when you feel less optimistic and unhappier than you would like.

2. At times, you may feel despondent, worried, guilty, and lacking in initiative. At these times you may feel bad about yourself and down on yourself.

3. You feel a mild sense of being trapped and defeated.

4. You may feel bitter and angry about the trap you are in but you can't see a good way out of your situation.

5. Whenever you try to find a way out, the solution would probably lead to self-criticism or criticism from others. This makes you feel agitated and frustrated about the situation.

6. You probably feel a little like a victim—and as though the predicament is not your fault. And yet you are not quite sure just who to blame or how to get out of it.

7. Periodically you may feel guilty and down on yourself about how things have worked out for you.

8. People with your profile are sensitive to criticism and reprimands, and other people's disappointments with you tend to hurt and wound you.

9. You may suffer from an occasional bad night's sleep or you may wake early in the mornings and not be able to get back to sleep.

10. You also may find that your sex drive and general energy level dips during times of stress and that you have to push yourself to get things done.

11. People with your profile have a tendency to verbalize hurt before they verbalize anger. When someone frustrates you, you may have a tendency to withdraw and become quiet rather than to express your anger openly.

12. This may relate to your wanting to be rational and fair and not wanting to express any anger unreasonably, so you withdraw and analyze your feelings to see if they are warranted.

13. Then, however, your anger may build up and lead to periodic temper outbursts after a period of hurt.

14. People with your profile are also very fair-minded.

15. Perhaps this relates to a childhood in which you felt unfairly criticized or judged.

16. You strive hard to treat others fairly and you get angry at instances of unfairness in others.

Background and Early Learning Experiences

Your present problems, may remind you of your childhood when your parents were quick to criticize, reprimand, or punish you. They may even have been humiliating in their treatment of you. Even though their criticism often seemed unfair, you probably tried to please them and be above criticism. But no matter what you did it may have been very difficult to get their approval.

At the present time you may be going through a similarly difficult situation in which you feel hopelessly trapped and unable to escape. You think you will be judged unfairly by others or judged by your own high standards. You may feel that to obtain approval is impossible: that no matter what you do, someone will always find fault.

You may feel extremely despondent. You cannot find any way out of this trap without feeling that you are a bad person, or without feeling that you are going to open yourself up to anger or humiliation from others. Your present predicament may make you feel hopeless about ever doing anything for yourself without being attacked and judged.

Self-help Suggestions

1. Whenever, in relations with others, you find yourself feeling hurt and becoming quiet, see if in fact you are not angry. Then try to express that anger.

2. *Long periods of silence are your way of retaliating for the hurts you suffer. This only prolongs your hurt and leads to others attacking you in return.*

3. *Whenever you find yourself withdrawing in anger, force yourself to verbalize your anger to the person who has upset you.*

4. *Try not to wait until you believe that you are completely justified in expressing your anger or resentment. Your anger may not feel one hundred percent right, but when you sense it at all, the best procedure is to express it before it builds up into more powerful negative feelings.*

5. *Don't wait until you feel you are completely justified in making your wants known. When you want something, try asking for it, even if you do not feel you have a right to it entirely. Others are free to tell you whether or not they want to comply to your wishes.*

6. *You do not have to work so hard always to be above criticism.*

7. *Sometimes people with your profile use alcohol as a way of relaxing and dealing with unhappiness. Try to avoid that; it may cause you additional problems. If you are using drugs or alcohol to feel better, discuss this with your therapist.*

CODETYPE 2-7/7-2

Descriptors

Concerns/Complaints: Worries over business, success, relationships, sex, responsibilities, health, somatic symptoms, heart, weight, losses of interest, increased stress, weakness, fatigue, personal adequacy and performance, fear of unpredictable loss.

Thoughts: Brooding, ruminative, obsessional, chronically worrisome, indecisive, anticipates problems, self-conscious, suicidal, slowed in tempo.

Emotions: Feelings of inadequacy, insecurity, inferiority, worthlessness; anxious, tense, nervous, depressed, guilt-prone, intrapunitive; need to achieve and receive recognition.

Traits/Behavior: Responsible, dependable, dependent, subassertive, introverted, docile, passive, perfectionistic, compulsive, can be suicidal.

Therapist's Notes

Clients with this profile feel anxious and depressed. They are in a constant state of anxiety—worried that disaster is just around the next corner. They are plagued with guilt and self-doubt and have a profound sense of insecurity especially around financial matters and responsibilities. The precipitating circumstance for evaluation and treatment is often an increase of responsibilities.

The hypothesis is that as children they experienced a single or a series of unpredicted and severe losses. Their response to past unpredicted losses is to anticipate every possible eventuality which may lead to a new loss and they are always protecting themselves against it. In some cases as children they were given too much responsibility and felt overburdened and overwhelmed. Rarely were they able to experience age-appropriate carefreeness. They were constantly on edge worrying about demands which were too burdensome for them to handle. They developed a hyper-responsible personality style, constantly worrying about their responsibilities and trying to protect themselves against some unpredictable disaster or failure.

Therapy should concentrate on helping them learn ways to relax and stop negative thoughts that interfere with ongoing functioning. Relaxation techniques are particularly useful with these patients. Implosion techniques are often useful to engage their fears of the unpredictable. These clients need to learn how to stop blaming themselves for their minor mistakes and to develop better self-esteem. They need to focus on their accomplishments rather than their failures.

Medication Notes

If the depression is secondary to prolonged and intense anxiety, one should consider anxiolytic medications including the benzodiazipines and buspirone. Beware of habituation as well as guilt and anxiety about taking medication of any kind. All anti-anxiety medications should be given on a time-contingent basis, probably no more than 6 months. This will give the patient time to learn other anxiety-lowering techniques.

Trazadone or a tricyclic antidepressant such as amitriptyline or imiprimine are indicated when depressive symptoms are disabling or when vegetative symptoms are present such as insomnia. If **Scale 8** also is elevated low doses of a non-sedating phenothizine (trifluoperizine) can relieve the debilitating sense of confusion and self-alienation.

FEEDBACK STATEMENTS

Issues—T-score: MMPI-1, ≥ 80; MMPI-2, NA (Not Applicable)

1. *You are going through a period of intense sadness and worry.*

2. *Very likely your mind races constantly, anticipating and worrying over every possible disaster that might lie ahead.*

3. *Perhaps, because you are so worried about what could go wrong, you tend to be a perfectionist who must try to*

account for every detail and make sure that nothing is left undone.

4. Right now you may be experiencing some headaches, neckaches, stomach upsets or other physical symptoms as a result of the stress you are under.

5. Physical symptoms such as constipation and backaches could be symptoms of the current stress.

6. It might be difficult for you to sleep well right now. Perhaps it is hard to fall asleep. Or, perhaps you may wake up with a jolt several times a night, filled with startle and worry.

7. During the day you probably push yourself trying to get everything done and are exhausted at the end of the day, spent of any energy to enjoy your spare time.

8. Your sex drive has probably decreased and your appetite may be affected by your worry and sadness.

9. It is hard for you to make decisions or think clearly right now and it is almost impossible for you to concentrate because your mind teams with possible disasters.

10. For you, guilt is a constant companion. If you enjoy something, you feel guilty. If you relax, you feel guilty.

11. If you think about the past, you feel guilty and blame yourself for so many things that you feel have gone wrong.

12. If you think about the future, you feel guilty because you anticipate making a mess of things.

13. Guilt and self-recrimination may make you feel so bad that at times you think dying is the only way you will ever get rest.

14. People with your profile are very responsible. You probably worry a great deal about your responsibilities—about your family, security, work, and finances.

15. Being self-assertive is very difficult for you because you are never quite sure you have the right to be assertive.

16. Generally, you are a person who follows the rules of society and who finds it exceedingly difficult to stand up to authority figures.

17. Because it is hard for you to assert yourself, people may use you and push you around. This only increases your sense of guilt and self-dislike.

18. It may be hard for you to relax and enjoy things because you are always on edge. If you relax and let your mind rest, you feel you are doing something wrong.

19. Perhaps you feel that you have never done enough or will never be really secure financially.

20. As a result, taking vacations and relaxing is very difficult for you.

Issues—T-score: MMPI-1, 70-79; MMPI-2, NA

1. You are going through a period of sadness and worry.

2. You may have difficulty getting to sleep or you may wake up mornings with a sudden jolt, unable to get back to sleep. With that the worries begin and life looks twice as bleak.

3. You may have a lowered interest in sex and disturbances in your appetite.

4. You probably spend considerable time analyzing yourself. You analyze the past, always trying to see where mistakes were made so that you can avoid them in the future.

5. When you analyze the past you keep remembering all the mistakes that you made. You blame yourself and are filled with feelings of guilt and recrimination at their memory.

6. People with your profile often develop symptoms of stress such as headaches, nechaches, stomach upsets, constipation, or backaches.

7. You may worry that your physical health is going to deteriorate, leading to further inefficiency.

8. You appear to be constantly on guard lest something go wrong. You are worried about some unexpected loss or that some overlooked detail will lead to disaster.

9. Because you are constantly on edge waiting for possible disaster, you may have learned to be a perfectionist: you want to be certain that every detail is attended to to protect against things going wrong.

10. You are wary of being too optimistic—if you allow yourself to get overly excited or hopeful about possibilities, you would only feel disappointed should the plans fall through or fail.

11. You probably find yourself feeling guilty a good deal of the time.

12. You feel guilty if you relax. You feel guilty about past mistakes and you even tend to feel guilty about what you failed to do to avoid those mistakes.

13. Sometimes people with your profile are so exhausted by guilt and anxiety that they will fantasize about ways of escaping. In periods of extreme despondency they may even think about how relieving it would be "just to be dead."

14. Often people with your profile become tense and anxious when problems arise around money and security at home or if problems occur at work around responsibilities.

15. Decision making is probably very difficult for you because you see every side of every problem and you see all the possible angles that could go wrong.

16. Very likely it is hard for you to concentrate: each time you start to think about one thing you are interrupted by thoughts of other things that could go wrong—by thoughts about what else you should be worried about. Worries encroach on worries.

17. Being self-assertive is also difficult for you because you don't like to "rock the boat."

18. You are a person who respects authority and who obeys the rules of society.

19. Standing up to an authority figure may be very hard for you and you generally dislike conflicts and work hard to avoid them.

20. You also are a very responsible person who takes all of your responsibilities extremely seriously, sometimes to the point that they exhaust you.

Issues—T-score: MMPI-1, 55-69; MMPI-2, NA

1. You are a person who is prone to worry, especially about responsibilities and making decisions.

2. You tend to be on guard for unexpected problems. This may be because you see all sides of a problem and tend to focus on the things that could go wrong.

3. Making important decisions can be difficult for you and when stresses accumulate your concentration may suffer.

4. You have a tendency to analyze your decisions to see where you could have avoided mistakes.

5. People with your profile experience guilt as a familiar companion.

6. More than likely you have a tendency to feel guilty whenever you relax, going over and over in your mind all of the things you feel you should be doing and worrying about.

7. Periodically, when stress accumulates, you may experience sleepless nights or you may awaken very early in the morning flooded with worries.

8. At these times your sex drive and appetite may be adversely affected, and your general level of energy and efficiency may diminish.

9. When stresses build you may develop symptoms such as constipation, headaches, neckaches, or backaches.

10. You can worry about everything—including concerns that your health and stamina are not what they should be.

11. You also may be somewhat the perfectionist: You want everything to be "just so" to minimize the possibility that something unexpected could go wrong.

12. People with your profile tend to be very responsible, especially about family, financial, and security matters.

13. Financial matters may worry you more than most people and you are not likely to take many serious risks.

14. When stresses at work accumulate you probably become tense and irritable and concerned about disaster, such as losing your job or disappointing your superiors.

15. You also are a person who finds conflict and asserting yourself generally unpleasant.

16. People with your profile respect authority and tend to follow the rules.

17. Consequently, it is often difficult for them to confront a person with authority even if they know the person has done something unreasonable or unfair.

18. Perhaps because of your caution about unexpected loss you may be seen by others as less than optimistic.

Background and Early Learning Experiences

People with your profile often had unexpected losses as children. Perhaps one of your parents died when you were young or perhaps your parents were divorced leaving you with an unreasonable amount of responsibility as a child. Childhood is meant to have periods of carefree play; perhaps you were deprived of such pleasant times. When children are burdened with too much responsibility they worry or escape into daydreams. They often try to anticipate problems to avoid making mistakes. You probably have continued to do this throughout your life, but right now you spend most of your time anticipating all the things that can go wrong. This makes you feel overburdened and unable to concentrate, think clearly, or make important decisions.

Self-help Suggestions

1. *Whenever you start to think about all of the things that may have gone wrong in the past, try to shut off the noise in your head and refuse to think about them. Going over and over past mistakes overloads you and does you more harm than good.*

2. *Try not to think through all the things that you ought to do. Just start by taking on one job that needs doing and finish it. Thinking clearly may be easier if you can accomplish one thing at a time, rather than getting caught up in a great whirl wind of duties where you try to remember everything and try to sort out their relative importance.*

3. *Whenever you finish or accomplish something, give yourself a reward. The reward may be just to sit down and read something pleasant or to do something pleasant just for yourself. Don't allow yourself to be driven directly to the next chore.*

4. *If something does go wrong, try not to blame yourself for the mistake. Rather, tell yourself that everybody makes mistakes and that it is alright for you to make a few yourself.*

5. *If you do have periodic stressful, anxious and worried times, make sure you are getting plenty of exercise which will relieve some of the tension.*

CODETYPE 2-8/8-2

Descriptors

Concerns/Complaints: Sadness, depression, tension, anxiety, physical illness, somatic symptoms, dizziness, forgetfulness, nausea, vomiting, fatigue, weakness, sleep disturbance, loss of control; fear of emotional abandonment and being "defective."

Thoughts: Unoriginal, unrealistic, confused, retarded, guilt-ridden, suspicious, obsessive, delusional, hallucinatory, suicidal, slowed speech, unable to concentrate, forgetful.

Emotions: Feeling pain, worthless, apathetic, indifferent, irritated, agitated, tense, resentful, hurt, depressed, alienated, anxious, isolated, tearful, withdrawn, sensitive to reactions of others.

Traits/Behaviors: Dependent, unassertive, unsociable.

Therapist's Notes

Clients with the **2-8/8-2** profile are depressed and will often feel "broken" or defective and unlovable. They complain of poor memory, an inability to concentrate and difficulty in making decisions or thinking clearly. They may also believe they are deteriorating in some way, somehow falling apart. The hypothesis is that they were raised in families where they were treated with coldness and indifference which they internalized as a negative self-image and "proof" of their being defective. The precipitating circumstance leading up to referral is usually the withdrawal of someone who was previously supportive and who ignores them or treats them with hostility or uncaring. These clients do no do well with explorative therapy and tend to experience the uncovering of their intimate reactions as confirming of their negative self-image. They do better with a nurturing and supportive approach that helps them to feel acceptable and likable. Relaxation techniques also are often useful.

Medication Notes

This group of patients is not homogeneous in their response to medication. Some respond well to a tricyclic antidepressant or trazadone which decreases their sense of defectiveness as the depression lifts. Others respond poorly to antidepressants, feeling an increase in their sense of agitation and confusion. In our experience patients who have this profile and a history of parental neglect and hostility tend to need a combination of antidepressant and phenothiazines in low dosage. In other patients antidepressants and anxiolytics work in combination.

FEEDBACK STATEMENTS

Issues—T-score: MMPI-1, > 80; MMPI-2, NA (Not Applicable)

1. *This is probably a very frightening time for you. You may feel sad, empty and disconnected from others. Furthermore you don't understand what caused these dark moods to descend on you.*

2. *You very likely feel hopeless and dejected and probably blame yourself for feeling so bad.*

3. *You also may feel tearful and despondent and figure that life is not worth living.*

4. *You may have many concerns about your body—that something is wrong with it—that you are deteriorating physically and somehow falling apart.*

5. *You may have headaches, stomach upsets, neckaches or other symptoms, but without these, you probably still worry that there is something going wrong with you and that you body is letting you down.*

6. *At present you are probably having difficulty with your thinking, feeling unable to solve problems effectively and to make decisions that you feel good about.*

7. *Very likely it is hard for you to keep your thoughts straight or know exactly how you feel.*

8. You probably have difficulty with your memory and attention. It is hard to concentrate because outside thoughts interrupt and intrude on what you are thinking.

9. Perhaps you also have some problems with your sleep, finding it difficult to get to sleep at night or waking too early in the mornings.

10. Upon wakening in the morning you may feel unrested and exhausted and find it hard to face another day.

11. You seem to spend a lot of energy trying to hold things together. You guard against intense feelings for fear that somehow you might fall apart.

12. The world of other people is also frightening to you. It is hard for you to relate to others and their reactions to you seem very confusing.

13. It is difficult for you to trust or get close to others because you can't trust how you see people or how they, in turn, see you.

14. Generally, it frightens you to let go of control, let people get to know you, or let yourself be emotional.

15. You are probably afraid that if you become vulnerable and let people get to know you, they may then humiliate or reject you.

16. You are very sensitive to anger or hostility from others and when you see that someone is angry with you it confuses you and you do not know exactly how to respond.

17. Getting angry back with people is also hard for you.

18. If someone upsets you, you probably do not let yourself respond, even though you may feel angry and deeply hurt.

Issues—T-score: MMPI-1, 70-79; MMPI-2, NA

1. Right now you are going through a period of sadness, confusion, and a feeling of aloneness.

2. You tend to get down on yourself. You think you aren't worthy of the love and acceptance you get from the people you care about.

3. You may also have dark moods when you feel negative, angry, and sad, but are not quite sure where these moods come from.

4. At these times you may feel hopeless about ever really being happy.

5. At other times you can bounce back and feel hopeful and even reasonably content.

6. You may periodically worry about your body and whether it is going to fall apart.

7. Some of the time you may find it hard to think clearly and make decisions because it feels like your head is filled with "cotton" or "wool."

8. At other times you may find your mind wandering or filled with intrusive or uncomfortable thoughts that are not related to what you are trying to concentrate on.

9. Your concentration has probably been affected by your recent sadness and you may worry about your efficiency or fear you are losing your memory.

10. You may have occasional sleep problems; either difficulty getting to sleep or perhaps waking early in the morning, long before you want to get up.

11. Upon awakening in the morning you may find yourself still tired and having to push yourself to get going.

12. Getting close to people is also somewhat frightening to you.

13. You experience concerns about feeling "good enough" to be liked, so you tend to be cautious about revealing yourself to people in case they reject or humiliate you.

14. *You are a very sensitive person; anger or hostility from others causes considerable distress.*

15. *If someone is angry with you, it tends to disorganize your thinking and it becomes difficult to mobilize your thoughts to protect yourself.*

16. *Generally, asserting yourself is quite difficult, and expressing anger when you feel it also is very difficult.*

17. *Letting go of control and expressing warm and positive feelings may frighten you.*

18. *There are times when you cannot trust your feelings or responses to others. This frightens you and makes you unsure of how you should act in a given situation.*

19. *It is as if you cannot quite understand why people respond to you in the way they do which leads you to mistrust your ability to comprehend social situations correctly.*

20. *Generally you try hard to be responsible and sensitive to others and you avoid conflict and hurting others.*

Issues—T-score: MMPI-1, 55-69; MMPI-2, NA

1. *Your profile is essentially normal. You are a sensitive, creative, and responsible individual.*

2. *Right now you may be feeling somewhat down and sad about some current predicament.*

3. *Perhaps you blame yourself and feel bad about yourself.*

4. *You may have periods when you feel a deeper sense of sadness—when you are "down on yourself" and wonder if you can be happy.*

5. *At those times you probably feel that there is something "not quite right" with you and that makes you unhappy and dissatisfied.*

6. Occasionally you may experience dark moods when you feel angry and alienated from others. Furthermore you don't know what causes these moods.

7. Then you want to push people away and be left alone.

8. Once in a while, when you are in these dark moods, your sleep may be affected. You may awaken too early in the mornings or you may get up feeling unrested in the mornings.

9. When you feel down you may even start to worry that you have some unknown physical illness.

10. Right now making decisions and thinking clearly is not as easy as it has been in the past.

11. Perhaps you feel your memory is not working as well as it did and that your concentration is not quite what it was.

12. You are sensitive to anger and hostility from others and if someone is hostile towards you it tends to confuse and upset you.

13. This makes you careful about who you will trust and confide in.

14. Being assertive is difficult for you because you dislike conflict.

15. If you feel angry towards someone you will more likely spend time thinking about it rather than expressing it.

16. Generally, letting go of your emotions is hard for you and you may find yourself expressing them in roundabout ways, rather than openly or directly.

Background and Early Learning Experiences

Early in life, people with your profile were often not provided the warmth and security they needed. Right now you may feel that someone previously supportive has withdrawn from you and is treating you in an angry, cold, and rejecting way. This may reawaken some old feelings from your childhood—times when you felt alone and disliked and had no one to whom to turn for understanding. When you were growing up, perhaps one of your parents treated you with angry silence or indifference. If that was so, you may be feeling that same anger and hostility from someone else right now. This is upsetting. It may make you feel hopeless about ever being acceptable or loved by someone again. Furthermore you blame yourself when people close to you withdraw.

Self-help Suggestions

1. Whenever you feel a dark mood sweep over you, see if you have been unfairly treated or treated in a mean or angry way. Try to confront the person who has treated you so badly. Tell them how you feel and what happened to make you feel that way.

2. Often medication can be useful in reducing the sudden surges of these moods and the periods of confusion and anxiety which follow. Discuss this with your therapist.

3. Whenever you feel depressed and alone try not to push your friends and family away. Tell them that you feel bad and that it is not your intention to withdraw or abandon them.

4. Try to stop your negative thoughts, especially, thoughts when you tell yourself that you are defective and undeserving of love and respect.

CODETYPE   2-9/9-2

Descriptors

Concerns/Complaints: Anxiety, depression, somatic symptoms, agitation, achievement, identity, self-worth, excessive alcohol use, possible encephalopathy.

Thoughts: Ruminative, aggressive, hypomanic, expansive, grandiose.

Emotions: Tense, anxious, moody, depressed, denying, alternating euphoria and depression.

Traits/Behaviors: Self-centered, narcissistic, impulsive, excitable, driven.

Therapist's Notes

Clients with this profile often are tense, jumpy, moody, and irritable. The mania of **Scale 9** conceals the symptoms of the depression of **Scale 2** but the optimism and expansiveness of **9** also are suppressed by the depression. The net effect is often abrupt changes of mood, from being happy, good natured, optimistic, and joking one moment to feeling angry, sullen, negativistic, and explosive the next. The central issue in therapy is generally their moodiness and irritability. They typically are achievement/failure oriented so that simple frustrations can easily precipitate bursts of explosive irritability. Profiles with T-scores over 80 are rare and are sometimes associated with a psychotic disorder, which may be paranoid or manic-depressive in character. A precipitating factor is often frustration in the accomplishment of an important task.

This profile also is associated with a high frequency of addiction to alcohol or other drugs to self-medicate the mood disorder. Frequently these clients were reared in families where they were constantly urged to achieve, but no matter how well they did they were either rarely or inconsistently rewarded. Therapy should concentrate on helping them distinguish between their own goals and wants and the goals and wants of others. Behavioral management of their mood swings can be a useful adjunct to chemotherapy.

Medication Notes

Medication is an important aspect to the successful treatment of patients with the **2-9/9-2** profile but they are very undependable, tending to regulate their own medications. A history suggestive of manic-depressive illness in the patient or in the patient's family would suggest lithium as the treatment of choice, especially if a history of significant mood swings exists.

Be aware that this profile is sometimes associated with organic illness. A careful neurological history, examination, and test battery for organicity should be conducted if you have any suspicion that the underlying process is a neurological disease. Psychotic *2-9's* tend to strenuously resist medication but respond well to phenothiazines as well as lithium.

FEEDBACK STATEMENTS

Issues—T-score: MMPI-1, > 70; MMPI-2, NA (Not Applicable)

1. *Right now you feel extremely moody, jumpy, tense, and irritable.*

2. *Most of the time you are optimistic and energetic but small set-backs can cause you to feel pessimistic and hopeless right away.*

3. *You appear to shift quickly from feeling extremely excited and positive to feeling very low and irritable. Minor issues take on giant proportions when you feel like this.*

4. *When you feel high, you are impulsive and over-commit yourself to too many tasks, activities, and projects. This invariably gets you into trouble.*

5. *When you feel low you are so despondent that you are self-defeating and destructive. You may give up on a worthy and important project. That only makes you feel worse.*

6. It seems that right now your energy level is exceptionally high. Your mind is racing, you make connections and see possibilities everywhere, you feel that nothing is impossible for you and you can do anything you want to do if you can just focus on a single one of these many possibilities.

7. At the same time you feel angry and irritable right now. You could easily explode at any small frustration—at anyone who stands in your way.

8. Others may complain that you are too ambitious and controlling. They find your interruptions and instructions annoying and unrealistic. They are uncomfortable and unhappy with your changing moods and do not understand why you act like this.

9. You have a need to be constantly on the move finding new undertakings and grand schemes. Rather than engage the pain of a recent failure or loss, you invest yourself in more and more projects. In fact your mood swings may be tied to some recent failure of achievement.

10. People with your profile often use non-prescription drugs and/or alcohol as a way of relieving their intense discomfort and moodiness.

11. However, drugs and alcohol may very likely aggravate your mood changes and your explosiveness.

Issues—T-score: MMPI-1, 55-69; MMPI-2, NA

1. Right now you are feeling somewhat tense, moody, jumpy, and irritable.

2. You may experience swings in your mood, from feeling optimistic with high energy to feeling pessimistic with low energy within a short period of time.

3. There are occasions when you have so much energy that you feel like there are dozens of opportunities that you

could undertake. Your mind races with these possibilities—and you would do them all if only you could
focus on a single project and carry it through.

4. Your energy level generally seems to come in spurts. At
times you over-commit yourself and take on too many
activities and at other times you procrastinate and have
difficulty getting things done.

5. Small set-backs loom large to you and then you are quick
to become pessimistic and even gloomy.

6. Right now you probably feel irritable and explosive,
especially when you are working on something and
someone interrupts you.

7. To others your moodiness may appear puzzling or even a
little frightening, and it may get you into trouble at work or
with loved ones.

8. It is important for you to be always productive and
working on new projects, and you feel down when you are
not excited about some new idea.

9. In fact most of your down times occur when you feel
unproductive or when someone or something is interfering
with your progress

10. People with your profile sometimes use non-prescription
drugs and/or alcohol as a way of relieving their tension.
You may very likely be prone to addiction and if you are
using drugs for the relief of stress, these will probably
aggravate your mood swings and your irritabilities.

Background and Early Learning Experiences

People with your profile frequently had parents who were
difficult or even impossible to please. You may have tried
desperately to obtain their approval but were rarely able to
satisfy them. No matter how well or how much you achieved
you probably sensed their disappointment. It is possible that
you responded to this by driving yourself to ever greater and

greater achievements. Right now you may be going through a period where you feel vulnerable to being disapproved of or worried that you will fail at something important. Failure and disapproval frightens you and makes you feel trapped in your agitation and ambition. Sometimes people with your profile have parents who also experienced mood swings; if so, you may have inherited this characteristic. Any history of head injury, periods of unconsciousness, or high fevers that may have preceded the onset of your moodiness also should be discussed with your therapist since neurological disorders also can produce mood problems.

Self-help Suggestions

1. It may be important for you to take medication to help you regulate your mood; you should discuss this with your therapist.

2. When you are working on something important, try not to over-react to small set-backs. Remember that you have a tendency to see even small problems as catastrophic.

3. Try to be realistic about how much time a particular project will require. Then give yourself more time than you think you need to finish that project before you start another.

4. Give yourself permission to fail sometimes. Try not to see failure as proof that you are no good.

5. When you do finish a project, reward yourself and enjoy your achievement rather than rushing on to a new project.

6. A regular exercise program is very helpful in discharging an excess of energy.

CODETYPE 2-0/0-2

Descriptors

Concerns/Complaints: Worry, unhappiness, feelings of inadequacy, insomnia, shyness, poor social skills, socially withdrawn, guilt and anxiety.

Thoughts: Indecisive, socially inept, poor self-image, personal inadequacies.

Emotions: Feeling timid, inferior, inadequate, unattractive, guilty, self-conscious, depressed; fearful of intimacy and emotional involvement, overinhibited, overcontrolled.

Traits/Behaviors: Shy, introverted, passive, unassertive, cautious, ruminative, self-effacing.

Therapist's Notes

Clients with this profile tend to be unhappy, withdrawn, and shy individuals who lack self-confidence and have limited tolerance for social and emotional relationships. The hypothesis is that as children they received very little warmth, affection, and physical contact. Usually their parents were not outwardly cruel and hostile but rather were withdrawn, socially inept, or retiring and limited in their ability to give or receive warmth and comfort themselves. In some cases the parents viewed the outward display of emotion as weakness and the child learned how to control feelings and emotional wanting. These clients typically have difficulty touching, holding, caressing, or kissing. The profile often reflects a stable personality pattern which can be quite resistant to change. Therapy should help the client who has children learn the pleasure of physical contact and, through the development of social skills, how to be more assertive and comfortable with others. They also could be helped to live with and accept a certain amount of shyness rather than putting themselves down for disliking or needing social interactions.

Medication Notes

Like other profiles with elevations on *Scale 2,* patients with a *2-0/0-2* profile benefit from antidepressant medication. However, they tend to be unusually sensitive to side-effects so medically induced changes in mood are apt to be disturbing and uncomfortable to them. They appear to have come to terms with their state so changes in it are disquieting. They generally do not want to take medications. Antidepressants will tend to be accepted more readily if given as a single bedtime dose adjusted to achieve a good night's sleep without feeling sedated or distressed by the anticholinergic effects (dry mouth, constipation, etc.) the next day. If anxiety becomes a chronic problem, buspirone, a non-sedating phenothiazine, or imiprimine usually brings relief without danger of habituation.

FEEDBACK STATEMENTS

Issues—T-score: MMPI-1 ≥ 70; MMPI-2, NA (Not Applicable)

1. *Your profile shows that right now you feel isolated, lonely, and sad most of the time.*

2. *You probably feel despondent and guilty and you spend a good deal of time feeling bad about yourself, as though you are not worth liking.*

3. *You might feel hopeless about the future and about ever being happy.*

4. *You may have difficulty getting to sleep, or you may wake very early in the mornings and be unable to get back to sleep.*

5. *You may feel guilty much of the time. Your energy may be low which makes it hard for you to get your work done without having to push yourself.*

6. *At the end of the day you may not have enough energy left to relax and enjoy yourself.*

7. Your sexual drive may have diminished and you may have problems with eating and with your weight.

8. People with your profile tend to have difficulty expressing their anger to others.

9. It is hard for you to confront people and to express anger or resentment openly. You may find yourself "stewing" unable to express your feelings directly.

10. You tend to avoid confrontations and that makes you feel guilty and angry with yourself. When you cannot express anger you may put yourself down and feel disappointed in yourself.

11. You are a very shy person so it is hard for you to reach out to others and make friends.

12. Even though you may feel warmth and affection towards others, it is uncomfortable for you to show your affection in verbal or physical ways.

13. Because of your painful shyness, you work hard to preserve your personal privacy and you avoid any situation where you have to relate to someone you don't want to.

14. You push yourself and spend all your energy getting your work done and have nothing left for fun and relaxation at the end of the day.

Issues—T-score: MMPI-1, 55-69; MMPI-2, NA

1. Your profile is that of a normal, healthy individual who is cautious, serious, dependable, and honest. Just now, however, you may feel somewhat isolated, even a bit sad and lonely.

2. Periodically you may feel despondent, guilty, and disappointed in yourself.

3. At times your unhappy moods can degenerate further into feelings of apprehension about the future: You fear you might not be happy or close to others.

4. Periodically you may have difficulty falling asleep, or you may wake early in the morning and be unable to get back to sleep.

5. People with your profile have difficulty dealing with anger. Confrontations tend to be difficult and painful for you, too, so if you avoid them, and don't speak up, others may take advantage of your silence.

6. It is often somewhat hard for you to reach out to others and make new friends.

7. Displays of physical affection and exuberance are uncomfortable for you. You like your privacy and guard it because you feel shy and uncomfortable with others. You dislike being trapped in a situation where you are with people to whom you cannot relate but also can not avoid.

8. These days, your energy may be lower than usual so that you expend it all on your chores and have little left at the end of the day for fun or relaxation. Getting your chores done drains you especially when you have to interact much with people.

9. Your childhood probably was not very playful or carefree. Children benefit from periods of carefree time but you may have had many adult responsibilities as a youngster, perhaps due to harsh classroom expectations or the loss or absence of a parent.

10. Your parents may not have expressed physical affection for you, or for each other, though they may have been loving in other ways.

11. You were probably allowed to be by yourself for long periods of time. When you made a point to interact with your parents they probably responded to you without physical warmth.

Background and Early Learning Experiences

Your childhood probably was characterized by early responsibilities and an absence of playful, carefree times. Children develop best when they have plenty of time for play, free from worry and unreasonable responsibilities. You probably did not enjoy those childhood experiences either because you were required to bear the burden of adult responsibilities, or because you received little emotional warmth from persons who cared for you. Your parents probably did not express verbal or physical affection. Even in times when you felt great distress they did not hold you and comfort you physically. You may have been left by yourself for extended periods of time. Rarely were you rescued from distressing situations or feelings unless you made a special effort to elicit their help. Their help was undemonstrative and emotionally dry and brisk. This in no way infers that they did not love you rather their style of showing affection and care was spare and economical.

Self-help Suggestions

1. Medication may be helpful if you are having trouble sleeping or if your energy and motivation is at a low ebb.

2. You were probably painfully shy as an adolescent and found it exceedingly hard to relate to your peers, especially to members of the opposite sex. This caused you pain when forming intimate relationships and probably increased your sense of guilt, anxiety, and uncertainty. Now it's time for you to forgive yourself for your natural inclination to shyness and privacy. Make an effort to strike a friendship with at least one other person who feels somewhat like yourself. Make a point of scheduling time to do something that will relax and entertain you—walks in the park, visits to a museum.

3. Give yourself permission to feel shy because there is much evidence that shyness is an inborn trait; people are born with different levels of shyness. However, try

to force yourself to join organizations with others who have similar levels of shyness and exert yourself to make friends who are like you.

4. Physical exercise is often useful for people with your profile. Regular physical exertion will help you feel more energetic and motivated.

5. Think about getting a pet that will allow you to express and receive affection. A pet may very likely help you with your feelings of loneliness and disconnectedness from others.

SCALE 3

Descriptors

Concerns/Complaints: Episodic stress induced headaches, chest pain, palpitations, abdominal pain, dizziness, weakness, fainting; receiving attention, acceptance, affection, unhappy home, work, marital situation, fears of emotional pain, possibly anxiety attacks, rejection by father.

Thoughts: Thinks positively, refuses to recognize obvious realities, may acknowledge physical problems but deny worries about them, otherwise worries, lacking in insight, talkative, alert, clever, enterprising, enthusiastic, possibly religious.

Emotions: Affectionate, emotional, feels fearful, generous, difficulty experiencing anger and expressing it directly, conversion symptoms, denying, repressing.

Traits/Behaviors: Infantile, immature, childish, demanding, self-centered, egocentric, narcissistic, exhibitionistic, extroverted, naive, suggestible, dependent, overactive; also empathic, friendly, responsive, sensitive, optimistic.

Therapist's Notes

It is hypothesized that **Scale 3** elevations are associated with a profound fear of psychological or emotional pain. It is assumed that clients with elevated **Scale 3** need to be liked and to avoid conflict. It is important for them to be seen by others as psychologically healthy. They will seek reassurance that they are likeable and will try to elicit it by flattering, rewarding and complimenting others. They tend to be positive in the face of adversity, anger or hostility, and they will often develop somatic symptoms when faced with stress or conflict. Often gestalt techniques together with implosion and systematic desensitization will help them face painful situations and unblock the anger and sadness related to frightening past events. It is helpful to look for what they explicitly deny because that is often at the center of their conflict. Be aware that these clients have difficulty remembering painful events. Eliciting catharsis is often helpful in extinguishing the strong fears that any negative feelings will overpower them.

Medication Notes

Rarely do "Spike 3" patients need medication. If they seek it for pain be aware of habituation. They are a poor risk for exploratory surgery, especially for complaints without a definite organic basis.

FEEDBACK STATEMENTS

Issues—T-score: MMPI-1, ≥ 70; MMPI-2, > 65

1. *Right now you feel very vulnerable to any kind of physical or emotional pain.*

2. *You may be going through a particularly stressful time trying to be brave and positive. You are afraid that negative feelings may overwhelm you.*

3. *Holding your feelings in and trying to stay positive, however, is putting stress on your body and you may be having all or any of the following symptoms: headaches, backaches, neckaches, stomach aches, nausea or dizziness.*

4. *These symptoms probably get worse as your stress increases and may change depending on what kind of stress you are under.*

5. *You tend to be an agreeable, even sentimental and romantic person who yearns for a life where people are kind and loving to each other.*

6. *You probably seek out situations where you can please others, make them happy and relieve them of suffering.*

7. *Very likely you work hard avoiding interpersonal difficulties or holding controversial views.*

8. Your discomfort with anger probably makes it difficult for you to confront people.

9. Consequently you may find yourself doing favors for others even when you would rather not. You don't want others to feel rejected, especially by you.

10. People with your profile are often seen as playful and childlike because of their extreme discomfort with the adult world of competition, greed and cruelty.

11. Serious and potentially painful responsibilities are something you avoid. You try to create situations that are pleasant, light, fun and enjoyable.

12. As a result, others may see you as naive, self-sacrificing and unrealistic.

13. You are easily influenced by other people's philosophies and think that you should think, want and do what they do.

14. Your willingness to entertain their suggestions, allows them to exert influence over you.

Issues—T-score: MMPI-1, 55-69; MMPI-2, 56-65

1. You have a number of strengths. You enjoy people, are kind and sensitive to people's feelings, and you like to make others feel comfortable and happy.

2. You are also an agreeable, perhaps even sentimental and romantic person who wants people to get along and not cause each other pain.

3. People with your profile typically deal with unpleasant and painful events by trying to stay positive and cheerful. You hope that the negative will just go away.

4. This tendency may lead those close to you to see you as a Pollyana.

5. Because of your tendency to look at the bright side of things and see the best in people, others also may see you as childlike and naive.

6. At times your unwillingness to see what is negative leaves you vulnerable to being exploited by others.

7. You are probably uncomfortable when you have to confront someone or be firm or angry with them.

8. It may be hard for you to say things that might hurt people's feelings so instead you end up doing something nice for them even when you don't really want to.

Issues—T-score: MMPI-1, 40-49; MMPI-2, 41-55

1. People with your profile tend to be very realistic and unsentimental in their view of the world.

2. As a result others may at times see you as honest, even to the point of being blunt.

Issues—T-score: MMPI-1, < 40; MMPI-2, < 41

1. People with your profile tend to be so grounded in reality that others see them as brutally honest.

2. This may mean that you are unable to ignore painful events even when it would be beneficial to do so.

Background and Early Learning Experiences for Elevated Profiles:

Rejection and anger from others are extremely painful for people with your profile. Perhaps as a child one of your parents was explosive or abusive and frightened you. Or perhaps you were subjected to periods of intense anger, or rejection by someone. In either case, your reaction very likely was to try to be brave, and to look for a positive outcome. Because you look for a positive outcome and because you are afraid of upsetting someone else, you fail to recognize your understandably negative feelings and anger. You may have learned to be totally unaware of your anger. Headaches, stomachaches, low back pain, or other physical symptoms are often caused by unfelt and unexpressed angry and negative feelings.

Self-help Suggestions

1. When you experience physical symptoms, such as headaches, backaches, stomachaches, etc., look to see if you are struggling with some angry feelings which are difficult to express. See if you are worried about confronting someone and do not want to do so.

2. Whenever you find yourself even mildly resentful or angry towards someone, try to express your feelings to them immediately even in small matters.

3. Rather than trying to make others feel better when you see them in distress, stop and ask yourself if you really want to offer help, or if you could even do so beneficially.

4. Try to see what is negative, as well as positive, in any given situation and try to balance the two extremes.

CODETYPE 3-4/4-3

Descriptors

Concerns/Complaints: Conflict over expression of feelings, episodic somatic symptoms, headaches, abdominal pain, blackouts, visual complaints, sexual, marital, family, legal problems, needing social approval and support, fearing rejection, suicidal thoughts, threats, and attempts.

Thoughts: Lacking in insight, poor judgment, dissociative, amnesic and possibly fugue episodes, suicidal when stressed.

Emotions: Poorly controlled, over-controlled, extrapunitive, discharging anger indirectly, periodically explosively, rageful, rationalizing, denying, dissociating, repressing, acting out, dependency and conflict, rarely anxious or depressed.

Traits/Behaviors: Passive-aggressive, immature, dependent, demanding, self-centered, egocentric, attention-getting, impatient, outwardly conforming, inwardly rebellious.

Therapist's Notes

Clients with this profile are sensitive to criticism, rejection, and lack of acknowledgement from others. They project their sensitivity onto others and so have difficulty with the expression of criticism to anyone else. In difficult face-to-face situations they say whatever is expedient to avoid negativity and to obtain approval. They are unaware of how they distort reality by lying and/or selective reporting. Generally they are over-controlled and out of touch with their motives and feelings. They can present a good public front, but will periodically discharge their anger in unpredictable and sometimes violent outbursts. The hypothesis is that as children they were subjected to parental discounts and rejections. The assumption is that the way they dealt with rejection was to deny it, to positivize it, to look on the bright side and at the same time shut-off caring towards their parents. They did this to protect themselves from emotional disappointments. They looked for the correct social role to play in order to avoid rejection and anger from their parents. They also learned to over-control their anger and deny that it could even exist.

Therapy should concentrate on developing trust and on recognizing and expressing angry and negative feelings. These clients assume that the therapist plays roles, which is often a projection of their own role playing and they have a difficult time trusting that they can express negative feelings without the therapist withdrawing from them emotionally. In order for trust to develop the therapist must actively engage in dealing with the transference on a regular basis. The client will need permission to express negative emotions or doubts about the therapy. If the therapist does not withdraw from hearing such doubts or negative emotions, then trust can develop. The client then may be amenable to explore painful childhood experiences and rejections.

Medication Notes

Patients with this profile tend to misuse drugs and alcohol. The anxiolytics, particularly the benzodiazapines, should be avoided. However, the anxiolytic, buspirone, may be helpful for patients who develop panic attacks that reflect their over-control. When medication is indicated for overwhelming anxiety, the non-sedating phenothiazines also may be helpful.

FEEDBACK STATEMENTS

Issues—T-score: MMPI-1, $\geq$ 80; MMPI-2, NA

1. *Your profile indicates you have a significant number of strengths. You are an adventurous, fun-loving person who fits in well with many different kinds of people.*

2. *However, right now you seem to be holding in a lot of your feelings, trying to be brave, staying positive, and looking on the bright side. But you are uncertain about your feelings and about how others feel toward you.*

3. You are a sensitive person, especially to any kind of rejection from others.

4. You probably find it hard to reject others or in any way say no to them because you find rejection so painful yourself.

5. You are a person who wants to guard others from painful experiences so you may find yourself having to tell "white lies" in order to protect other people's feelings.

6. You tend to conform to society's values and expectations but at the same time you are somewhat of a rebel who hates to be controlled.

7. Perhaps as a way of dealing with these two parts of your personality, you may mix with very diverse groups of friends.

8. Some of your friends may be very conforming and some very likely are on the fringes of society.

9. If that is not the case, then at least you feel comfortable dealing with people who are very different, both those who conform and those who deviate.

10. Being in a situation where people in authority have power over you makes you extremely uncomfortable.

11. You have learned to be a survivor and it is difficult for you to let go and be vulnerable with others without feeling that you are going to be abandoned or let-down.

12. You generally want to please people and see the best in them.

13. Perhaps for this reason you tend to deny anger or fail to recognize when you are angry with others until at some point you explode.

14. These angry outbursts may frighten you and probably terrify others because they come out of nowhere and are very intense.

15. You are a person who is able to "read" what people want of you and you are able to fit into the roles that people expect.

16. In fact you are very skillful at playing those roles that society demands of you. You find it important to be seen as doing a good job of fitting in.

17. People with your profile are usually very good at selling and will often gravitate towards jobs where there is contact with people and a minimum of structure.

18. You are very aware of etiquette and the proper way to behave even though you may not always behave that way yourself.

19. However, being skillful at role playing may make you feel very much alone, because then no one really knows you and you may not even know yourself.

20. People with your profile sometimes experience powerful attacks of anxiety.

21. You may be taken off guard by the anxiety and not know why it erupts, but it is often the result of feeling that people are not telling you the truth, or are somehow manipulating you.

22. If you experience anxiety that seems to come out of "nowhere," then this may be because you work so hard to play the right role that you are not aware of your negative feelings until they finally over-power you.

23. Anxiety also may erupt when you feel that people are lying to you, which may relate to your own tendency to tell people what they want to hear so that they will respond with what you want to hear.

24. Often people with your profile are seen as charming and attractive to the opposite sex.

25. Sometimes you may get into trouble with the opposite sex because your freewheeling, easygoing attitude may be interpreted as insincere.

26. However, letting go of control and being emotionally spontaneous and intimate with others may be difficult for you.

Issues—T-score: MMPI-1, 70-79; MMPI-2, NA

1. You are going through a period right now where you are feeling vulnerable to rejection or being discounted.

2. You feel frightened, tense, and unable to explore the full range of your emotions.

3. You are probably struggling to hold in feelings of anger or sadness because you are afraid these feelings will be socially unacceptable.

4. You tend to be a sensitive person, especially to anticipated rejection or being discounted by others.

5. Because rejection is so painful you find it hard to reject others; especially when you identify with them.

6. It is probably hard for you to say no to people when they ask you for favors. You may tell them "white lies" in order to protect them from your anger or rejection.

7. You are a complex person: you are both a conformist and a rebel.

8. You conform to being very sensitive to social norms and values. For example, you may pay attention to etiquette and do things in the right and proper manner.

9. However, you also refuse to conform. You dislike being controlled and are somewhat suspicious of people with authority.

10. Consequently, you may go through life doing the right things and playing the right roles but at the same time you have outlets for your non-conventional behavior.

11. Perhaps these outlets are in having friends who come from "the fringes" of society or perhaps there are a number of unconventional things you do that few people know about.

12. Being skilled at role playing and in fulfilling others' expectations of you may leave you feeling isolated and alone.

13. Your close friends may not even know you and you may even sometimes wonder if you really know yourself.

14. People with your profile often do well in sales. They know what to say to make people feel good and they tend to understand the needs and feelings of others.

15. However, people with your profile cannot always tell when they are angry.

16. You tend to ignore your negative feelings and look on the bright side of things. You don't want to engage in negative thinking.

17. As a result, your anger will often build up over time and lead to an eventual uncontrollable outburst which even frightens you.

18. However, you rarely get angry. When you do, it is typically provoked by a specific person in your life and you get over it soon.

19. Other people may feel somewhat bruised and even terrified by the intensity of your angry outbursts, even though they are short-lived and you are quick to regain control.

20. Sometimes people with your profile experience brief anxiety attacks.

21. These attacks may result from denying their negative feelings and their efforts to get along with people. Then periodically they feel that people cannot be trusted.

22. Or sometimes attacks will occur because they are struggling to deny their anger, when in fact they are very angry.

23. People with your profile are often seen as charming and attractive by members of the opposite sex.

24. However, being emotionally spontaneous and vulnerable, and letting go of control, is probably difficult for you.

Issues—T-score: MMPI-1, 55-69; MMPI-2, NA

1. You are a person who is sensitive to rejection and being discounted by others.

2. You may be going through a period right now where you anticipate rejection or you have recently been rejected by someone.

3. Because rejection and negative feelings are painful for you, you have learned to be cautious about direct confrontations with others.

4. You probably try hard to please people and you find creative ways to say "no" when people ask for favors.

5. This may mean that at times you selectively report or tell "white lies" in order to protect other people's feelings.

6. You are aware of society's rules and values and you balance these with your own needs for non-conformity and individuality.

7. However, you dislike being controlled and you have a distrust of people in authority.

8. People with your profile like to work with other people and in jobs which allow a variety of social roles.

9. You may be interested in sales where you are able to rehearse various roles in a variety of situations.

10. Being skillful with roles may lead you to wondering if anyone really knows you.

11. This may leave you feeling lonely even though you may have many friends.

12. You probably work hard at being positive. You look on the bright side of things, and sweep unpleasant feelings "under the carpet."

13. This may lead to periodic angry outbursts, but once you have released your anger you probably bounce back and forget the incident.

14. However, others around you may be somewhat frightened by the intensity of your anger and their response to it may linger long after your explosion has blown over.

15. People with your profile may experience anxiety when they are angry and unaware of it.

16. You may become anxious too, when you doubt other people's honesty, because you tend to assume that people are not always honest with you since you are not always direct with them.

17. People with your profile are sometimes seen as attractive by members of the opposite sex because they come across as easygoing and charming.

18. However, in a committed relationship it is a little more difficult for you to be vulnerable and express your feelings openly.

Background and Early Learning Experiences

Your tendency to be cautious about letting go of control and being vulnerable to others may relate to a childhood *where one of your parents treated you with disrespect or in a harsh and authoritarian manner. This may have included severe spankings or angry rejections which left you feeling humiliated and abandoned. The pain of this may have instilled in you a distrust of authority and a sensitivity toward protecting others from feelings of pain or of being rejected themselves. Your parents also may have had a tendency not to confront people with their anger but rather expressed it in roundabout ways.*

Self-help Suggestions

1. *Work on being clear and direct. Don't tell people what you think they want to hear.*

2. *Think more about what you believe rather than what you think might please others. This may help you feel less distant from people and also may help you believe in them when they tell you something.*

3. *Think also about what you do want rather than what you think you should want in order to be socially acceptable.*

4. *Work on not telling "little white lies" in order to protect people. When you tell such lies you often end up wondering whether people are telling you "white lies" in return. Then you are never quite sure just who is telling the truth.*

5. *Remind yourself to explore your negative feelings whenever you feel mildly irritated or upset. Remember that your negative feelings are like the tip of an iceberg. Most of your negative feelings are still submerged and difficult to access.*

6. *When you are feeling mildly irritated, "pretend" that you are really angry so that you can practice knowing and expressing your feelings.*

7. *When you are angry towards others, allow yourself that feeling rather than trying to look positive and cheerful. Remember that when you deny anger it will later erupt in unpredictable and uncontrollable outbursts.*

CODETYPE 3-6/6-3

Descriptors

Concerns/Complaints: Tension, anxiety, headaches, abdominal pain, chronic family and interpersonal problems, difficult knowing and getting close to.

Thoughts: Thinks positively, difficulty accepting psychological basis of interpersonal conflicts, denial of anger, hostility and suspiciousness, resentful, lacking in insight, little self-understanding.

Emotions: Denying, rationalizing, projecting, hypersensitivity to criticism.

Traits/Behaviors: Egocentric, self-centered, narcissistic, naive, Pollyannaish, defensively uncooperative.

Therapist's Notes

Clients with this profile are afraid of being criticized, judged, and rejected. They project themselves as conforming and cooperative and deny their sexual and aggressive impulses. They often were model children, frequently "teachers pets," and the favorite child of the opposite-sex parent. They experience little, if any, anxiety or self-doubt. The hypothesis is that as children they were subjected to strict and demanding discipline. They learned to try to please others to avoid criticism and judgment. They also learned to avoid pain by denying it and putting on a cheerful face. They often have a great deal of pride, which makes it difficult for them to discuss themselves and reveal their feelings.

Therapy should concentrate on helping them recognize and express anger and resentment, and generally be more assertive. Insight therapies could help them re-engage some of the painful and humiliating reprimands and punishments which occurred in their childhood. If they could unblock their rage and learn to retaliate when attacked, they could learn that the feeling and expression of anger does not necessarily lead to overwhelming negative consequences. Therapy should move cautiously to avoid their feeling criticized, judged, or ashamed of their background experiences.

Medication Notes

Patients with this profile rarely admit psychological distress so they tend not to seek psychotropic medication. If they are disdainful of psychotropic drugs (elevation on *Scale 6*), they tend to be prone to dependency on medication (elevation on *Scale 3*). Sometimes they experience anxiety attacks as their denial collapses and paranoid sensitivity increases. At these times they are cautious about any medication that interferes with their vigilance. Low doses of trifluoperizine are useful in these cases.

FEEDBACK STATEMENTS

Issues—T-score: MMPI-1, $\geq$ 80; MMPI-2, NA (Not Applicable)

1. *Right now you may be going through a time when you feel that somebody is out to get you, perhaps to humiliate you, or somehow to hurt you emotionally.*

2. *Perhaps you are in a situation where you feel vulnerable to being criticized or perhaps you are in a relationship which you are afraid you may lose.*

3. *You seem to be trying very hard not to be angry or unjust. You want to avoid expressing feelings for which you could be ashamed.*

4. *At the same time you are feeling vulnerable and even hurt by what is going on. At times you are confused about whom to trust.*

5. *You probably also are feeling quite tense right now and may be experiencing headaches, neckaches, stomachaches, backaches or other physical symptoms.*

6. You are a person who strives to be above criticism and avoids doing things that will lead to rejection, disapproval, or criticism.

7. Very likely your expectations are exceedingly high and you are tough on yourself when you do not live up to your standards.

8. You may put a lot of "shoulds" on yourself and work very hard to do everything in the best possible way.

9. It is important for you to be seen as a pleasant, healthy, and cheerful person.

10. Consequently, most of the time you give people the benefit of the doubt and do not like to see their negative behaviors.

11. At rare times you can explode. You can be angry especially with people who you believe do wrong things.

12. When you do express anger, it probably is in the form of sharp verbal remarks or you may even break things, but only after you feel that you have been mistreated enough.

13. Once you do let yourself become angry, it is probably very difficult for you to trust the person who has hurt you.

14. For you anger and hurt go side by side. If somebody frustrates you it often hurts you as well as makes you angry.

15. You are a person for whom being meticulous about your social responsibilities is very important.

16. If you were to do something, even by accident, that was not socially acceptable, it may humiliate you terribly.

17. Having other people angry with you, especially if they are people you respect, is very humiliating and can be painful beyond imagination.

Issues—T-score: MMPI-1, 70-79; MMPI-2, NA

1. Right now you may be afraid of being rejected or humiliated.

2. You appear to be dealing with this by looking on the bright side and trying to live your life beyond criticism or judgment.

3. Your profile suggests that you have high standards for yourself and that generally you work hard to be above criticism.

4. You also tend to be a little hard on yourself if you break your own moral standards.

5. You are probably feeling tense right now with symptoms such as headaches or neckaches that result from holding in your feelings and trying to control them.

6. It is important for you to be seen as cheerful, polite, contented, and cooperative.

7. You are uncomfortable with confrontations unless you believe that you are justified and have the "right" to confront someone.

8. Consequently, most of your irritations and frustrations tend to get "swept under the carpet."

9. It is hard for you to express anger, even when you are extremely frustrated.

10. Very likely you will analyze your feelings until you think you have the "right" to be angry. Then when you are finally angry it is usually accompanied by a sense of hurt.

11. When your feelings are hurt, it takes you a long time to get over it.

12. When you do finally express anger, it may be so intense that it will alarm you or those around you.

Issues—T-score: MMPI-1, 55-69; MMPI-2, NA

1. *You are a person who may have high standards and who tries to be above criticism.*

2. *It is probably important for you to be seen as cheerful, polite, and contented.*

3. *You may work hard to please others and not "rock the boat."*

4. *You have a tendency to ignore the negative aspects of people and to give them the benefit of the doubt.*

5. *It is probably hard for you to become angry unless you feel completely justified.*

6. *Generally, you probably find confrontations with others difficult.*

7. *Sometimes people with your profile will bottle up negative feelings and then express them in short, sharp, and angry outbursts.*

8. *You are a person with high self-expectations and you think others should have high expectations as well.*

9. *Most people see you as cooperative, conscientious and very much of a team player.*

Background and Early Learning Experiences

Very likely, even as a child, it was important for you to be cooperative and conscientious. As children, people with your profile were often liked by their teachers because they worked hard to please and they were very well behaved. Perhaps your parents were very strict and demanding in their discipline and held high expectations of you. You may have tried to please them and be above criticism because their reprimands were so painful to you. You probably still try to avoid being criticized or judged, especially on issues which you feel are socially or morally reprehensible.

Self-help Suggestions

1. *Give yourself permission not to do everything perfectly all the time.*

2. *You have a tendency to analyze all your emotions to ensure they are rational and fair before you let yourself fully engage them. Consequently, once you are angry, it is the result of an accumulation of angry feelings, so it becomes hard for you to forgive and forget. As soon as you feel anger allow yourself to admit it to yourself, even if you decide not to express it to others.*

3. *Remember also that you can be angry with someone without blaming them.*

4. *Allow yourself to explore what you **"want"** in a given situation, rather than always thinking about what you **"should want"** in order to be above criticism.*

CODETYPE 3-7/7-3

Descriptors

Concerns/Complaints: Worries, tension, anxiety, various physical and psychosomatic ailments, occasional insomnia.

Thoughts: Worrisome, lacking in insight, little concern about physical symptoms, excessive self-criticism.

Emotions: Denying, repressing, unresolved dependency needs.

Traits/Behaviors: (None available.)

Therapist's Notes

Clients with this profile are "worriers" who think ahead to every possible eventuality and try to anticipate them. If they have a number of responsibilities, then they are quick to feel guilty unless all responsibilities are taken care of and that, well in advance. They also wish to be liked, to avoid people being angry with them, and to have others approve of them. They dislike confrontations and will deny anger or resentment towards others rather than risk the discomfort of their own negative feelings. They are prone to develop somatic symptoms under stress. Their responsibilities are most important to them and the precipitating circumstances of referral often will center around some anticipated angry confrontations, or a threat to their emotional or financial security.

The hypothesis is that their fear of anger and unpredictable events stems from a childhood in which one of their parents, or a sibling or peer, was periodically explosive, physically attacking, or rejecting towards them. The unforeseeable anger was so frightening that they learned to over-protect against it by thinking ahead for possible eventualities in order to anticipate and pre-empt them by being meticulously nice and acquiescing. These clients are very amenable to standard behavioral therapy procedures. Relaxation and thought stopping are particularly useful. Assertiveness training, helping the patient role-play and expressing anger also would be useful.

Medication Notes

Patients with the **3-7/7-3** profile often respond well to anxiolytic medication. Beware of quick dependency on any pain or anxiety reducing medications.

These patients rarely exhibit psychotic symptoms though they can experience somatic concerns and debilitating anxiety. Elective surgery in these patients may result in unexpected, disturbing, and significant psychological and emotional sequelae.

FEEDBACK STATEMENTS

Issues—T-Score: MMPI-1, ≥ 80; MMPI-2, NA (Not Applicable)

1. *You have a number of strengths. You are a person who takes your responsibilities very seriously.*

2. *You are a sensitive and non-hostile person who likes to please people and avoid hurting their feelings.*

3. *You are thoughtful and attentive to the details of inter-personal relationships.*

4. *You also are cautious about things going unpredictably wrong, so you are very attentive and careful.*

5. *It appears that right now some of your strengths may be working against you. Although you attend to detail, it seems that now you are seeing danger and unpredictable catastrophe almost everywhere.*

6. *You may feel that you must be constantly on "guard," worrying about every possible thing that could happen.*

7. *People with your profile will sometimes experience headaches, backaches, stomach upsets, or other symptoms which are often related to stress.*

8. If you do experience physical symptoms, this will tend to confirm your belief that you have to be on guard against some unpredictable catastrophe.

9. People with your profile frequently have great difficulty facing conflict of any kind. Confronting someone may cause you days of anguish and worry.

10. It may affect your sleep and cause you almost constant anxiety over long periods of time.

11. The support of your friends is very important to you. You will spend a good deal of time making sure that they like you and checking up on the status of their feeling towards you.

12. Disapproval from any of your friends is often enough to overwhelm you with anxiety.

13. You may find yourself bending over backwards to give in to your family and friends to the point where most people would be angry.

14. Your discomfort with anger and confrontation may mean that you go out of your way to please those around you, reminding them of their strengths and good qualities and ignoring their weaknesses and poor qualities.

15. Making decisions and being able to concentrate for any period of time also is very difficult for you.

16. Most of the time it is almost impossible for you to feel that you are worth liking, and yet the approval of others is important to you.

17. You probably feel guilty most of the time, whether it is because someone seems annoyed with you or whether you feel irritation with someone else.

18. You probably also feel guilty about all the things you are not doing that you feel you are supposed to do.

19. Recently your responsibilities may have accumulated to the point of being almost unbearable.

20. It also is possible that someone who was previously supportive is rejecting you and so you are feeling very frightened and alone.

Issues—T-score: MMPI-1, 70-79; MMPI-2, NA

1. You have a number of strengths. You test as a sensitive and thoughtful person who works hard to avoid confrontations and hurting other people's feelings.

2. You are thoughtful, attentive to details, and caring about others.

3. During stressful times you are prone to developing some headaches, backaches, stomach upsets, or some other physical symptoms.

4. Your sensitivity to people and your attention to details may cause you problems, especially around not wanting to confront others if there is a possibility of someone getting angry.

5. You may find yourself glossing over things that upset you and even holding down your anger.

6. Conflicts are uncomfortable for you so occasionally a friend or family member may make demands on you which you find hard to resist even though you may want to.

7. You also may have a tendency to worry about some unpredictable event occurring which could cause you additional problems.

8. Generally you are a responsible person, concerned about family, financial and emotional security.

9. You enjoy being liked and you try to make other people feel liked in return.

10. If stress ever becomes too severe, you may suffer from an occasional sleepless night or, in rare cases, a lessened interest in sex.

11. Although you tend to be psychologically healthy, you are prone toward guilt around unfinished responsibilities and around expressions of anger.

12. When stresses accumulate, making decisions and concentrating may be difficult for you.

13. If you are seeking help of any kind because of a recent problem, it is likely that the problem involved some issue around your security or some issue around confrontations or anger.

Issues—T-score: MMPI-1, 55-69; MMPI-2, NA

1. Your profile is well within the normal range and reveals you as having many strengths. You are a sensitive, thoughtful person who works hard to avoid confrontations and hurting people's feelings.

2. You are thoughtful, attentive to details, and caring about other people's concerns.

3. During stressful times you are prone to developing headaches, backaches, stomachaches, or some other physical symptoms.

4. You may have occasional problems around not wanting to confront others, especially if there is any chance of them or you getting angry.

5. At these times you may find yourself glossing over things that upset you and even trying deliberately to hold down your anger.

6. Conflicts are uncomfortable for you so occasionally people will make demands on you which you find hard to resist even though you may want to do so.

7. You also may have a tendency to worry about minor things and things that are unpredictable also could cause you problems.

8. Generally you are a responsible person, concerned about your own and your families financial and emotional security.

9. You enjoy being liked and you try to make other people feel liked in return.

10. During stressful periods you also may suffer from an occasional sleepless night or, in rare instances, a lessened interest in sex.

11. You may be prone toward developing guilt around unfinished responsibilities or around feelings of anger.

12. As stresses accumulate, making decisions and concentrating may be difficult for you.

13. If you are seeking help for a recent problem, it is likely that the problem involved some issue around your security or some issue around confrontations or anger.

Background and Early Learning Experiences

You probably always have been sensitive to anger and hostility. Perhaps one of your parents was unpredictably "explosive" so that you were constantly on edge anticipating something frightening and potentially harmful happening to you. This may have instilled in you a caution about confrontations and you make an effort to please people who are angry with you rather than risk their hurting or disliking you. It is possible that you experienced a frightening illness as a child which left you feeling less confident in your ability to handle unpredictable situations in general.

Self-help Suggestions

1. From now on think about a problem, come up with a solution, and then stop thinking about the problem until it is time to solve it.

2. *Remember, you have the power to think about things you want to think about and to turn off thinking about things you do not want to think about.*

3. *People with your profile can be helped through relaxation techniques. Perhaps buying a relaxation cassette tape, or taking a few minutes every day to stop and think of a pleasurable relaxing scene, together with focusing on deep breathing, could help you feel less anxious.*

4. *Try to recognize when you are getting angry and then learn to express your anger directly. You will see that it does not have "dire" consequences.*

CODETYPE 3-9/9-3

Descriptors

Concerns/Complaints: Episodic attacks of acute distress, anxiety, chest pain, palpitations, headaches, interpersonal conflicts, conversion symptoms, fear of rejection and failure.

Thoughts: Hostile, verbally aggressive, anger toward domineering mother, superficially open, optimistic, thinks positively.

Emotions: Denying, repressing, dependency conflict, labile, feeling irritable, hostile.

Traits/Behaviors: Gregarious, outgoing, socially visible, dramatic, energetic.

Therapist's Notes

Clients with this profile are generally seen as energetic and optimistic with a high drive and a high need to perform, achieve, and earn praise and recognition. They have difficulty focusing on their feelings for fear of facing negative emotions, and are always planning new activities and seeking out opportunities in which to achieve and gain approval. During childhood they were frequently raised by domineering parents who demanded achievement as a prerequisite for approval but who then gave approval or rewards irregularly. Their central conflict is in needing approval and resenting the control they perceive from those who provide it. They are usually unaware of their anger, tending to over-control and deny it, however they will have infrequent angry outbursts directed toward a specific target. They fear failure which could lead to rejection or disapproval by others, and try to avoid it by constantly taking on more and more projects. They crave approval and fear failure.

Therapy should help them distinguish between their own wants and desires and what they think they ought to do to gain the approval of others. They need to reward themselves for what they achieve and not drive themselves to produce even more.

They need to recognize their negative feelings and express them promptly to prevent eventual explosions. They will benefit from dealing with their ambivalence towards their parents, whose values they actually share. They need to develop a positive self-image. Their tendency to boast reflects their underlying insecurity.

Medication Notes

Patients with this profile have a high incidence of alcoholism. Be wary of using any medication with addictive potential. Signs and symptoms of mania can be controlled with Lithium or Haloperidol. Patients with elevated *3-9/9-3* profiles resist any medication which sedates or slows them down. Sometimes *9-3* profiles are associated with brain damage so if any history of head injury exists, a careful neurological evaluation is advised.

FEEDBACK STATEMENTS

Issues—T-score: MMPI-1, > 80; MMPI-2, NA (Not Applicable)

1. *Your profile shows that currently your energy level is exceedingly high. Your mind is probably racing with thoughts. You have periodic surges of energy which cause you to over-commit yourself and take on a great number of tasks and activities.*

2. *Your mind may be racing so fast that it is hard for you to concentrate on a single topic for any length of time. You can see the connections between all your thoughts which causes your mind to race faster than you can express them.*

3. *In fact your energy is so high right now that it may be getting you into difficulties. You may be buying things, doing things, committing yourself to things that later, when your energy subsides, you will regret.*

4. *Your extreme optimism and reluctance at the present time to look at anything unpleasant may mean that others*

become impatient with you and feel that you are being unrealistic.

5. Right now it is exceedingly hard for you to admit that you may be bothered by anything, and you may be sweeping a lot of unpleasant issues under the carpet. You look at the bright side of life and often deny that anything is troubling you.

6. You often don't know when you are angry with people because of your tendency to sweep unpleasant things under the carpet. This causes your anger to build up and leads to periodic explosive outbursts.

7. When you do explode you seem to feel better and go on as if nothing had happened. You may even be surprised that the person with whom you were angry now feels hurt or angry with you.

8. People with your profile are usually ambitious. Your ambitions and goals changed direction a number of times, often just at the point when you were about to be or were successful.

9. You probably are very demanding of those around you. You want everyone associated with you to be the very best, which may put tremendous pressure on your family, friends, or co-workers.

10. If people are critical of you and you feel that you do not deserve it, you can become very angry with them.

11. You may be going through a period right now where you feel vulnerable to failure so you have stepped up your efforts to achieve a greater sense of accomplishment.

12. You hate it when people have power over you and you probably work toward a position of autonomy. Authorative figures who are critical or controlling can be especially hard for you to work with.

13. If you use drugs and/or alcohol, your tendency to explode, and you propensity to over commit yourself may get worse. In fact, if you are taking any chemicals, you may find yourself becoming exceedingly angry and explosive and doing things which you later seriously regret.

Issues—T-score: MMPI-1, 70-79; MMPI-2, NA

1. Your profile shows that currently your energy level is very high. You are probably involved in numerous projects, some of which you are going to have a difficult time finishing.

2. You tend to work in spurts. You let things pile up and then you try to finish them all at once. You have a tendency to overcommit yourself to too many tasks and activities.

3. Because your energy is so high the world probably moves too slowly for you. If people take what seems to you a long time to express themselves, you will want to interrupt them, finish their sentences for them, or walk off before they have finished.

4. Right now your impatience is high. It is hard for you to work at a task if the reward or success is not immediate.

5. You may become angry easily when you feel held back or prevented from keeping your schedule.

6. You probably are very ambitious and success is very important to you. You work hard to be successful and you enjoy approval for doing so.

7. You may have many creative ideas but have difficulty attending to detail or finishing projects.

8. People with your profile have very high standards and demand perfection from themselves and from family members and co-workers.

9. *You like to tell people about your achievements and you enjoy telling others how much you approve of their efforts when they achieve as well.*

10. *Criticism or disapproval hurts you greatly and makes you angry.*

11. *Perhaps because you are a perfectionist and ambitious as well as impatient, you have changed goals a number of times in your life and seem to be looking for excitement and challenge constantly.*

12. *Perhaps a fear of failing drives you toward trying harder and harder to achieve a greater and greater sense of success.*

13. *People with your profile will typically see the connections between their thoughts and may talk ahead of themselves making it difficult for others to follow them.*

14. *Right now your mind seems to be racing so that it may be difficult for you to finish what you are saying before switching to another topic.*

15. *It is very important to please the people you love or care about but you may find yourself promising things you cannot fulfill.*

16. *People with your profile have a need for independence. You do not like to be controlled and you prefer to work on your own, though you like to be around other people.*

17. *Conflicts with authority figures are likely to center around their abilities or performance because you feel better qualified than they are. Often the people whose approval you most want are also the people who make you the most angry.*

18. *Often, because of their high energy, people with your profile will use drugs or alcohol as a way to relax. This is dangerous and could easily result in a drinking or dependency problem.*

19. *Right now you want to deny that anything is bothering you. You have a tendency to ignore unpleasant events and feelings.*

20. *You try to stay positive while your angry feelings accumulate. Then you explode, often at a specific person. While you may quickly recover, you are often surprised at how hurt or angry that person became.*

Issues—T-score: MMPI-1, 55-69; MMPI-2, NA

1. *Your profile shows that you have a high level of energy, optimism, drive, and ambition.*

2. *You tend to work in spurts, you let things pile up until you decide to get them all done at once and then you can get impatient with people if they stand in your way.*

3. *Because of your high energy, you may become a little impatient with people who take a long time to say something. Perhaps you finish their sentences for them, leave the room before they finish talking, or interrupt them with a counter response.*

4. *You like to do things quickly and move on. Very likely you get impatient with how long things take because the world seems to move a little slower than you do.*

5. *You are a person who has a tendency to over-commit to too many tasks and activities, some of which you then find difficult to finish.*

6. *You tend to see the big picture and brush aside the detail. Probably you have found someone who is good at taking care of the loose ends and details that you leave behind.*

7. *You are probably seen as a cheerful individual, positive and optimistic.*

8. *However, this may mean that you ignore unpleasant, negative events and feelings which accumulate and may lead to occasional angry outbursts. If so, you probably get*

over these eruptions quickly and even forget what led up to them.

9. It may surprise you when those who witnessed your anger are more hurt and upset than you think is reasonable.

10. You tend to have high standards and expectations for yourself, and you may demand that friends, family, and co-workers all conform to similar levels of energy, work output, and excellent standards.

11. Very likely you work hard to avoid failure, and you enjoy approval. Disapproval or criticism makes you angry and upsets you. You tend to approve of and reward the work of others which results in a return of their approval and their recognition of your own good work.

12. You tend to see how things are interconnected, and when you are excited you may rush ahead making it difficult for others to follow your thoughts. Others may see this as changing the subject.

13. Although you tend to conform and want to achieve in ways that others can appreciate, you also resent being controlled. This may cause conflicts because the people who you like to please also may be the people who you feel have power over you.

14. People with your profile are constantly looking for challenges and excitement. This may mean that you change goals periodically, especially if you are frustrated with your current project.

15. People with your profile often like to work with other people such as in jobs related to sales. You are convincing and charming with your high energy so you are likely to be successful, but these same characteristics may make you erratic in performance.

16. You may use drugs and/or alcohol as a way of relaxing. This may cause uneven surges of energy, during which time you over-commit yourself or become angry or explosive.

Background and Early Learning Experiences

People with your profile often grew up in homes with rather domineering parents who constantly urged them to higher performance no matter how well they did. The parents could never give whole hearted approval and insisted there was always room for improvement. The parents also may have held back on promised rewards as a way of punishment. This makes it very difficult for you to enjoy your own successes because you probably internalized your parents voice. This causes you to push yourself towards greater accomplishments. Perhaps you are afraid to enjoy your successes for fear you will stop driving yourself, or you may be afraid that you won't be good enough to be liked unless you are very successful.

Self-help Suggestions

1. *When you find yourself thinking about taking on a new project, stop for a moment and consider the possibility that you may be frustrated and impatient with your current situation or task.*

2. *You probably are a person who thrives on rewards and approval, and punishment, anger or criticism makes you angry. You have a tendency to deny your accomplishments and not reward yourself for having achieved them. Plan immediate and small rewards for whatever you accomplish.*

3. *Do you hear your parents voice constantly challenging you and urging you to do better? You can stop that voice and think about your successes.*

4. *If your high drive and energy is causing you to over-commit your time or overspend your money, medication may substantially help you return to a normal level of relaxation and sleep. Discuss this with your therapist.*

5. *If you are using drugs and/or alcohol, these will seriously aggravate your mood swings and your*

explosive episodes. It is very important for you to stop using all chemical agents.

6. *You may have a difficult time knowing when you are angry and sad because whenever you are confronted with these feelings, you try to be positive and optimistic. Your sad and angry feelings will eventually overwhelm you. Try to become more immediately aware of your frustrations and express your feelings. Don't escape into new activities which may only get you into further trouble.*

SCALE 4

Descriptors

Concerns/Complaints: Resents rules, customs, regulations; disregards social standards and consequences of actions; experiences school, work, family, marital, legal problems; possibly overt or covert fighting; asocial, antisocial behavior, excessive use of alcohol and drugs; fear of caring, interpersonal trust.

Thoughts: Enterprising, self-confident, spontaneous, impulsive, unpredictable, rebellious, hostile, easily bored.

Emotions: Insensitive, shallow, superficial, intellectualizing, rationalizing, blaming, acting out.

Traits/Behaviors: Immature, self-centered, narcissistic, manipulative, impulsive, unreliable, irresponsible, antisocial; also sociable, adventurous, assertive, energetic, enterprising.

Therapist's Notes

Clients with elevations on *Scale 4* are survivors. They are afraid to invest themselves emotionally in relationships and they are afraid to commit themselves to long-term goals. The hypothesis is that due to overwhelming stress in their childhood where they had no-one to turn to, they developed the coping mechanism of numbing out their vulnerable feelings in order to survive. Often they had an authoritarian parent who would respond to them without empathy so they depended on their own resources. In the absence of such a childhood the patient may currently be going through an adjustment reaction characterized by numbing out feelings in order to cope with a prolonged stressful situation. The client is likely to suppress vulnerable and emotional feelings in order to protect against disappointments. Clients, though often superficially charming, will often present as cool, aloof, distant, and hard to engage in the therapeutic situation.

A vital part of the psychotherapeutic process requires constant work on the client/therapist relationship to keep the client engaged or involved. This is because the client has a tendency to feel that a therapist cannot be trusted—that the therapist is playing a game. This is a projection of their own view of the world as a place where most people play games and do not really care about one another.

Gestalt techniques are most useful and most likely to succeed. They force the clients to engage feelings in hypothetical but realistic situations. Addressing the therapeutic relationship at every opportunity is also very important. Clients with this profile show some response to insight therapy in which they re-engage the painful experiences of being emotionally abandoned as children. This enables them to reactivate their emotional responsiveness.

Medication Notes

Medications are generally contraindicated for patients with **Scale 4** elevations. A likelihood is that they will abuse medications. While they may complain of depression this is more a feeling of emptiness and alienation rather than a sense of sadness and loss. In rare cases, especially if the K scale is over 65 T, they may complain of anxiety attacks. These episodic anxiety attacks may be due to a kind of paranoia, reflecting a projection of their own mistrust onto others. In such instances medication will not relieve the anxiety.

FEEDBACK STATEMENTS

Issues—T-score: MMPI-1, $\geq$ 80; MMPI-2, > 75

1. *People with your profile are very independent and rather uncomfortable working for others.*

2. *They prefer to have full control and have difficulty sharing authority, or trusting and confiding in others.*

3. Right now it is difficult for you to care about others and you don't want to get involved with them for fear they will disappoint you or let you down.

4. Perhaps recently you were in a difficult situation and you counted on someone. They let you down and severely disappointed you. Now you want to protect yourself—you don't want to count on anyone again and so you will keep your distance and stay uninvolved and emotionally numb. That way you hope to avoid a repetition of that pain.

5. You are probably a survivor. You learned to take care of yourself at an early age.

6. This may have left you with a cynical view of the world in which real love and caring doesn't exist.

7. Right now you may feel bored. You may have self-defeating thoughts, such as giving up on something before you have even given it a chance to work.

8. You also may feel angry, bitter, and defeated in your relationships.

9. You have a low tolerance for frustration and you may find yourself restless and impulsive especially when stressed.

10. People with your profile also have difficulty expressing anger about what bothers them. Instead they come across as being constantly irritable and sarcastic.

11. Often they will view the world as a cruel and heartless place. They fear that if they are not vigilant and should become vulnerable, others will use them and take advantage of them.

Issues—T-score: MMPI-1, 70-79; MMPI-2, 66-75

1. You are a person who loves adventure and new challenges.

2. You are somewhat of a rebel: uncomfortable with rules and regulations. You want to do things your own way.

3. People with your profile are often interesting conversationalists and storytellers.

4. They will frequently exaggerate and embellish their stories for the sake of entertaining others.

5. Your profile shows that you are easily bored and so you look for excitement.

6. This may mean turning to alcohol and drugs or getting into fights, but it also means doing other risky and dangerous things.

7. You have a tendency to be spontaneous to the point of showing poor judgment.

8. You have little patience for the moment-to-moment details of everyday life.

9. People with your profile have a low tolerance for frustration.

10. They like immediate gratification. They want what they want, and they want it right now.

11. This difficulty with waiting for things probably leads you to impulsive and hasty acts which often get you into trouble.

12. In some cases this can lead to problems with the law and to problems with other authorities as well.

13. You distrust people in authority and have difficulty working with them.

14. You may even have difficulty staying with any one job, because of this.

15. Being manipulative and not always telling the truth is alright with you, since that is your way to survive.

16. People with your profile often have numerous relationships with the opposite sex, but there is little real intimacy or satisfaction.

17. In fact, letting yourself really care about someone is difficult because you do not expect people to care about you.

18. As a result you tend to see the world as a "dog eat dog" place.

19. Even though you may be experiencing a number of difficulties in your life right now, most of your problems stem from your relationships rather than from overwhelming anxiety or low self-esteem.

Issues—T-score: MMPI-1, 55-69; MMPI-2, 56-65

1. You have a number of strengths. You are an independent and self-sufficient person who likes excitement and challenge. Right now, however, you may be cautious about letting yourself care too much for others.

2. You may be protecting yourself emotionally, keeping your distance for fear of being disappointed.

3. People with your profile often have a view of life that a "person is ultimately alone in the world," and that real intimacy and emotional sharing is rarely achieved.

4. You also tend to be a survivor. People with your profile tend to turn to their own resources rather than to others for help when they are in trouble.

5. Anger may be a problem for you in that you sometimes don't see it building up and you may express it by being verbally cutting and sarcastic.

6. You value spontaneity in yourself and in others which may periodically lead you into trouble because you have not thought through all of the consequences of your spontaneous acts.

7. People with your profile do not usually complain of anxiety and self-doubt.

8. Generally most of their difficulties lie in their relationships.

9. Their concerns will typically arise when others make demands on them—hem them in—make them feel trapped.

10. You are generally an independent person who enjoys taking charge of situations.

11. You are an excitement seeker and you like challenge and change.

12. You may become easily impatient and restless in situations where you feel constrained by the responsibility of painstaking details.

13. You are probably uncomfortable in highly structured environments where authority figures have considerable control.

Issues—T-score: MMPI-1, 40-54; MMPI-2, 41-55

1. You are not a rebellious person. You can tolerate significant levels of frustration.

2. Manipulative and pushy people may be able to take advantage of you and exploit you because you will not want to resist them.

3. People closest to you may become overprotective because of your reticence to stand up for yourself.

4. People with your profile are often slow to anger and tolerant of frustration and pressures.

5. This may mean that you do not stand up for yourself, allowing others to manipulate you into situations that can make you uncomfortable.

Issues—T-score: MMPI-1, < 40; MMPI-2, < 41

1. Your profile suggests that you are a person who has loyal, stable, and long-standing relationships.

2. You can tolerate a lifestyle that is based on routine.

3. You rarely feel bored and you do not have to take risks in order to feel a sense of excitement.

4. It is important for you to follow the rules of society and you rarely resist authority figures unless they blatantly break common rules of decency.

5. Your acceptance of your fate may mean that you are somewhat passive and unassertive.

Background and Early Learning Experiences for All T-scores Over 50

People with your profile often grew up in environments where they had to care for themselves because the authority figures in their lives could not be trusted to meet their needs. Perhaps one or both of your parents were alcoholic or violent or so demanding that when you were vulnerable in some crisis you could not turn to them. Their response would only make things worse. That is why you are still cautious about trusting authority figures.

You may remember specific occasions in your childhood when you were particularly disappointed. You may have faced a serious crisis and there was no one to whom to turn for help or understanding. Or perhaps in adolescence when you needed your parents support or permission to do something, they used their authority arbitrarily or in ways that were detrimental to you.

Self-help Suggestions

1. At the present time you are probably pushing people away from you and not letting anyone get very close. If others do reach out to you, notice how you "numb" yourself to their approach. Try to allow people to be warm to you without pushing them away.

2. When you get bored and look for excitement, find things to do that are not dangerous, illegal, or destructive.

3. Explore, with your therapist, how serious your drinking or chemical use is right now, so that you can learn ways to control it.

4. When you set a goal, try to give yourself small rewards along the way so that you don't think of quitting before you have given it a real try. When you feel bored, visualize the good feeling you will have when you finally succeed. This might help you stay focused.

5. Find ways to express your anger before it starts to build instead of letting it accumulate and explode. Exercise or an active sport, for example, is a good outlet for your anger.

6. If you notice yourself being sarcastic and cynical, that is usually a good measure of your anger. Learn to express that anger directly by saying how you really feel rather than talking about it indirectly through sarcasm, or the criticism of others.

7. When others say flattering or complimentary things to you, or when people say how much they care for you, don't discount what they are saying and assume that they are playing some game and being dishonest.

8. Observe your tendency to do or say whatever is convenient, whether you believe in it or not. Watch how you "bend the truth" and say what you think someone wants to hear. Then you end up feeling that no one tells the truth and this leaves you feeling alienated and lonely.

CODETYPE 4-6/6-4

Descriptors

Concerns/Complaints: Interpersonal relations, especially with opposite sex; social adjustment, legal, work, marital problems, anger control; occasionally asthma, hay fever, headaches, hypertension, chest pain, blackouts, drug usage, addiction, alcoholism, possibly conflict with same sex parent.

Thoughts: Evasive, defensive, refuses to admit difficulties, hostile, suspicious, litigious, poor judgment, critical.

Emotions: Feels tense, irritable, angry, resentful, hostile; over-sensitive to criticism, explosive, poor impulse control, rationalizing, repressing, projecting.

Traits/Behaviors: Self-centered, demanding, aggressive, belligerent, sullen, rigidly argumentative, manipulative, seen as obnoxious.

Therapist's Notes

Clients with this profile feel angry, alienated and resentful. They are suspicious of people's motives and are vigilant of being exploited and emotionally abandoned or let down. They anticipate anger from others and often elicit it with their argumentative attitude. The hypothesis is that as children their parents were arbitrary and critical and that whenever the child developed trust in them, the parents would humiliate and degrade them. They developed a hypervigilance about fairness, a caution against authority, and a tendency to argue as if all communication was a competition for control. They are quick to accuse others to protect themselves against anticipated criticism and control. They are wary of attacks on their autonomy or pride.

Therapy should concentrate initially on building trust. In order to maintain the therapeutic relationship an important procedure is to deal with transference issues and to give permission to the patient to express anger, hurt or rejection towards the therapist. These clients will expect the therapist to abandon or withdraw from them if they express anger, and if this doesn't occur, then they begin to develop the trust that was lacking in their early parental relationships. Help them to find ways to express their intense inner rage, and their wants and hurts directly, rather than storing them up until they feel resentful.

Medication Notes

As with other profiles with elevation on **Scale 4** these patients have a tendency to abuse drugs and alcohol. The addiction potential of most anxiolytics (especially the benzodiazipines) is sufficiently great to seriously question their therapeutic value with these patients. Medication is indicated if the patient is extremely paranoid and angry. In these cases low doses of a nonsedating phenothiazine such as trifluoperazine may be useful.

FEEDBACK STATEMENTS

Issues—T-score: MMPI—1, ≥ 70; MMPI-2, NA (Not Applicable)

1. *Your profile shows that you have some solid strengths. Generally being an independent person is important to you.*

2. *You are a survivor. You rely on your own resources to deal with the difficulties of daily life.*

3. *You are a person who works hard to be rational, fair, and analytical, and you spend a lot of energy trying to understand exactly why people react the way they do.*

4. *You also are an extremely sensitive person and are able to sense other people's angry feelings quite easily.*

5. *At the present time you may find yourself so afraid of being exploited that it is hard for you to know who is for you and who is against you.*

6. Sometimes you may wonder whether you are being unnecessarily vigilant and at other times you may wonder if you are being vigilant enough.

7. This may be a very confusing and frightening time for you. You feel vulnerable to attack and afraid that you will not be able to defend yourself.

8. You want affection and intimacy but you are probably afraid to respond to this need, to give up control, and to be caring of others. You are afraid that others will exploit your feelings and use them against you.

9. You tend to express your wishes in indirect ways. You feel that those closest to you ought to know how you feel, and give you what you want without having to ask for it. This may cause you to be angry and disappointed with those closest to you.

10. You value fairness and presently you feel unfairly treated yourself. When you see unfairness, it fills you with anger and you want to intervene and put things right.

11. Very likely you feel so vulnerable right now, that you will do anything to protect yourself. You are a survivor which means that you will bend the rules to protect yourself against being hurt, wounded, or unfairly treated.

12. Because of painful rejection or unfair treatment by parental or authority figures, you are vigilant for any transgressions by people with authority. You have a strong fear of being controlled.

13. You may find yourself resentful of people who have power over you. You may feel constantly vigilant against anyone who has control over you and has the power to attack you.

14. Generally you try to be rational so that people around you cannot criticize and attack you. You have an excellent memory in an argument in order to prove that you did not start the argument, that you were not to blame and that you were just trying to defend yourself.

15. *You try to understand everybody's viewpoint and withhold your anger unless you feel completely justified. When you feel justified you may become extremely angry, perhaps even rageful—smashing things, or at least wanting to smash things.*

16. *Once you allow yourself to become angry with someone, you may try to be forgiving, but it is hard to give up your resentment because your wounds feel so deep and painful.*

17. *People with your profile will often use words like "should" and "ought." This is because they feel they can not make demands on others unless they have the right to do so.*

18. *They hate to have other people make demands on them.*

Issues—T-score: MMPI-1, 55-69; MMPI-2, NA

1. *Your profile is within the normal range. It reflects a number of healthy strengths. You test as a person who is independent and sensitive.*

2. *You believe in drawing on your own resources and you tend to approach problems in a nontraditional and innovative way.*

3. *It is important for you to be rational, fair, and analytical so that you do not cause others unfair or unnecessary pain.*

4. *You probably are sensitive to the feelings of others. You value an exciting lifestyle.*

5. *Right now you are feeling cautious about being exploited or unfairly treated by others.*

6. *This is because you have been disappointed in the way others have treated or taken advantage of you.*

7. *You may find yourself constantly vigilant, protecting yourself against being taken advantage of or exploited and abandoned.*

8. Generally fairness is important to you, perhaps stemming from a childhood in which one of your parents was quick to reprimand and criticize you unfairly.

9. Very likely you are a person who wants and values intimacy but is reluctant to return it because you fear that expressing your care will give others control over you. Consequently in intimate relationships you may feel apprehensive.

10. You find it difficult to express your wishes directly because you fear that others will let you down or abandon you.

11. You are a person who values independence and you don't want authority figures to tell you what to do.

12. At times when someone is very forceful with a point of view, you are easily drawn into an argument.

13. This may stem from your need for fairness and balance and your irritation with abuses of power.

14. Although you may often express anger in a healthy and appropriate manner, you have a tendency not to express it directly when you feel vulnerable about an issue.

15. You may store up resentments, trying to analyze your feelings to ensure that they are fair and rational.

16. At these times your anger and frustration may build until you feel justified in expressing it. This leads to periodic expressions of anger followed by difficulty in forgetting the associated hurt.

Background and Early Learning Experiences

People with your profile often grew up in homes where the parents were at times humiliating, controlling, and arbitrary. Perhaps one parent was even physically threatening or abusive in attempts to discipline you. You probably felt let-down numerous times by those in authority, which caused you to lose trust in them. Perhaps some authority figure you trusted unfairly controlled and degraded you. You may have developed rational and analytical ways of dealing with your feelings, holding them back and refraining from exposing yourself to protect against unwarranted accusations and retaliations. Now when you care about someone, you fear that they will have power over you. This leads you to fear becoming too close with people you care about.

Self-help Suggestions

1. Right now you are feeling angry and resentful. Look for ways to express that anger without taking it out on others. Wait until your anger has subsided so that you can effectively tell people who have hurt you.

2. Learn to express your wishes directly rather than couching your needs in justifications. Tell people what you want rather than telling people what they owe you because you deserve it.

3. Learn to express your hurt feelings as they occur. Try to remember that others are not out to hurt you. Just because you may feel hurt and wounded does not mean that this was the intention.

4. Remember that you have a tendency to be argumentative. You may even find yourself arguing a point of view that you don't even believe.

5. As a bond begins to form, observe how you hold back in relationships to protect yourself against let-downs. Don't demand proof of love everytime you find yourself anxious about a relationship. You get frightened when you care about someone. You fear that being vulnerable they will have power over you and then they will abuse it. Your demand for proof of affection may elicit the very anger you feared most and will confirm your view that all relationships are difficult and conflicted.

CODETYPE 4-7/7-4

Descriptors

Concerns/Complaints: Tension, headaches, abdominal pain, fatigue; personal, social, legal problems, self-worth; alcohol use, sexual activity, home and marital conflicts.

Thoughts: Brooding, ruminating, self-condemning, regretting.

Emotions: Feeling inferior, resentful, rejected, tense, moody, irritable; insensitive to feelings of others; repetitive acting out followed by remorse, regret, self-pity; under controlled.

Traits/Behaviors: Immature, impulsive, insecure, dependent.

Therapist's Notes

Clients with this profile are insecure, dependent, but often ambitious and competitive. They act impulsively to reduce their tension and gratify their desires rather than postpone any short-term goals for long-term rewards. Clients with elevations on *Scales 4* and *7* will "bend the rules," "selectively report," "disinform," or turn to chemical substances as a way to immediately relieve anxiety. However, this usually leads to guilt, further anxiety, and a repetition of the cycle. In some cases this appears as a pattern of impulsive, regrettable behaviors, followed by guilt, anxiety, and more acting out to relieve the guilt.

The hypothesis is that as children they were raised by parents who were inconsistent on every level including the setting of limits. Often one parent was very indulgent and the other depriving and unpredictable. Frequently, when one parent was unfairly punitive, the other parent reacted with over-indulgence. Sometimes the same parent alternated between unpredictable explosiveness and over-indulgence due to guilt.

Therapy should concentrate on helping the client identify anxiety producing situations that lead to impulsive, acting-out behaviors. New adaptive behaviors are needed to replace acting-out behaviors that lead to cycles of guilt. These clients must learn how to confront painful situations directly, rather than in a manipulative and passive/aggressive manner.

Medication Notes

Psychotropic drugs are best avoided for the majority of these patients. Medication with abuse potential leads to dependency. Nonaddictive drugs tend to be taken in an unreliable manner. Medication requires careful monitoring. Anxiolytics should be given on a time contingent basis rather than on an anxiety reducing basis. Buspirone may be an exception. Anti-depressants with anti-anxiety qualities such as imiprimine are useful when **Scale 2** is also significantly elevated.

FEEDBACK STATEMENTS

Issues—T-score: MMPI-1, > 70; MMPI-2, NA (Not Applicable)

1. *Your profile indicates that you are a person who is constantly on edge, worried, and on guard, in fear that some unpredictable event will cause you to feel disappointed and abandoned.*

2. *There are so many thoughts running through your mind that it is hard to concentrate and think clearly.*

3. *When your anxiety builds, you may make impulsive choices to relieve your anxiety.*

4. *However, impulsive choices and decisions often result in feelings of guilt and worry. This increases your anxiety and leads to another round of impulsive behavior.*

5. *Some of your impulsive acts, like drinking, unwise purchases, getting involved in illicit sexual relationships, and other such behaviors, may have serious consequence for you.*

6. *Very likely you will stay involved in relationships that are supportive and help relieve your anxiety, even if they are not emotionally satisfying.*

7. *You will find yourself wanting to be taken care of and reassured, though the reassurance does not last very long and does not take away that nagging sense of anxiety.*

8. *Often, for people with your profile, the relationships that help them with their anxiety also are the ones that they worry about the most.*

9. *People with your profile have difficulty with interpersonal conflicts and being assertive.*

10. *Very likely, whenever you become anxious, you find yourself becoming manipulative or somehow presenting the truth in its most favorable light in order to avoid someone's anger or rejection.*

11. *You may even find yourself telling a lie in order to avoid anger from others.*

12. *You are afraid of other people's anger, but you have difficulty expressing your own anger as well.*

13. *When anxiety or anger has built up and you can no longer hold back you may explode and do something impulsive.*

14. *You may avoid conflict by doing most anything, no matter how self-defeating.*

Issues—T-score: MMPI-1, 55-69; MMPI-2, NA

1. *Your profile is essentially normal and healthy. However, it shows that when you become anxious you have a tendency to impulsive actions which you might regret later.*

2. *When this happens you may worry and feel guilty about what you have done, which leads you to becoming tense and increases the likelihood of another impulsive act.*

3. As your profile is normal, you may only have these tendencies when tension and anxiety build up.

4. Generally you find conflict difficult and confrontations uncomfortable.

5. Whenever you are faced with a serious problem, you may find yourself doing something manipulative or finding some other way to avoid confronting the problem.

6. For example, you may find yourself "selectively reporting," that is, not reporting the whole truth in order to avoid an immediate painful consequence.

7. You may go through periods where you feel guilty and anxious, followed by periods where you could care less.

8. Generally you avoid situations that might make you angry or cause somebody to be angry with you.

9. When you finally do feel angry, you may behave impulsively due to the build-up of tension.

10. After your angry outburst, you may feel guilty and remorseful.

Background and Early Learning Experiences

People with this profile often grew up in homes where there was a great deal of uncertainty and anxiety. Perhaps one of your parents would occasionally explode with anger that frightened you and left you feeling alone or abandoned. The other parent would then feel guilty and try to make it up to you. Life felt uncertain, alternating between periods of harsh discipline and periods of being spoiled and over-indulged. This may have instilled in you a tendency to "grab" for whatever you could—whenever you could, especially when you felt worried or tense, without regard to the possible consequences.

Self-help Suggestions

1. *Pay attention to situations that make you anxious. Instead of waiting until your anxiety builds and then acting out impulsively to relieve it, plan more suitable ways to reduce your anxiety. Remember, you have a strong tendency to do almost anything to feel better when you experience anxiety, and it is difficult for you to think clearly at these times.*

2. *Learn some ways to stop your thoughts. Frequently your mind will race around as you think of all the things that could go wrong at a particular time. Worrying is an attempt to foresee the future, and account for all possibilities in any given situation. Learn ways to stop worry when it seems to be going nowhere.*

3. *Identify situations in your life that typically cause you a great deal of conflict. Rather than selectively reporting, being manipulative, or acting impulsively to relieve the conflict, learn to face it directly and be more assertive. Tell people what you want rather than feeling you have to manipulate them indirectly.*

4. *Remember, you have a tendency to avoid anxiety at any cost with no plan of how you are going to pay for the consequences of your action. Usually after you have impulsively acted to reduce tension, you feel guilty if your actions have not been productive. Learn more adaptive tension-reducing behaviors which you can practice on a daily basis such as exercise.*

CODETYPE 4-8/8-4

Descriptors

Concerns/Complaints: Fears, unhappiness, trusting others, being harmed and rejected, accepting responsibility, relating interpersonally, conforming socially, family, work, legal, sexual, anger problem; excessive alcohol use, drug abuse.

Thoughts: Confused, indecisive, unpredictable, obsessive, odd, bizarre, vicious, sexual, suspicious, self-defeating, hostile; suicidal; radical social, political, religious views; poor judgment, rebellious, antisocial, argumentative.

Emotions: Feeling inadequate, inferior, insecure, easily threatened; distant, withdrawn, inappropriate, worried, unhappy, empty, moody, distrustful, unempathic; rationalizing, projecting, withdrawing, acting out.

Traits/Behaviors: Unpredictable, nonconforming, impulsive, withdrawn, schizoid, paranoid, antisocial, hostile.

Therapist's Notes

Clients with this profile often feel depressed and confused. They may complain of "black moods," difficulty concentrating and making decisions, intrusive and disturbing thoughts, and low self-esteem. The "black moods" are feelings of emptiness that arise when the client numbs out emotions because of stress. The hypothesis is that this profile is a defensive response to a childhood characterized by neglect, hostility, and uncaring. As children these clients felt defective and unlovable. Often their parents had pushed them away emotionally and they experienced the rejection as proof that somehow they were damaged, defective, and broken. Confused by these thoughts and a negative self-image, they escaped into fantasy and survived often by lying, cheating, manipulating, and in adolescence by sexually acting out.

Explorative and insight therapy is usually contra-indicated. These clients seem to benefit from a supportive approach, specifically dealing with their fears that the therapist will dislike and reject them. Expect a number of tests of trust and the taking of periodic breaks from therapy. Once the tests are passed, the breaks will lessen and the client will make a more definite commitment. These clients do rather poorly in group therapy because of their tendency to see others as wearing masks. They are unable to identify the feelings of others. They have extreme difficulty in opening up and revealing themselves for fear that they will be humiliated and rejected, recapitulating their childhood experience with their parents.

Medication Notes

To find a suitable medication for the client with a **4-8/8-4** profile may be very difficult. They can be very anxious but the addiction potential of anxiolytic and sedative-hypnotic medications is quite significant for these patients, and must be avoided when the MacAndrews alcohol scale is significantly elevated (over raw score of 25). Care also should be exercised when prescribing antidepressants because these drugs may precipitate decompensation into a florid psychosis. What the patient may call or describe as "depression" is really a profound sense of numbness and emptiness. Antipsychotic medication may be necessary especially if a diagnosis of schizophrenia is made or if a drug-induced psychosis results from stimulant abuse or street drugs such as PCP. Low doses of trifluoroperazine are useful for the anxiety associated with this profile.

FEEDBACK STATEMENTS

Issues—T-score: MMPI-1, ≥ 80; MMPI-2, NA (Not Applicable)

1. *Your profile shows that currently you feel a great deal of tension, confusion, and anxiety. Nevertheless you have a number of strengths. You are a person who wants to be independent and rely on your own resources.*

2. *You seek original and creative solutions to problems.*

3. *Generally you are creative and imaginative and probably spend a good deal of time in fantasy.*

4. You are not a person who "follows the crowd." You seek out your own way and your own solutions.

5. However, at the present time some of your strengths are not working for you and may even be working strongly against you. Your profile suggests that trusting others and feeling connected to others is very difficult.

6. You feel people are "wearing masks" so it is hard for you to "puzzle out" how they feel about you. That makes it difficult for you to know what to make of them.

7. It seems that right now you are somewhat disconnected from others and afraid to trust, let go, and care about others for fear that you will be let down and rejected by them.

8. At times, your world feels like a scary place and you are probably spending a lot of time and energy thinking of ways to protect yourself.

9. Perhaps much of the time you are preoccupied with how to avoid being humiliated and rejected by others.

10. You may be experiencing periods of "black moods" where you feel alone, empty, and disconnected from everything and everyone around you. That makes it hard to become involved in anything and/or to feel interested, excited, or hopeful.

11. The world may feel unpredictable and unmanageable and you may be feeling somewhat out of control.

12. Even when things seem to be going well you may feel a sense of dread and fear that something bad is about to happen.

13. All of this makes you feel bad about yourself. You don't feel good about yourself or feel that others could possibly like or respect you.

14. You may have encased yourself in a self-protective armor. You keep people at a distance for fear that they will get too close and then humiliate and reject you.

15. Even though you may have some real successes in your life, you continue to doubt your abilities. You feel that you have tricked or fooled people into believing in you and fear that any moment they will discover who you really are.

16. Although having sexual relationships with the person you love is important to you, your sexual relations may leave you feeling dissatisfied and somehow alienated and alone.

17. Often people with your profile confuse aggression and sexuality. That means that they may become involved in relationships that are angry and hateful as well as exciting and sexual at the same time.

18. Although your ability to fantasize is an aspect of your creativity, some aspects of your fantasy leave you feeling uncomfortable and tense.

19. Perhaps you are fantasizing about what may be wrong with you or about what could go wrong.

20. These bad feelings interfere with your ability to make decisions and resolve problems.

21. Even reading these comments may be difficult for you. You will want to blame yourself and feel that there is something terribly wrong with you.

Issues—T-score: MMPI-1, 70-79; MMPI-2, NA

1. Your profile shows that you are experiencing a great deal of tension, confusion, and anxiety. Nevertheless you have a number of strengths. You are a person who wants to be independent and rely on your own resources.

2. *You seek creative and unusual solutions to problems.*

3. *Since you are very creative and imaginative you spend time in fantasy, exploring different ideas and solutions to problems. You are not a person who follows the crowd.*

4. *At the present time some of your strengths are not working for you and may even be working against you which makes the world seem a frightening place to be.*

5. *Everyone seems to be wearing a mask and you cannot understand what they are feeling or be empathic with them.*

6. *You feel like you are on the outside and you do not belong to any one or any group.*

7. *Most of the time you feel vulnerable to being rejected and humiliated so it is hard to relax and feel safe with any one group.*

8. *Often "black moods" sweep over you and you feel empty, alone, irritable, and angry.*

9. *Even though you may try to understand what causes these moods, you cannot link them to any external reality.*

10. *At these times you may find yourself pushing people away, snapping at them and keeping them at a distance because you feel so frightened, vulnerable, and alone.*

11. *Because of these feelings, communicating with others is difficult.*

12. *You have such a difficult time understanding what other people are thinking and feeling that you often misjudge their messages and are surprised by their reactions.*

13. *It is hard for you to relate or communicate with others in a way that works for you or for them.*

14. *Intimacy is important to you, so you may become sexually involved in relationships that end up making you feel dissatisfied or used or even humiliated. This may be because you misjudged or misinterpreted the others' intentions.*

15. *Right now you may feel that the world is somewhat frightening, the future feels unpredictable and something terrible may happen at any moment.*

16. *Even when things seem to be going well for you, you may still experience a sense of dread and fear as if some dark and ugly event may happen.*

17. *Much of time you feel as though you are not in control of your world or your feelings.*

18. *One of your strengths is your ability to fantasize and be creative, but at times your fantasies are so disturbing and uncomfortable that it interferes with your ability to think clearly and make decisions.*

19. *Reading these comments also may be difficult for you. You may blame yourself and feel that there is something terribly wrong with you.*

20. *You often doubt your abilities, even though you may be quite successful. You feel that you have somehow fooled others into believing that you are better than you really are.*

Issues—T-score: MMPI-1, 55-69; MMPI-2, NA

1. *Your profile suggests that your problems are not too severe. It shows that you may well be able to make some changes that will work better for you. You have a number of strengths. You are independent and you look for creative and unusual solutions to problems.*

2. *You probably also are creative and imaginative, as well as unconventional and nonconforming.*

3. *There are times, however, when your strengths might work against you. Your ability to address problems with imaginative and creative solutions may make it difficult for you to communicate with others who do not think in the unusual ways that you do.*

4. *Your way of thinking may make it difficult to relate easily with others in a mutually satisfying way.*

5. *There are times when you may find it hard to know how others are going to react to you and you may even be surprised at their responses to you.*

6. *You like to rely on your own resources, but this indicates that you have some difficulty trusting others and developing emotional bonds. You fear that being vulnerable may lead to eventual abandonment and humiliation.*

7. *During times of stress you may feel uncertain and confused about how others are responding to you. People seem to be wearing masks so that you cannot understand exactly what they are feeling.*

8. *Another of your strengths is your non-conformity. However at times this may cause you to feel on the outside. You don't feel a sense of belonging to a group of people you can trust and care about.*

9. *People with your profile occasionally experience "black moods" when they feel empty and disconnected from others, and they are not sure from where these feelings came.*

10. *These moods are not so much a sense of sadness but a sense of emptiness and aloneness.*

11. *When you have these moods, you may feel irritable and angry and will push people away. You won't want to reach out to people.*

12. *You are cautious about revealing yourself to others too quickly because sometimes you fear that you are not quite*

worthy or good enough to be accepted by others, even the people that you most trust and care about.

13. At these times you fear rejection so you may push people away to protect yourself from their possible rejection.

14. Even when things are going well for you, stress may make you feel that your world is unpredictable and that you are not totally in control.

15. At these times you may experience a sense of anxiety, as if some dread thing is about to happen, but you do not know where these feelings come from.

16. Periodically you may doubt your own abilities even though you may be successful in a number of areas. You have a vague, disquieted sense that somehow you don't deserve these achievements.

17. Generally you are a person who is very sensitive to hostility and any anger or hostility from others tends to confuse or disorganize you.

18. People with your profile tend to have exciting and romantic sexual relationships. Sometimes it is hard to be vulnerable to your partner unless you are feeling particularly safe. But if you are, your relationships can be very satisfying.

19. Most of the time you function well and your imagination does not interfere with your concentration.

20. However, when stressed you may find it difficult to concentrate because then you daydream and your mind wanders unproductively.

21. These daydreams and fantasies can be uncomfortable and disturbing.

Background and Early Learning Experiences

Often people with this profile grew up in homes where they were treated with humiliation, rejection, and anger. You probably were a sensitive child who had no one to whom to turn when distressed and you withdrew into your thoughts as a way of escaping from threatening situations. You may have been ignored most of the time except when you were being punished and then you may have been treated severely.

Very likely you were seen as the "bad apple" in the family, so that when anything went wrong you were blamed. Perhaps to survive you stopped feeling and sought some different but workable routes to escape. This may have involved pushing people away emotionally, or lashing out at people to protect yourself and avoid more hurt and humiliation.

Self-help Suggestions

1. Remember your struggle as a child. You did what was necessary to survive and the very fact that you survived as well as you did is a testimony to your strength. Don't put yourself down for the way you handled things. Try to see your present fear of trusting others as an understandable reaction to your experience as a child.

2. If you find yourself daydreaming about unpleasant and uncomfortable things, learn to switch off the unpleasant thoughts and fantasies. They go nowhere and just make you feel worse.

3. Write a list of things that you have done well and that make you feel good. When you have a black mood and feel empty and alone, force yourself to read your list of accomplishments. Perhaps it has been raising a child, or finishing a particular project. Concentrate on the things you have done well, rather than constantly thinking of your failures.

4. Try not to push others away with anger when you are in one of your dark moods. Learn to express your fears of rejection and humiliation to those you love.

5. Learn to ask people how they feel and try to believe them. Try not to assume that everyone is wearing a mask and

deliberately misleading you about how they think and feel. Try to express your feelings honestly even though this is difficult. You fear that others will walk all over you if you are not in control and hiding your feelings.

6. *You have learned to manipulate others in order to survive and get what you want, but that leaves you feeling alienated and lonely, convinced that everyone else plays life by the same rules. Learn to ask for what you want and trust that, with time, you might learn to believe that others can be trusted to treat you well and tell you the truth about how they feel.*

CODETYPE 4-9/9-4

Descriptors

Concerns/Complaints: Transgresses social, legal, moral, decency standards; tests limits, takes risks, seeks excitement, acts impulsively, defies authority; deceives and manipulates others; deficits in judgement, conscience, empathy, and commitments; chronic legal, family, marital, work problems; alcohol, drug use and abuse; probable lying, fighting, delinquent and criminal activities; periodic emotional outbursts.

Thoughts: Self-centered, self-serving, selfish, pleasure and excitement seeking; talkative, argumentative, hostile, ambitious, self-defeating.

Emotions: Feeling angry, enthusiastic, resentful, hostile, irritable; uninhibited, arousal-seeking, empathy lacking, shallow and superficial; rationalizing, blaming, intellectualizing, acting out, "numbing out."

Traits/Behaviors: Extroverted, energetic, impulsive, immature, irresponsible, unreliable, untrustworthy, dependent, selfish, self-indulgent, narcissistic, acting out.

Therapist's Notes

Clients with this profile tend to be self-centered, vain, impulsive, excitement seeking, and sometimes lacking in conscience. They are often in trouble, either with the law, with other authority figures, or with people in their close relationships. Superficially charming with an easygoing style, they can quickly become impatient and belligerent when confronted or crossed. They are seen as skillful manipulators, who verbalize their dislike of people who lie, while at the same time "selectively reporting" or lying to stay out of trouble. Constantly seeking the "adrenalin rush" of a new challenge, they frequently have chaotic personal lives with many interpersonal conflicts. The hypothesis is that this profile results from an interaction of a specific genetic temperament and their learning experiences.

Frequently these clients were reared by one parent who was authoritarian and unreasonable and one who was indulgent and weak. Their early relationships with the authoritarian parent presumably led to a disrespect but fear of authority and a "numbing out" of feelings in order to survive. They responded to being treated arbitrarily by "playing the game" of the person they saw as unreasonable, yet constantly resisting any attempts to control them.

Therapy should concentrate on helping them to see how their constant rationalizing, selective reporting, and manipulating leave them feeling empty and alone. They tend to see the world as a "dog-eat-dog" place, where only the "top-dog" will survive. Their projection onto the therapist of their own mistrust and transgressions suggests the need for constant attention to the transference relationship.

Medication Notes

Medication should probably be avoided for patients with elevated **4-9/9-4** profiles. Some may have a history of drug abuse, and they seldom have symptoms for which medication is therapeutically helpful. However, if mania is a significant problem, lithium is the drug of choice.

FEEDBACK STATEMENTS

Issues—T-score: MMPI-1, $\geq$ 80; MMPI-2, NA (Not Applicable)

1. *Your profile suggests that you have a number of strengths. You are a person who prides yourself on being unconventional.*

2. *You may be an innovator, a leader and not a follower.*

3. *You value your independence and you are quick to ask "why" rather than being compliant and doing things according to rules.*

4. People with your profile can be charismatic and brave and adventurous.

5. They also are often seen as charming and friendly by others.

6. However, underneath your own friendliness you probably see the world as a "dog-eat-dog" place where you need to be in position of power to avoid others taking advantage of you.

7. It is hard for you to be vulnerable to others, or to allow others to see your anxieties and worries because you tend to see people as playing a role and as not being trustworthy.

8. It is generally easy for you to give advice to others, but it is hard for you to take it in return.

9. Your profile also suggests that you are a person who is in need of constant excitement. You love the "adrenalin rush" of danger and of challenges.

10. People with your profile hate "the 9 to 5 scene" where they are controlled by rules, regulations, and orders of others.

11. You are a person who loves a challenge but you tend to lose interest once you have conquered something, or if it involves attention to detail.

12. Generally impulsive, you will "go for what you want" typically, without thinking about consequences until after you have acted.

13. Even though this tendency may involve breaking rules, it is hard for you to stop doing something that is exciting, even risky.

14. Generally you may have difficulty following through on long-term goals, preferring the thrill of taking immediate action.

15. People with this profile often have severe difficulties with authority figures because they see them as arbitrary and unreasonable.

16. Occasionally you may feel some fear towards people you do respect but if you see them as less "powerful" than you, then you not only lose respect for them but you may even resort to manipulating them.

17. You test as a nonconformist, a rebel, someone who likes to do things their own way irrespective of established rules or etiquette.

18. You may consciously flaunt convention and enjoy the shock value of being different.

19. Because you hate conventionality, dislike authority, and distrust others, you may experience periods of loneliness when you may feel few people know you and there are very few people in whom you can confide.

20. People with your profile are often seen as "survivors." Perhaps because of this you rarely allow your conscience to stop you from doing something. You tend to "go for what you want," sometimes irrespective of other people's feelings.

21. Although you may say that you dislike people who lie, you are very good at "selectively reporting" yourself, that is, telling others only what they need to hear in order to create the right impression.

22. People with your profile are generally easy-going and even charming until someone gets in their way, confronts them, or crosses them. Then they can become extremely angry and their anger can be expressed in ways that can sometimes have severe repercussions.

23. Perhaps when people cross you, you smash things, or do other destructive things that end up backfiring on you.

24. People with your profile often become involved in drugs and/or alcohol as a way of relaxing and generating more excitement.

25. However, invariably this will lead to serious lapses of judgment and increasing dosages of either/or both in order to keep your excitement level high.

Issues—T-score: MMPI-1, 70-79; MMPI-2, NA

1. Your profile suggests you have a number of strengths. You are unconventional and independent.

2. You are probably always looking for new ways of doing things, rather than doing them the conventional way and following the rules.

3. You are more of a leader than a follower and you test as being energetic and "a survivor." People with your profile can be leaders, heroes, daredevils, and explorers and innovators.

4. You probably are a person who loves thrills and excitement.

5. In fact, you enjoy the "adrenalin rush" of a challenge so much that you would have considerable difficulty working in any situation that is confining.

6. You would probably avoid "the 9 to 5 scene," preferring work that allows you a lot of freedom and a great deal of stimulation.

7. Enjoying a challenge, you may have difficulties in your personal and job relationships if they are in any way boring or confining.

8. You have a tendency to "go for what you want" and think about the consequences later. This may even involve breaking the conventions of your group and at times even the rules.

9. People with your profile also are often seen as charming and easygoing until they are frustrated or until someone crosses them. At that time they may become explosive and irritable, leading to actions which frequently work against them.

10. People with your profile often have difficulty trusting others.

11. You are especially distrustful of authority figures, seeing them as potentially arbitrary and unreasonable.

12. This may be because they see the world as "dog-eat-dog" place, where in order to survive they have to seek positions of power and be the "top dog."

13. You dislike people having power over you but you can tolerate it if the person is someone you respect, especially if you also see them as highly intelligent.

14. However, if you cannot respect them, then it is hard for you to conform to their rules, and conflicts with them could lead to disruptions in your social and work relationships.

15. You generally need a lot of freedom and you enjoy working with a number of people as long as you are not confined one-on-one with anyone for too long a period of time.

16. You are a nonconformist who enjoys doing things your own way. You can enjoy the shock value of doing things differently.

17. It may be hard for you to be vulnerable to others, to let them know your feelings because you fear that they will somehow use them against you.

18. People with your profile often have many acquaintances but it is harder for them to have long-term friends they can trust.

19. Periodically, you may feel pangs of loneliness as you realize that few people know you because you are so skillful at playing a role and avoiding intimacy.

20. Although you may dislike people who lie, you are very skillful at reporting events in such a way as to create the impression you want to create by "bending the truth."

21. You also are clever at manipulating people and getting them to do what you want.

22. While this may help you become a leader, it is something that can get you into trouble, because people may feel used by you.

23. People with your profile also often become involved with drugs and/or alcohol as a way of relaxing, as well as increasing their excitement and stimulation. This can be addicting however.

Issues—T-score: MMPI-1, 55-69; MMPI-2, NA

1. Your profile is within the normal range, and reveals a number of strengths. You are an excitement seeking and fun-loving person.

2. You tend to look for new ways of approaching problems and you are likely to ask questions about traditional claims to authority.

3. You tend to be more of a leader than a follower and you are probably a "survivor" in the sense of relying on your own resources to satisfy your needs.

4. Very likely you are also independent and dislike authority figures telling you what to do.

5. You also enjoy the excitement of new challenges and situations, and you think in terms of the "big picture" rather than little details.

6. You are also uncomfortable in situations that confine you to structure and routine.

7. You generally dislike to feel controlled in any way and you seek situations in which you have autonomy and freedom.

8. You may see yourself as a nonconformist (perhaps even at times a rebel), liking to do things your own way.

9. You like the occasional excitement of going "against the stream" or "setting the pace" for others to follow.

10. People with your profile, while generally easygoing and friendly, can become irritable when frustrated or crossed.

11. You have a mild tendency to see the world as a place where you have to guard against being vulnerable because others may take advantage of you.

12. You tend to see situations in heirarchical terms; where people are either "above you" or "below you."

13. People with your profile often are involved in supervisory related jobs that allow them contact with others while not confining them to the traditional "9 to 5 scene."

14. People with your profile usually love a challenge, which occasionally can lead to trouble, because you might "bite off more than you can chew."

15. You have a tendency to work in spurts of energy; letting things pile up and then suddenly working on them all at once.

16. You also have a tendency to distrust authority figures, demanding that they prove themselves as more capable than you before you will respect them totally.

17. In situations where you feel that people above you are not more capable than you, then it may be very difficult for you to follow their rules or instructions completely, and you may have occasional "brushes" with them.

18. *Although respecting some basic laws and morals may be important to you, occasionally you will bend the laws and even "selectively report" in order to satisfy your needs, especially if you think the laws are "stupid" or if you think, "the end justifies the means."*

19. *You probably are good at manipulating others and getting them to do what you want and occasionally you may use that skill to further your aims.*

20. *Periodically you may experience loneliness because of your tendency to be a "survivor" and not to trust or open up to others easily.*

21. *At times you can be impulsive, going for what you want without always thinking through all the consequences.*

22. *Often people with your profile make many acquaintances, though the friends that they completely trust are not as plentiful.*

23. *People with your profile are sometimes addiction-prone; enjoying alcohol and/or drugs as a way of relaxing and relieving their boredom.*

Background and Early Learning Experiences

People with your profile were often active, energetic, and inquisitive children. One of your parents may have been authoritarian and strict, and treated you arbitrarily and with disrespect. From an early age, you probably resisted and resented your parents and responded to them by "numbing out" normal, vulnerable feelings of childhood and relying on your own resources. You became "street smart" in the sense of being able to manipulate others to satisfy your needs. Although you once may have been a "good" student at school, conflicts with authority have since been a problem. Your profile is often referred to as a "survivor" profile, because people with it learn from an early age to survive when there is no one to whom to turn for understanding and support.

Self-help Suggestions

1. *Try to find legal and/or non-dangerous ways of getting the "adrenalin rush" to which you are probably addicted. Perhaps because you have spent so many years "numbing out your feelings," you may have developed a feeling deficit. If so, your response to this deficit may be to look for anything that would give you an immediate high—often ignoring the dangerous and immoral aspects of your behavior. Find ways that you can get the "rush" without getting into trouble.*

2. *Try to set a goal and then reward yourself after you have completed each small step on the path towards that goal. Remember, you respond well to reward and poorly to environments where you receive no reward or punishment. Try to set goals with rewards along the way, to keep you involved and interested in future oriented goals.*

3. *Take time and observe how you tell people what you think they want to hear rather than what might be true. See if you notice how, this distances you and alienates you from people and leads you to assume that everybody is playing a game and telling you what you want to hear in return.*

SCALE 5

Descriptors For Men: High T-scores

Concerns/Complaints: Gender identity, aggression, performance, personal appearance, confrontations, relationships, possibly role adjustment.

Thoughts: Aesthetic, artistic, literary, cognitive, logical, insightful, understanding, introspective, idealistic, imaginative, creative, curious, inner-directed, intelligent, socially perceptive, tolerant, wide interests.

Emotions: Warm, caring, sensitive, expressive, empathic, self-controlled; sublimating, suppressing, introjecting, possible reaction formation.

Traits/Behaviors: Passive, submissive, dependent, unconventional, talkative, effeminate, dramatic, affected; also sociable, ambitious, colorful, interesting.

Descriptors for Men: Low T-scores

Concerns/Complaints: Physical, mechanical and sexual activities, athletic prowess, toughness, survival, self-protection, possibly doubts of own masculinity and traditional masculine-feminine views.

Thinking: Practical, thrill-seeking, unoriginal, inflexible; work, sports, outdoor life, mechanics, activity related, narrow interests.

Emotions: Unempathic, unexpressive, contented; idealizing, displacing.

Traits/Behaviors: Aggressive, adventurous, competitive, outgoing, relaxed, independent, jolly, cheerful, coarse, crude, vulgar, possibly dramatic.

Descriptors for Women: High T-scores

Concerns/Complaints: Gender identity, self-assertion, work and social relations, possible role adjustment.

Thoughts: Practical, logical, calculating, self-confident, work, sports, hobbies, achievements, mechanical, scientific, business, and outdoor activities, rejects traditional feminine views.

Emotions: Uninhibited, unemotional, may have difficulty appropriately channeling aggression; sublimating, introjecting, possible reaction formation.

Traits/Behaviors: Assertive, aggressive, competitive, masculine, tough, coarse, unfriendly, dominating; also vigorous, energetic, outgoing, confident, balanced, colorful, interesting.

Descriptors for Women: Low T-scores

Concerns/Complaints: Family, home, friends, relationships; assertion, privacy, security, violence, appearance, being taken advantage of; possibly doubts of own femininity and traditional masculine-feminine views.

Thoughts: Conscientious, capable, insightful, caring, understanding, cynical, unimaginative, unenthusiastic, constricted.

Emotions: Feeling capable, competent, considerate; caring, empathic, sensitive, emotional.

Traits/Behaviors: Modest, idealistic, intelligent, forceful, easy-going, unprejudiced, complaining, fault-finding; also may appear passive, submissive, yielding, self-pitying, coy, helpless, seductive, manipulative.

Therapist's Notes Related to Men

The hypothesis is that *Scale 5* measures a person's gender identity and not their sexual preferences. The higher the elevation the more the individual identifies with values, interests, and behaviors stereotypic of the opposite sex. **Scale 5** elevations for men suggest a close boy-mother (or female surrogate) childhood relationship in which the mother confided in the boy and discouraged displays of "masculine" aggression. The boy-father (or male surrogate) relationship is assumed to have been less close, intense, or present.

Issues— Men T-score: MMPI-1, $\geq$ 90; MMPI-2, $>$ 78

1. *You are a man who rejects culturally stereotypic male values and your relationships with women reflect your rejection of the "macho male" image.*

2. *You enjoy being around women and you enjoy feminine things, such as clothes, fashions magazines, jewelry, and cosmetics.*

3. *Men with your profile tend to be nonaggressive and non-competitive.*

4. *You probably enjoy cultural, verbal, and aesthetic interests but not traditionally masculine ones.*

5. *For example, you may not enjoy hunting, fishing, or playing poker.*

6. *The state of your environment is probably also more important to you than to most people, and everyday practical matters are of a lesser interest than music and art.*

7. *You have a tendency to be passive in your relationships, waiting for others to take the initiative and make the first move.*

8. *This may translate into "hanging back" in relating to people and waiting to see if you are going to be accepted and liked before you approach someone who interests you.*

9. *You may or may not have sexual relationships with men. But whether your relationships are sexual or not, you care*

a great deal about the men with whom you are close and you tend to be very nurturing and emotionally involved in these relationships.

10. Men with your profile typically dress stylishly, expressively, impeccably, and well.

11. They are "fussy" about their appearance and will attend to themselves with great care.

12. You enjoy and like to please women, and you enjoy talking about your relationships and feelings with women you are close to.

Issues—Men T-score: MMPI-1, 80-89; MMPI-2, 68-77

1. Men with your profile are quite often verbal, inquisitive, and introspective.

2. They will enjoy arts, music, opera, and ballet but will have virtually no interest in traditionally masculine activities such as hunting, fishing, and repairing things.

3. You have a tendency to be somewhat passive in your relationships in general.

4. Perhaps your sensitivity to rejection by others leads you to wait for others to make the "first move."

5. You enjoy and like to please women, and you enjoy talking about your relationships and feelings with women you are close to.

6. You also care about men and you may be involved in a number of close male relationships.

7. You can be very comfortable around men, listening to them share their feelings, and being warm and physically expressive toward them.

8. However, you tend to dislike aggressive or competitive men and you will try to avoid them.

9. Appearances, overall, are important to you.

10. How things look and how they feel to you are often more meaningful than their cost, function, or utility.

Issues—Men T-score: MMPI-1, 70-79; MMPI-2, 58-67

1. You are a man who publicly may spurn the traditionally masculine role of dominance and aggressiveness.

2. You probably enjoy being around women and pleasing them, and you try hard to avoid being rejected by them.

3. Talking about your feelings and your relationship with women is necessary and meaningful to you.

4. Men with your profile also have relationships with men which are close, meaningful, and open to discussions of feelings and issues.

5. Your relationships with men, as with women, are important to you.

6. Appearances, overall, are important to you, even as much as the way something works or the purpose it serves.

7. You are a person who may enjoy some competitive sports and aggressive activities as long as nobody gets hurt, balancing these with cultural, verbal, and artistic pursuits.

8. When it comes to expressing yourself, you are more likely to do so verbally than physically, and you are generally capable of maintaining good impulse control.

9. Men with your profile often will enjoy professions or work positions which involve thought and contemplation, but which also may include a nurturing or caretaking role.

Issues—Men T-score: MMPI-1, 55-69; MMPI-2, 43-57

1. Men with your profile usually have a good balance between their "masculine" and "feminine" sides.

2. You have some cultural, verbal and aesthetic interests but you also enjoy some traditionally masculine interests.

3. You can be as comfortable in your relationships with men as in your relationships with women.

4. Men with your profile typically enjoy indoor as well as outdoor activities, both as a participant and as an observer.

5. They like sports and the challenges of physical and competitive activities.

6. Matters of practicality do not weigh more heavily than those of appearance for you.

7. You try to balance how something looks and feels with what it costs and how useful it may be.

Issues—Men T-score: MMPI-1, 40-54; MMPI-2, 28-42

1. You tend to be a practical man who has less concern with aesthetics and how things appear, and more for how they work and how much they cost.

2. Your interests tend to be traditionally masculine, such as in hunting, fishing, working on cars, and building and repairing things.

3. You probably hold fairly traditional views of men and women, perhaps seeing women as "the weaker sex" and men as "the stronger sex."

4. This does not mean that you see women as inferior to men, but that you have traditional views of male and female relationships.

5. Often for men with your profile "actions speak louder than words."

6. You probably find discussing issues or talking about problems less appealing than actually "doing something about them."

7. You may find it particularly difficult to discuss feelings, problems, and common experiences with those to which you are closest.

8. Men with your profile typically enjoy physical contact, outdoor activities, and competitive sports, and they have a definite interest in who "wins" and who "loses."

Issues—Men T-score: MMPI-1, < 40; MMPI-2, < 28

1. You are a practical, down-to-earth man with "male" interests and a traditional view of male and female relationships.

2. This may mean that you see men as the "stronger sex" and women as the "weaker sex," believing that men are the "breadwinners" who should earn the living and protect the family, and women are "housewives" who should raise the children and take care of the home.

3. Most men with your profile prefer being their own boss and doing things in their own way.

4. They can work well with men, but rarely with women.

5. Women, for them, have feelings they don't understand and concerns about feelings that interfere with tangible results.

6. Outside of work you probably enjoy hunting, fishing, and the out-of-doors and building, repairing, and making your own things.

7. You also enjoy watching and participating in highly action-oriented, competitive, and aggressive adventures.

8. Men with your profile tend to be security and preparedness conscious.

9. Often they will join organizations advocating self-defense, survival training and gaining of weaponry skills.

Therapist's Notes Related to Women

Scale 5 elevations for women suggest a close girl-father (or male surrogate) childhood with the girl playing with boys, being a tomboy, and participating in activities traditionally confined primarily to boys. The girl-mother (or female surrogate) relationship in this instance is assumed to have been less close, present, or intense. Also a genetic component may be related to **Scale 5.** Men with elevations tend to have been nonaggressive and sensitive as boys, whereas women with elevations tend to have been independent, practical and adventuresome as girls.

Issues—Women T-score: MMPI-1, $\geq$ 65; MMPI-2, $\geq$ 70

1. Women with your profile tend to be independent, competitive, and pragmatic and have a variety of tangible and verbal skills.

2. You enjoy male companions, are comfortable around men and traditionally masculine activities, and can accept and positively identify with many male values.

3. You may in fact be more at ease with men friends than with women friends.

4. You are a woman for whom time, practicality and functionality are probably much more important than art, music, or literature.

5. You are not an "image" conscious person interested primarily in fashion, fads, or style.

6. You also are a woman who cannot see not doing something for the reason that "only men do it," or "women never do it."

7. For example, you may thoroughly enjoy motorcycles and cars, working on them, talking about them, racing and driving aggressively; or you may equally enjoy sports, science, business, or politics.

8. Women with your profile tend to be assertive in their relationships with people, and can often be comfortable asserting their personal and sexual wants in their relationships with men.

9. Most likely you are not a person who will spend much time talking about feelings and you have little interest in discussions of personal or family matters.

10. You may feel that in most instances "actions speak louder than words," or you would just rather be outdoors engaged in some physical activity.

Issues—Women T-score: MMPI-1, 55-64; MMPI-2, 60-69

1. You are a woman who may enjoy many traditionally "masculine" interests and activities.

2. For example, you may like cars and understand how they run.

3. You also may like to drive fast and aggressively, and will take some risks in search of adventure.

4. You also may like sports, science, business, and politics, and to a lesser extent music, art, and literature.

5. Women with your profile are often assertive in their relationships with people.

6. Most likely you can be as comfortable in your relationships with men as in your relationships with women.

7. You probably can accept and positively identify with many male values, and be a little more at ease with men friends than with women friends.

8. You probably are not a person who particularly likes to talk about her feelings, or who enjoys "gossip" or discussing personal or family matters.

9. More likely you would rather be "talking shop" or outdoors engaged in some physical activity.

10. Practicality, functionality, and your own time and energy are probably more important to you than how things look or appear.

11. You are not a particularly "image" conscious person, and your surroundings whether at home or work do not always have to be attractive or pleasing.

Issues—Women T-score: MMPI-1, 45-54; MMPI-2, 51-59

1. Women with your profile typically have a good balance between practical and aesthetic interests. They like being attractive and stylish to reflect themselves, and yet see the importance of being practical.

2. You can enjoy equally relationships with women and relationships with men.

3. You can accept men's interests and values as complimentary to your own.

4. You probably are a person who expresses herself verbally and avoids physical confrontations whenever possible.

5. Yet, you also are assertive, forthright, and not easily intimidated.

6. It is probably important to you to spend some time talking about your feelings and relationships, since your life would feel empty if you didn't take the time to do so.

7. However, getting practical things done is also important to you.

Issues—Women T-score: MMPI-1, 30-44; MMPI-2, 40-50

1. Women with your profile tend to be both practical and idealistic.

2. You have a good balance between your masculine and feminine sides.

3. You enjoy beauty and attractiveness, but also can have interest in physical or mechanical things, and in how things work.

4. You are a person who likes gentle and sensitive companions who can relate to the complexity of your feelings and ideas, but also you can enjoy companions who are "doers."

5. Talking about feelings, accomplishments, and relationships with family and friends is important to you and may occupy a significant part of your time.

6. Generally you are enjoy a balance between romantic ideas and practical matters.

Issues—Women T-scores: MMPI-1, < 30; MMPI-2, < 40

1. Women with your profile are family oriented, enjoy close friends, and will cherish a number of relationships.

2. Most likely you thoroughly enjoy talking with friends and relatives about your daily activities, your feelings, and the emotional events in your life.

3. In fact, talking about feelings and relationships probably occupies a very important part of your time.

4. Women with your profile often have a romantic fantasy of a "knight in shining armor," or of a "strong man" who would come along and sweep them right off their feet.

5. However, in reality this desire would most likely conflict with their dislike of the "macho male" who may be unwilling to discuss any personal feelings.

6. You are a woman who may have difficulty asserting herself, especially with dominant men and it may be hard for you to relate to men who do not have the balance between strength and gentleness that you enjoy.

7. Past hurts or failures in sex, marriage, business, and family life may lead you to fears of being further exploited, especially by men and you may find yourself ambivalent or distrustful of future relationships with them.

8. Often women with your profile will seek out women with compatible-values or gay and sensitive men for close friends.

9. You have a strong awareness of beauty, style, fashion, and design.

10. Your personal belongings, privacy, and having a special place of your own to decorate and adorn are all very important to you.

11. You probably have little interest in financial, computational, or mechanical matters and dealing with them can be emotionally draining.

SCALE 6

**Descriptors: For Clinical Cases, or
Patients Showing Poor Adjustment,
and/or Under Considerable Stress**

Concerns/Complaints: Trust, people's motives and thoughts; being misunderstood, unfairly criticized and treated, fear of moral and physical attack.

Thoughts: Suspicious, opinionated, argumentative, rigid, lacking in insight, moralistic, self-righteous, disturbed thinking; possible ideas of reference, delusions of persecution and grandeur.

Emotions: Feeling angry, mistreated, resentful, picked on; antagonistic, harboring grudges, touchy, overly sensitive, self-dissatisfied, projecting, rationalizing, externalizing.

Traits/Behaviors: Argumentative, stubborn, self-centered, undependable, evasive, hypersensitive, lacking in social skills, self-righteous, distrustful, suspicious, grandiose, paranoid; also curious, investigative, questioning, discriminating.

**Descriptors: For Normal Cases,
or Clients Showing a Good Adjustment,
and/or Under Minimal Stress**

Concerns/Complaints: Self-confidence, worry, fear of criticism and judgement.

Thoughts: Inquisitive rational, fair-minded, perceptive, insightful, decisive, wide-interests, clear-thinking.

Emotions: Affectionate, sensitive, soft-hearted, sentimental, loyal, trustful, generous, worrisome.

Traits/Behaviors: Frank, cooperative, kind, trusting, intelligent, industrious, energetic, poised, submissive, dependent.

Therapist's Notes

The hypothesis is that **Scale 6** elevations are associated with a fear of attack on one's abilities, behaviors and beliefs, as well as the domination over one's will. Clients with prominent **Scale 6** scores have been subjected to varying degrees of attack, criticism, and judgment. The assumption is that the higher the score the more extreme, the more will-breaking, and the more humiliating the attack has been. These clients need to trust that their therapist will not try to humiliate or control them. They are very perceptive and have a "sixth sense" as to whether a person is frightened or intimidated by them, or is not telling them the truth.

Many techniques can be effective with them once basic trust has been established. Giving them permission to be angry and empathizing with their sensitivity to criticism and humiliation will be vital in the initial stages of therapy. Encouraging insight and engaging their rage at having been criticized and humiliated unfairly also is useful. Typically these patients did not allow themselves to retaliate against criticism with anger for fear that it would lead to further attacks and criticism. They try to live their lives in avoidance of criticism and judgment.

Now they need to learn how to stick up for themselves before their anger accumulates and explodes in a self-justified, rationalized, and often uncontrolled outburst. They need to learn how to relax and accept criticism from others without feeling hurt and rejected.

Medication Notes

If paranoia is a clinical concern a non-sedating phenothiazine such as trifluoperazine or perphenazine is the drug of choice.

FEEDBACK STATEMENTS

Issues—T-score: MMPI-1, $\geq$ 70; MMPI-2, $\geq$ 66

1. *Right now you are feeling extremely sensitive to criticism, attack, or judgment.*

2. Either it is your own self-judgment that you are possibly trying to avoid or you are involved in a situation in which you feel that someone is about to criticize or judge you.

3. You may feel so vulnerable right now that it's hard to know who you can trust.

4. At times you may not be able to tell if someone wishes to give you a hostile message, but doesn't want to admit it to you.

5. In any event, criticism hurts and frightens you terribly and you try hard to avoid it.

6. You are a person who values honesty, integrity, and truth.

7. You also are very cautious about revealing to others your deepest thoughts and feelings.

8. This is probably because you fear you may reveal too much and your self-revelations will be used against you.

9. You also are very sensitive about what is right, fair, and just and are cautious about transgressing other people's boundaries. If others invade your boundaries, you can become very tense and angry.

10. Your interpersonal sensitivity is very high. You are wary of being a victim of someone else's power. This makes you very cautious and concerned about the motives of others.

11. If you care about someone deeply, it frightens you because you feel vulnerable to them. You fear that this gives them control over you and then they may hurt you.

12. You are an extremely loyal person so that when you care about people you stand by them and support them in every way.

13. However, should they ever let you down, deceive you, or hurt you, it is very hard, if not impossible, for you to ever trust them again.

14. *People with your profile have difficulty expressing their anger until they can feel fully justified in doing so.*

15. *In the meantime they will often analyze their anger away, or they may wait until they feel they have "every right" to be angry. Then they express it in an angry way.*

16. *There are times when you become so angry that it is hard for you to forgive the person who you see as the source of your anger and who has frustrated or hurt you.*

17. *Being rational and fair is also extremely important to you, and you expect others to be this way as well.*

Issues—T-score: MMPI-1, 55-69; MMPI-2, 56-65

1. *Your profile is essentially normal and it reveals a number of strengths. You value being alert, rational, and analytical and you are generally an inquisitive person.*

2. *You value honesty and fairness and you are sensitive to other people's feelings.*

3. *Because you are a sensitive person, your feelings are easily hurt especially if you feel manipulated or treated unfairly.*

4. *Right now you may feel cautious about revealing yourself in case something you say may be used against you.*

5. *Once you trust someone, you are very loyal to them.*

6. *You appreciate truthfulness and you always try to do the right thing.*

7. *Right now you are feeling anxious about being evaluated, criticized, or judged.*

8. *Periodically you may wonder whether someone is "trying to give you a message" behind what they are really saying.*

9. Expressing anger is often difficult for you until you feel completely justified for feeling the way you do.

10. More often than not you will probably feel hurt before you feel angry.

11. People with your profile are quite sensitive to being controlled in any way.

12. In your relationships you may suddenly pull back to avoid caring too much. Caring makes you feel vulnerable to being dominated and controlled.

13. You are cautious about others taking advantage of you, but you are also cautious about not invading the rights of others.

14. Pushy and manipulative people especially make you angry.

Issues—T-score: MMPI-1, 40-49; MMPI-2, NA

Your answers to some of the questions were markedly different than those of most people and suggest the following two possibilities.

A. 1. If you have not experienced severe psychological difficulties then you are probably seen by others as mature, serious, and reasonable.

   2. You also would be seen as trusting, loyal, and compassionate.

   3. In fact, your tendency to trust the motives of others may at times lead others to see you as rather naive and impressionable.

   4. Generally you face life situations in a balanced and self-controlled manner.

B.   1. *However, if you have experienced severe psychological difficulties, then you are probably cautious about trusting others in case you are unfairly criticized or judged.*

      2. *You also would find yourself avoiding confrontations and seen by others as sensitive and easily hurt.*

      3. *Generally you are shy and feel that if you reveal to much to others, they may use it against you.*

      4. *If others invade your boundaries, you can become very resistant and angry.*

Issues—T-score: MMPI-1, < 40; MMPI-2, < 40

1. *Generally you feel extremely sensitive to being criticized and judged.*

2. *You also are feeling vulnerable right now so that it is hard for you to know just whom you can trust.*

3. *Very likely there are times when you cannot tell if someone wishes to give you a hostile "message," but does not want to admit it to you.*

4. *You also are very cautious about revealing to others your innermost thoughts and feelings.*

5. *There are times when you probably become so angry that it is hard to forgive a person who has hurt you.*

6. *Being rational and fair is extremely important to you and you expect others to be this way as well.*

Background and Early Learning Experiences

People with your profile often were reared in households where their parents were controlling and judgmental. As a child you may have felt unfairly and unjustly criticized and attacked. Perhaps one of your parents was critical and domineering and would lecture and criticize you even for minor mistakes. Perhaps this parent also was quick to reprimand and find fault with you. If that is true, you could easily feel cautious about ever doing anything that would lead to being unfairly treated or criticized. At present you may experience some fears of being criticized which makes you feel very tense and cautious. It reawakens your vulnerability to being dominated and controlled.

Self-help Suggestions

1. At times when you feel you are being criticized unfairly, remember that not all criticism is negative and that not all negative criticism is intended as a personal attack on you.

2. When you feel hurt, irritated, or angry with someone, try giving yourself permission to express that anger or hurt rather than first analyzing your feelings to see if you are justified in having them before you can express them.

3. Try expressing your anger as you feel it, so that it will not get "bottled up" inside and discharged in periodic angry outburst. It will be easier for you to forgive the people who have hurt you, if you express your anger toward them right at the time that the hurt takes place and not a long time after the fact.

4. If you find yourself feeling mildly criticized by someone, observe to see if your feelings get hurt and you withdraw rather than standing up to argue your case.

CODETYPE 6-8/8-6

Descriptors

Concerns/Complaints: Trust, tension, worry, depression, self-esteem, self-confidence, personal security, contact with reality, social and emotional avoidance, possibly suicidal.

Thoughts: Unusual, unconventional, indecisive, over-ideational, circumstantial, tangential, unpredictable, confused, disorganized, fragmented, incoherent, autistic, bizarre, suspicious, grandiose, delusional, hallucinatory; difficulty attending, concentrating, remembering; poor judgment, daydreaming.

Emotions: Feelings of fear, anxiety, apathy, inadequacy, inferiority, guilt, depression, unreality; angry, resentful, inappropriate, phobic, withdrawn, isolated, regressed, moody.

Traits/Behaviors: Shy, schizoid, paranoid, lacking social skills.

Therapist's Notes

Clients with this profile often are confused and bewildered. They feel alone in a hostile world and unable to read accurately other people's reactions to them. At the same time they often are invaded by their own strange and frightening thoughts, and go through life bottling-up their feelings for fear of exposing themselves and being attacked and humiliated. Periodically they may inappropriately "explode" which leads to angry and fearful responses from others. The effect is as if they feel constantly under siege and yet unable to process what is happening to them. The profile may have a genetic component. When the T-scores are over 70 the patient may be diagnosed as psychotic and/or schizophrenic.

The hypothesis is that during childhood these clients experienced will-breaking hostility and humiliation from adults upon whom their security depended. Frequently they grew up in broken families with little supervision and caring, and whenever they were given support it was in a hostile and degrading manner. Many were "babied" and "put-down" by siblings and parents, which led to a negative self-identity.

Major life transitions are very stressful to them, and can lead to psychotic episodes. Any threats of violence should be taken seriously, especially with the profile elevated over 80. At this elevation medication is indicated, though these patients will be suspicious of any medication that deprives them of their vigilance. Therapy should concentrate on building trust, providing support, and "reparenting." These clients are suspicious and afraid of the humiliation of being dependent.

Intensive and uncovering psychotherapy approaches are best avoided because these clients are already overloaded, easily disorganized, and see insights as confirming of their negative self-concept. They need help to express anger in an appropriate and modulated way and will benefit by "telling the therapist off" because it helps them to see that no disastrous consequences occur. Often they store-up rationalized resentments and ruminate about how they can retaliate, but they rarely will express anger for fear it would expose them to further humiliation and anger of others in return. They also need help in skill training and in restoring their self-esteem.

Medication Notes

The non-sedating phenothiazines are generally the drugs of choice for patients with this profile. If **Scale 2** is elevated and the patient complains of depressive symptoms, antidepressants may be given but with great care because of the possibility of precipitating a psychotic episode. If **Scale 9** is also significantly elevated, the patient will show a better response to the butyrophenone, haloperidol, or to the anti-manic medication, lithium.

FEEDBACK STATEMENTS

Issues—T-score: MMPI-1, ≥ 70; MMPI-2, NA (Not Applicable)

1. *(Patient's or client's name), your profile suggests that you are going through a very difficult time right now. Generally you are a person who has a number of strengths. For example, you are a creative and sensitive person.*

2. It has always been easier for you to escape painful situations by turning to your inner-world of fantasy rather than to confront people.

3. However right now your sensitivity, creativity, and imagination may be working against you.

4. At the present time it seems that little in life is giving you pleasure and that most of the time you are feeling very alone, empty, and unhappy.

5. If this is true then perhaps the world is confusing to you right now and it is hard to connect with others or to communicate with them in a meaningful way.

6. Other people may seem to "wear masks" so that it is difficult to read what is going on with them and what they are really thinking or feeling.

7. Most of the time you may live with a good deal of fear and confusion because the way others respond to you seems so peculiar and hard to understand.

8. Perhaps you are feeling that other's are hostile towards you, or at least that they are harboring hostile intentions and feelings towards you.

9. Some of the time you may feel an empty numbness but at other times a deep rage boils within you.

10. It is hard to express the anger because you do not want to expose yourself and have others attack you in return.

11. Occasionally when you feel that hostility and anger from others is reaching dangerous proportions, you may find yourself lashing out in order to defend yourself.

12. At these times you may think of violent ways to defend yourself, and you may meticulously plan ways to get back at your enemies and eliminate them forever.

13. It may be hard for you to figure out what is real and what is not so that it is difficult to open yourself up and let people know what you are thinking and feelings.

14. Much of the time you probably blame yourself, feeling that you are defective, that there is something wrong with you, and that you are seriously "broken" or damaged inside.

15. It is as if the thoughts inside your head are so loud that you can hear them as voices talking to you.

16. Sometimes these voices may be telling you to protect yourself and get rid of your enemies, and at other times the voices may be telling you to destroy yourself.

17. In either case, the world seems bleak, confusing, and frightening right now.

Issues—T-score: MMPI-1, 60-70; MMPI-2, NA

1. (Patient's or client's name), your profile is within the normal range and it reveals that you may be a creative, sensitive, and highly imaginative person.

2. There are some times, however, when you may feel somewhat empty, alone and disconnected from others.

3. These times occur when you are stressed because someone is angry or upset with you, or perhaps when you are angry and upset with others.

4. It is at these times that you may find it hard to read other people, and to trust your ability to know what others are feeling toward you.

5. Sometimes you may find yourself unsure as to whether you are reading a situation correctly, or whether you are exaggerating it in some way.

6. People's anger and hostility may be so painful to you that you work hard to avoid it.

7. Sometimes when you are in conflict with others you become confused, tense, and agitated.

8. At these times your thoughts may become so loud that your concentration is disturbed and your ability to think clearly is impaired.

9. When some conflict has occurred between you and those who are closest to you, you may wonder how angry they are with you or whether you can trust your perception of what is going on.

10. Generally it is hard for you to become angry because you do not want others to lash out at you and accuse you of being angry for the wrong reasons.

11. You try hard to think through your feelings to make sure that they are above criticism, before you express any kind of reaction yourself.

12. Once you finally do become angry, it is often the result of feelings accumulated over time which then come out in sharp and angry ways, and may often be expressed in symbolic ways.

13. After you have expressed anger you may feel guilty and worried, feeling that perhaps you now have to protect yourself because you are going to be paid back for having shown how upset you really feel.

Issues—T-score: MMPI-1, 50-60; MMPI-2, NA

1. (Patient's or client's name), your profile is well within the normal range. It reveals a person who may be creative, and imaginative and when stressed resorts to creative and imaginative solutions.

2. You also are a person who is sensitive to anger and criticism.

3. Your sensitivity can mean that occasionally you get down on yourself when you feel that you are disappointing people who are important to you.

4. Your sensitivity also can mean that at times you feel disconnected from others, especially if you sense that they harbor any kind of resentment towards you.

5. At these times it is hard for you to respond to them or engage them because you dislike the prospect of facing their anger or annoyance.

6. Because you are a sensitive person, whenever you feel stressed you may become confused and have trouble knowing whether to trust your intuitions or whether to doubt them.

7. Generally you avoid confronting people and getting angry until you feel that you are justified in doing so.

8. This may mean that anger is allowed to build until it shows in short, sharp, and angry expressions when you finally have "had enough."

Background and Early Learning Experiences

People with your profile often were extremely sensitive as children. They were sensitive to uncaring, anger, and put-down, and grew up in an environment where they experienced a great deal of hostility. Perhaps one of your parents was particularly harsh or even cruel at times, especially when you did something displeasing. Perhaps you were subjected to the harshness of siblings or friends as well. If so, very likely you learned to avoid situations where you feel vulnerable to people having control over you or in some way being able to evaluate and criticize you. You may have escaped into daydreams as a way of "numbing" yourself to the pain of humiliation.

Perhaps right now you are feeling vulnerable, alone, and sensitive to being criticized and harmed. Perhaps someone who was previously supportive has withdrawn and you are feeling angry, hurt, and frightened. This may be reminding you of your childhood when you felt frightened but unable to turn to others for support because you feared humiliation.

Self-help Suggestions: T-score Over 70

1. *Often medication can help to take away that sense of dread and anxiety. Should your thoughts become so loud that you hear them as voices, perhaps medication can help you to feel calmer and think more clearly. There are types of medicines available that can help you to think more clearly without taking away your ability to see clearly what is going on around you, and you should discuss this with your therapist.*

2. *At first it may be very hard for you to trust your therapist because right now it is hard for you to trust anyone. It will be important to discuss this with your therapist as well.*

3. *If your therapist makes you angry it will be important to tell him or her, so that you will know that you will not be attacked or humiliated for expressing your feelings. People with your profile have often "swallowed their anger" in order to avoid being picked on and degraded. Perhaps you and your therapist can work on ways that you can express your anger when you feel it, so that it does not bottle up inside and lead to your becoming tense and confused.*

4. *Although right now you are probably feeling terrible, it is important that you do not blame yourself and see yourself as defective or "broken." These feelings you are experiencing now are normal for someone who has been through the kind of pain and stress that you have been through, however with help you can feel better.*

Self-help Suggestions: T-score Between 60 and 70

1. *Remember that when you are confronted with anger or hostility, it is hard for you to think clearly and organize*

your thoughts. At these times do not put yourself down but try to be kind to yourself.

2. *Whenever you feel angry, give yourself permission to express anger in a clear and direct way. Do not spend time ruminating and analyzing your anger to see if you are justified in feeling it because then you are likely to store resentments, leading to episodic and revengeful angry outbursts. You are a sensitive person and you dislike cruelty. However, when you allow yourself to store up angry feelings, then you may express them eventually in cruel ways. Probably because you have been so hurt you want to make sure that others will experience the same intensity of pain. This can come across as cruel and may push people away from you. Learn with your therapist how to express anger as you feel it, with the intensity that you feel it, rather than allowing it to build up over time.*

Self-help Suggestions: T-score Between 50 and 60

1. *If someone is angry with you or if you are angry with someone, try not to become so frightened and realize that nothing "bad" is going to happen simply because of anger.*

2. *Learn to recognize when you are irritated with someone and express it as you feel it rather than trying to analyze it away. If you perceive that someone is angry with you, try to confront the person with the anger at the time you perceive it.*

CODETYPE 6-9/9-6

Descriptors

Concerns/Complaints: Tension, stress, criticism, moral justification, intimidation, needing affection.

Thoughts: Ruminative, obsessional, overideational, suspicious, hostile, self-aggrandizing, grandiose, irrelevant, perplexed; possibly incoherent, disoriented, delusional.

Emotions: Tearful, anxious, irritable, angry, agitated, trembling, excitable, projecting.

Traits/Behaviors: Dependent, egocentric, restless, excitable, energetic, manic, paranoid.

Therapist's Notes

Clients with this profile appear tense, distractable, perhaps also suspicious and agitated. They are especially vulnerable to criticism or judgment from others. Clients with T-scores **over 80** will present more florid, manic, and paranoid symptoms; as for example, exhibiting grandiose and elaborate fantasies as to who is the source of their troubles. Their paranoia tends to be fixed and rational rather than diffused; they feel that specific people are "planning to get them." These patients are difficult to interview because of their distrust, and they are security-conscious and fearful of any attempts to control them.

The hypothesis is that they were reared in families where one or both parents were critical, judgmental, and domineering. As children they felt they were expected to live up to unrealistic expectations; when they failed they felt criticized, reprimanded, and humiliated. Possibly they tried to avoid criticism by pursuing unrealistic goals which would allow them to be above it.

The precipitating circumstance is usually a perceived attack or criticism from a loved one. Typically, they deal with stress by first feeling maligned and victimized and then counter-attacking the person criticizing them. They are rarely intro-spective and they are often unaware of their motivations or of their maladaptive behaviors.

Therapy should focus on establishing trust and validating the pain of being criticized and judged. Attempts to analyze the cause of their disturbance often will be seen as an attack on them and will result in angry retaliatory behavior. Help them see that the behavior of others' is not always an attempt to punish them, and how they assume others "must know what they are doing" when their actions hurt them. Help them to recognize their anger and learn ways to express it. Also help them distinguish between what their wants are as distinct from their internalized-parents' wants and expectations.

Medication Notes

Psychotropic medication is an important component in the treatment of patients with elevated *6-9/9-6* profiles. However, many are fearful of medication. Their rigid and often over-whelming need to be seen as virtuous, rational, and controlled renders them disdainful of drugs. Also, they are fearful of being slowed down and depressed. Initial low doses and thorough discussion of drug-related symptoms and side-effects often increases the patient's acceptance. Lithium can be the drug of choice, particularly when *Scale 9* is the more elevated of the two. If effective, the paranoid symptoms will subside as soon as the manic symptoms come under control. If the paranoid symptoms do not subside, a phenothiazine may be added or substituted.

FEEDBACK STATEMENTS

Issues—T-score: MMPI-1, $\geq$ 70; MMPI-2, NA (Not Applicable)

1. *(Patient's or client's name), your profile reveals that you have a number of strengths. You are interpersonally sensitive and you work hard to avoid hurting other peoples' feelings.*

2. *You also are very energetic and ambitious.*

3. You are a person who has exceedingly high standards and you work hard to do things well.

4. You value fairness and rationality and you spend a good deal of time and energy making sure that your feelings, thoughts, and behaviors are exemplary and beyond reproach.

5. At the present time one of your greatest strengths, your sensitivity, may be working against you. Your profile suggest that right now you are feeling extremely vulnerable to being criticized, judged, or attacked by others.

6. Criticism and judgment are very painful to you and it seems that you feel trapped in a position where someone dislikes you or somehow "has it in for you."

7. This criticism and judgment may be making you very tense, agitated, and even confused.

8. It also is possible that the person judging you so severely right now is yourself.

9. Perhaps you are in a position where you feel that others might judge you, and you are anticipating the criticisms and attacks and somehow preparing for them.

10. However, this tension about feeling vulnerable to criticism is making you feel very unprotected and frightened.

11. Generally you are a person who likes to live at peace with others and tries to avoid anger.

12. You work hard to analyze your feelings to ensure that they are "justified" before you ever express them.

13. There are periods when you do not express resentment and anger because it wouldn't be fair and reasonable to do so.

14. However, when you do feel justified in expressing anger, it is sometimes too late to express it in a calm and rational

way, and it comes out in a sharp and perhaps even a physical manner.

15. Another of your strengths is your ability to be rational, to be analytical, and to think things through.

16. However, right now, your mind is racing trying to analyze how to protect yourself in what you see as dangerous and an emotionally vulnerable situation.

17. There are probably times when you cannot be sure whether you are seeing things clearly or whether you are just being too sensitive, which is confusing and even frightening to you.

18. People with your profile often feel uncomfortable with emotions that they see as "irrational." For example, being jealous may appear as a "useless emotion" to you.

19. However, right now you may be feeling jealous and frightened that something of yours is unfairly going to be taken away from you, or perhaps you feel that you are about to lose someone who is particularly close to you.

20. It seems that you are feeling extremely tense and energized by these events but at the same time angry, and perhaps even confused.

21. You may be lashing out at your enemies as a way of protecting yourself.

22. You tend to value a moral and just way of behaving and may become angry if you feel that people are doing things that you would consider as unfair and unreasonable.

23. When other people do what you believe is wrong, you may be quick to tell them off and that can get you into trouble.

24. You are a person who probably takes a great deal of pride in the way you look and dress, and being attractive to the opposite sex, is an important part of your self-image.

Issues—T-score: MMPI-1, 60-70; MMPI-2, NA

1. (Patient's or client's name), your profile is within the normal range and reveals that you have a number of strengths. You are an energetic and ambitious person.

2. You tend to be optimistic, hard working, and perfectionistic and you value analytical and rational thought.

3. It is important for you to do things well and you have high standards for yourself.

4. You are sensitive to others and you value fairness and honesty.

5. It also is important for you to be independent and you have a good deal of pride.

6. Your strengths can sometimes work against you. Your sensitivity may mean that your feelings are easily hurt when others are critical of you.

7. It seems that right now you are feeling somewhat vulnerable to being criticized, judged, or perhaps evaluated in some way.

8. It may be your own criticism that you are experiencing or perhaps you are in a situation where you feel that "all eyes are on you" and that performing "perfectly" is vital.

9. You are a person who dislikes becoming angry unless you feel fully justified to be so.

10. Generally, you tend to analyze your emotions to see if they are fair and reasonable and if you have the "right" to have and express them.

11. This may mean that occasionally you will analyze your emotions away.

12. While this can be useful, it may backfire on you in that anger and resentments get stored, leading to periodic

angry outbursts and the build-up of hurt and resentful feelings within you.

13. *Perhaps because you value being rational so much, it is hard for you to accept certain feelings within yourself. For example, the feeling of jealousy may be one that you find difficult to tolerate.*

14. *Perhaps right now you are experiencing some fears that something important to you is going to be taken away from you unfairly or even arbitrarily, and this may be contributing to your present state of feeling tense, vulnerable and suspicious of people's motives.*

15. *You are a person with high standards, and you try hard to do what you believe is morally right and just.*

16. *You also have a high degree of pride so behaving in the appropriate way is important to you.*

17. *Because you try hard to do the "right thing," you can become angry and irritated when you see people breaking moral codes that are important to you.*

18. *People with your profile often take pride in the way they look and dress.*

19. *Your relationships with others are important to you and you probably spend at least a moderate amount of time on your personal appearance.*

Issues—T-scores: MMPI-1, 50-60; MMPI-2, NA

1. *(Patient's or client's name), your profile is well within the normal range. You exhibit a number of strengths. You are a sensitive, energetic and ambitious person.*

2. *You also have high standards and you work to avoid criticism and judgment from others.*

3. *You value fairness and being rational.*

4. Your profile also suggests that you are somewhat cautious about being criticized or reprimanded by others.

5. People with your profile tend to avoid expressing anger until they feel "justified" in doing so.

6. Consequently, you have a tendency to analyze your thoughts to ensure that they are reasonable and fair, which means that you may allow anger and resentments to build up and then express them in periodic angry episodes.

7. Once in a while this may even mean an angry explosion.

8. This tendency to analyze may interfere with your being able to spontaneously express your feelings leading to a build-up of hurt and resentment over time.

9. Because of your high standards you may be a little tough on people who break the moral code that you believe is the right and just one to have.

10. It is important for your self-image to be attractive to others and you probably ensure that by being appropriately dressed and groomed, and by caring about your appearance.

Background and Early Learning Experiences

People with your profile often grew up in homes where great demands were placed upon them. Perhaps you had an extremely critical parent who would lecture and humiliate you whenever you made a mistake or did something wrong. Throughout your life you have worked hard to achieve, to do things well, and to be above criticism. You may even remember specific times where you thought you had done a good job, only to be humiliated and criticized. Perhaps you became extremely angry but were unable to retaliate and defend yourself because you felt that it would only make things worse. You may have developed a lifestyle of avoiding criticism, seeking approval, and trying to do the right thing to avoid being humiliated.

Self-help Suggestions

1. *Give yourself permission to make mistakes. You have high standards and you tend to be self critical. It is probably hard for you to forgive yourself for any minor mistakes. Often you become so tense about doing things perfectly that it may interfere with your long-term goals because you may change goals whenever you see yourself unable to achieve perfection in any particular area. People with your profile often see every side of every issue and so it is hard for you to let yourself "rest" and give yourself approval for things you have done well.*

2. *Learn to distinguish between your goals and those of your parents and others.*

3. *Try to concentrate on doing what you want versus what you think you should do.*

4. *Give yourself rewards for the things you have done well. Do not focus on your mistakes or imperfections. See the balance between what you have done well and what you are not pleased with.*

5. *Give yourself more rewards when you do accomplish something successfully. Try not to get into the trap of goading yourself to greater and greater achievement as others may have been doing to you. If you work with people, try to reward them when they have done something successfully, rather than noticing what they have not done well.*

6. *Learn now to recognize when you are feeling angry. You have a tendency to confuse anger and blame. The difference between anger and blame is an important one. For example, if you are planning a picnic one day and it rains you may be angry but no-one is to blame. Often you will become frustrated by people's actions and they are not to blame for causing you the frustration. Allow yourself to express anger when you feel frustrated in a way that is not blaming of others. Give yourself permission to express the anger and tell other people when they have made you angry.*

7. *Try to express anger as it builds rather than analyzing your feelings to ensure they are "above criticism." When you analyze your feelings and do not express your anger until you feel you are justified, your anger builds until you are often so angry that your anger frightens others and even yourself.*

SCALE 7

Descriptors

Concerns/Complaints: Worrying, concentrating, making decisions, self-confidence, social relations; possible fatigue, exhaustion, insomnia; fear of failure and unexpected events.

Thoughts: Moralistic, self-conscious, self-derogatory, introspective, ruminative, self-critical, indecisive, self-doubting, difficulty concentrating.

Emotions: Feeling inferior, insecure, apprehensive, anxious, guilty; moody, agitated, soft-hearted, sentimental, trustful; rationalizing, undoing, intellectualizing, magical thinking.

Traits/Behaviors: Anxious, worrisome, high-strung, rigid, obsessive, ritualistic, perfectionistic, compulsive, dependent, reliable, formal, hard to get to know; also conscientious, persistent, methodical systematic, organized.

Therapist's Notes

The hypothesis is that *Scale 7* elevations are associated with a profound fear of unpredictable events. The assumption is that clients with elevated *Scale 7* scores were constantly teased and humiliated as children. Or perhaps they experienced some unpredictable and catastrophic event which led them to overprotect against unanticipated future events by planning and worrying. Worrying is seen as trying to predict the future by thinking ahead of all possible eventualities. These clients are amenable to almost any form of therapy. Implosion techniques in conjunction with insight therapy can be particularly useful. So also deconditioning these patients to the original unpredictable and frightening experiences will be helpful.

Medication Notes

Anxiolytics are useful but should be given on a time-contingent basis rather than on a symptom reduction basis. They are then motivated to set treatment goals.

FEEDBACK STATEMENTS

Issues—T-score: MMPI-1, $\geq$ 70; MMPI-2, $>$ 65

1. *Right now you are feeling constantly on the alert, as though danger lurked around every corner.*

2. *You worry about what could happen next; one unforeseeable event could occur and throw everything into a state of mayhem and disaster.*

3. *It is hard for you to think clearly, remember things, or concentrate, because you are constantly distracted and fretful about details.*

4. *You may find yourself making "mental lists" of all the things you have to worry about to avoid some unpredictable catastrophe.*

5. *Because your mind is constantly working and fretting, it is hard for you to make decisions.*

6. *People with your profile often develop a number of habits or superstitions that serve to reduce their anxiety.*

7. *Perhaps doing things repetitiously in a certain way has always worked for you so you are loathe to change your habits even though the benefits of doing such things are not immediately obvious.*

8. *You may have some fears of certain situations, people, or things, and you aren't even sure why that is. But avoiding these people or things helps to make you feel better.*

9. *Your profile suggests that you are extremely cautious about ever making a mistake that could lead to humiliation or shame.*

10. *You tend to be a careful, thorough, and persevering person who attends to every detail.*

11. You may be an ambitious person demanding a great deal from yourself and berating yourself over missed opportunities and achievements.

12. Other people's success may leave you feeling guilty as if you should have succeeded too.

13. It is not that you are jealous of others' but rather that you tend to see their success as proof of your own failing.

14. Confrontations with others that might lead to anger are frightening and you tend to avoid them.

15. You are reluctant to be angry with others and it is difficult for you to approach others if you think they will be angry with you.

16. Being angry with others causes you to feel guilty, tense, and uncomfortable.

17. Consequently being assertive is generally difficult for you and you may allow others to "push you around" or take advantage of you.

18. You are not inclined to take risks and you tend to avoid dangerous, challenging or even exciting situations.

Issues—T-score: MMPI-1, 55-69; MMPI-2, 56-65

1. You have a tendency to be anxious about what might go wrong.

2. Sometimes your anxiety is bad and other times you feel quite relaxed and free of worry.

3. Sometimes you may also make mental lists of possible disasters.

4. At times your anxieties grow so intense that it is hard to take on any new responsibilities. Others may not see how burdensome your worries are for you.

5. Decision-making is difficult for you, especially important decisions.

6. You may have found a certain way of handling situations that minimizes your anxiety. You may be reluctant to change this routine even if it is not the most effective way to handle the stress.

7. You are not a risk-taker and you are cautious about anything that is not a "sure thing."

8. You also are a thorough person with a good deal of ambition and drive to achieve.

9. The success of others can leave you wondering whether you have done well enough yourself.

10. You value things being done in a correct and thorough manner.

11. You are cautious about any detail going wrong, especially one that could lead you to feeling ashamed of yourself or humiliated because of your carelessness.

12. You generally dislike anger and confrontations.

13. When you have to confront someone you probably become anxious and tense.

14. To avoid confrontations and anger, you try to find ways of appeasing and placating others.

Issues—T-score: MMPI-1, 40-49; MMPI-2, 41-55

1. You tend to be self-confident and responsible person who can adapt to various situations without a great deal of worry and discomfort.

2. Even if you make a mistake or overlook an important detail you rarely feel guilty.

3. Others generally see you as relaxed, easy-going and a person who does not have many disabling fears.

4. You also are seen as efficient and comfortable with yourself.

5. It is easy for you to handle novel situations and to meet deadlines without feeling much stress.

6. You value success and enjoy achievements which give you power, status and recognition.

7. Whenever you are recognized for an achievement, you are not a person who feels "I do not deserve this."

8. Generally you are able to relax without feeling guilty that all of your chores are not done.

Issues—T-score: MMPI-1, < 40; MMPI-2, < 41

1. You are a person who is determined not to allow anxiety and worry to interfere with your relaxation and enjoyment.

2. You may allow important deadlines to pass or overlook important details which often leaves others to be angry with you and perhaps even call you "lazy."

3. Your lack of worry or guilt may make others judge you as indifferent, too laid back, or even undependable and irresponsible.

Background and Early Learning Experiences

People with your profile often were reared in homes where they were subjected to unreasonable or unexpected and frightening events. Sometimes they were given too much responsibility as children, or their parents were "explosive" or they were constantly teased by older siblings or by classmates at school. This led them to be constantly on edge and vigilant. They tried to protect themselves from the unexpected by analyzing and predicting the future and thereby avoiding any future painful event. They learned to dislike all surprises, even those with pleasant and joyful connotations. This continuous effort to anticipate and then prevent all that could go wrong is worrying. You probably have been doing this for a long time and it can be exhausting.

Self-help Suggestions

1. Whenever you find your mind racing ahead thinking of all possible eventualities, try and "stop your thoughts" and concentrate on one problem at a time.

2. Make a list of all the things that you worry about, and then take one worry at a time and see if you can do something about it. Forget about the other worries as you concentrate on the one.

3. Whenever you find yourself tense with your mind vigilantly attentive, take some time and think of a peaceful and relaxing scene. Take a couple of deep breaths and tell yourself to relax even further.

4. When something does go wrong, try not to punish and blame yourself as a bad person. Once something happens, accept it and move on.

5. Once you make a decision, do not go back over it and reanalyze it. Stick to your decision and leave it along.

6. When you first realize that a confrontation with someone is coming, give yourself permission to be angry and deal with the person as soon as you can. Try not to feel guilty afterwards.

CODETYPE 7-8/8-7

Descriptors

Concerns/Complaints: Worries, tension, stress, nervousness, depression, insomnia, sex, relationships, personal adequacy and achievement, suicide, excessive drinking, possible drug abuse.

Thoughts: Self-doubting, indecisive, introspective, obsessive, ruminative, confused, difficulty concentrating; possibly panicked, bizarre, delusional, shut-in.

Emotions: Feeling inferior, inadequate, insecure, anxious, fearful, nervous, guilty, agitated; possibly depersonalized, inappropriate, withdrawn.

Traits/Behaviors: Shy, withdrawn, poor interpersonal and social skills, passive-dependent.

Therapist's Notes

Clients with this profile are anxious, worried, and self-doubting. They fear unexpected arousal, shock, or startle, but most of all unexpected humiliation or embarrassment. Often they appear as obsessive and compulsive with a poor self-concept and low self-esteem. Some will feel defective, broken, or empty. Many are afraid of relationships.

The hypothesis is that as children they were sensitive and slow to mature, and they may have exhibited some personal peculiarities that reflected this; such as a quickness to cry or a slowness to warm up to others. This left them vulnerable to being teased and criticized which instilled in them a sense of inadequacy and of being somehow defective, broken, and different. Clinging and dependent behaviors were rewarded by attention and nurturing by their parents but they felt humiliated for being babied and overprotected. They reacted to teasing by worrying and trying to avoid situations where they might be teased again.

As adults they continue to worry which makes it difficult for them to concentrate, trust their decisions, and have self-confidence. Insights from therapy will depress them and tend to confirm their sense of inadequacy and low self-worth. Intensive, insight-oriented therapies can be disorganizing to these clients. In the initial stages of therapy, such methods are not indicated. These patients can, however, benefit from relaxation, desensitization and assertiveness-training. They need help to express anger, develop a better self-image, and gain self-confidence.

Medication Notes

Medication is often an important component in the treatment of the patient with an elevated **7-8/8-7** profile. Patients with a schizoid or schizophrenic disorder will often respond to a non-sedating antipsychotic medication while those who are neither schizoid nor schizophrenic will respond more favorably to an anxiolytic or an antidepressant. A bedtime dose of imiprimine will often control the disturbing intrusive thinking so commonly seen in patients with this profile. If the antidepressant mobilizes affects to an uncomfortable level, adding a non-sedating phenothiazine usually makes the patient comfortable and able to engage in the therapeutic process.

FEEDBACK STATEMENTS

Issues—T-score: MMPI-1, ≥ 70; MMPI-2, NA (Not Applicable)

1. *Your profile indicates that you feel a great deal of distress currently. However, you do have a number of strengths. Generally, you are a very analytical person.*

2. *You are probably creative and have an unconventional and creative way of approaching problems and solving them.*

3. *You are someone who usually attends to details.*

4. *Generally you are not a person who enjoys controlling and dominating others.*

5. You are considerate, sensitive, and cautious about hurting people's feelings.

6. You also are cautious about making mistakes and you are not a person who takes many risks.

7. One of your strengths is your sensitivity to people.

8. However, right now that sensitivity may be working against you. Any criticism seems to hurt you terribly and may even make you feel like a complete failure or like you are hopelessly defective.

9. People with your profile are cautious about ever getting angry with anyone in case it hurts the other person's feelings.

10. Right now it seems almost impossible for you to let yourself be angry and express anger to people who are frustrating you.

11. You fear that if you did express anger, you would feel very guilty.

12. Your profile indicated that most of the time you seem to feel a great deal of fear, anxiety, and doubt. Your mind races ahead of you. This may disrupt or interfere with your sleep.

13. You probably spend a great deal of time analyzing all the things that could possibly go wrong in your life, but you are not coming up with answers that feel safe or helpful.

14. It is probably very difficult for you to concentrate and make decisions.

15. Whenever you try to read anything or concentrate on anything you keep getting interrupted by frightening thoughts, of things that have horrible consequences.

16. It seems that you spend so much time thinking about what might be wrong with you that it is hard to concentrate on anything else.

17. *Most of the time you feel a constant sense of dread and guilt.*

18. *It is as if you are always blaming yourself for all of the things that have gone wrong. You feel you deserve to be punished—that, especially, you deserve all of the bad things that happened to you.*

19. *If people praise you or say good things about you, you feel undeserving and that if you accept people's praise, you will eventually be found out and humiliated.*

20. *Because you tend to put yourself down so much it is probably hard for you to reach out to people and make friends.*

21. *Perhaps you assume that if you do, people will see you as defective and somehow broken or damaged.*

22. *It is especially difficult for you now to relate to the opposite sex because you feel so inadequate and unlovable.*

23. *If someone of the opposite sex cares about you, you may even wonder what is wrong with them because they like you or are interested in you.*

Issues—T-score: MMPI-1, 55-69; MMPI-2, NA

1. *Your profile is within the normal range. It reveals that you have a number of strengths. You are an analytical person who looks at problems in a creative and unusual way.*

2. *You also tend to be good with details and generally sensitive.*

3. *You are cautious about making mistakes and you do not take needless risks.*

4. *Your profile also shows that you are vulnerable to worrying about things going wrong unpredictably.*

5. You spend energy analyzing the future to make sure that no unforeseen detail could lead to your feeling humiliated and bad about yourself.

6. Your analytical strengths, however, can sometimes lead you into trouble, especially when you start analyzing the past to see which mistakes you should have avoided.

7. While you may think that analyzing the past is useful, you only end up kicking yourself for mistakes which you can do nothing about.

8. You do not feel confident in new situations.

9. This may hinder you in your relationships. It is difficult for you to be spontaneous and friendly with people. You are afraid to be open and vulnerable because you think you may be found weak or lacking in some manner.

10. Generally people with your profile are cautious about getting angry and confronting others.

11. You have a tendency to rely on your analytical powers and consequently you may analyze your negative feelings away.

12. If and when you do get angry, you probably feel remorse and guilt.

13. People with your profile feel guilty much of the time.

14. You may experience guilt when someone praises you or when you feel that you do not quite deserve this praise.

15. You also may experience guilt when things go wrong, blaming yourself because you should have known better and prevented it.

16. During times of stress it becomes particularly difficult for you to concentrate.

17. During these times you may find yourself interrupted by thoughts about all the things that could go wrong—or all the mistakes you could make. "How can this go wrong?" and "How will I mess this up?"

18. All of this makes it difficult for you to relax and enjoy members of the opposite sex.

Background and Early Learning Experiences

As a child you were probably very sensitive—quick to cry and somewhat slow to "warm up" to others. Sensitive children are far more likely to be teased and put-down by their siblings and peers; this may have happened to you. If you were quick to cry or if you were cautious about new situations, you may have been teased about it. This may have been humiliating to you, and you may have tried to now show it. Even when your parents were supportive you may have felt self-conscious or humiliated, feeling that you were different because you needed special care.

Self-help Suggestions

1. You spend a great deal of energy thinking about all the things that could go wrong in the future and all the mistakes you have made in the past. You have control over what you think about. Thinking about these things does absolutely no good. It exhausts you, and leaves you feeling bad about yourself. Learn how to "stop thinking." Give yourself permission not to think about the past. Once you have made a decision, no matter how small it is, let it go. Do not go over and over your decision in your mind looking for what could possibly go wrong.

2. People with your profile often respond well to medication that slows the racing thoughts. Initially you may feel bad about needing to take medicine, and you may even feel guilty, as if you are somehow escaping from what you deserve. However, medication often helps people subjected to humiliation and put-down regain their natural strengths and abilities.

3. *Try to assert yourself on small issues with friends and family with whom you are most comfortable. Learning to stand up for yourself in small ways can help you learn to assert yourself later over more important issues.*

4. *Write down several self-affirming statements and read them to yourself at least two or three times every day. For example, write down statements such as "I am a good person," "I deserve to be loved," "I do have some strengths," "I am analytical and I have unusual ways of solving problems," and "I am not 'run of the mill.'" Your therapist may give you other statements to repeat as well.*

5. *Learn how to express your anger and frustration rather than analyzing your feelings. You have good analytical abilities but sometimes they work against you. By not expressing your anger you isolate yourself from people so they do not really have the chance to know you. You end up blaming yourself and feeling defective. It is a vicious cycle. You do not express your feelings, people do not get to know you, and you feel bad about yourself because you do not feel connected to others. You can break this cycle.*

SCALE 8

Descriptors

Concerns/Complaints: Anxiety, panic, terror, confusion, identity, alienation, security, sexuality, personal crises, communicating, perceiving, feeling, evaluating, relating; fear of hostility, being different, rejected.

Thoughts: Withdrawn, secretive, inaccessible, idiosyncratic, different, divergent, unusual, original, unconventional; fears, sex, hostility, ambivalence, indecision, resentment; difficulty attending, concentrating; poor judgment, possibly disoriented, delusional, hallucinations.

Emotions: Feeling anxious, fearful, dissatisfied, unhappy, incompetent, inferior, unaccepted, alienated, isolated, rejected, misunderstood; regressing, depersonalizing, isolating, withdrawing.

Traits/Behaviors: Moody, secretive, eccentric, stubborn, opinionated, shy, aloof, reclusive, withdrawn, confused, bizarre, schizoid, uninvolved, immature, impulsive; also, adventuresome, spontaneous, peaceable, generous, conscientious, high-strung, creative, imaginative.

Therapist's Notes

The hypothesis is that **Scale 8** elevations are associated with a childhood of being despised and rejected by a person upon whom life and security depended. Perhaps in some instances the child expressed some peculiar habit or eccentricities or was physically inept which led others to express anger, hatred, and resentment towards him or her. The assumption is that the child in an act of self-protection, would shutting down, that is, not think or not pay attention, which would lead in turn to faulty cognitive and emotional functioning.

Therapy with these clients should concentrate on helping them feel comfortable at the moment. Reconstructive methods are usually disorganizing and are counterindicated. Achieving insight often leads these clients to feeling even more alien and defective. These clients are very sensitive to hostility and will require a warm, interactive, and positive therapeutic relationship.

Medication Notes

Patients with elevations on **Scale 8** frequently need psychotropic medications but the type of medication depends on the other scale elevations. If **Scale 2** is elevated an antidepressant is usually indicated. Antidepressants should be monitored very carefully when **Scale 8** is elevated because some of these patients can become extremely agitated and anxious, even psychotic when given antidepressants, particularly the tricyclics. When this happens often what is necessary is to discontinue the antidepressant and add a major tranquilizer. If **Scale 7** is elevated with **Scale 8,** an anxiolytic is frequently essential. Benzodiazapines in moderate dosages are often very satisfactory.

FEEDBACK STATEMENTS

Issues—T-score: MMPI-1, $\geq$ 80; MMPI-2, $>$ 75

1. *Right now the world is a very frightening place for you.*

2. *You are probably feeling very separate from others and it is hard for you to know how others feel toward you.*

3. *You are probably confused about your own thoughts and moods, and wonder if there is something really wrong with you.*

4. *It seems that right now you feel bad about yourself, you feel unworthy and not worth liking.*

5. *Perhaps you feel that if people get too close to you and come to know you, they will somehow discover that something is wrong with you and reject you.*

6. Your profile suggests that at times you have dark moods which seem to swell up in you for no apparent reason.

7. These moods probably make you feel very empty and angry and you want to get away from people.

8. Very likely you spend a good deal of time day-dreaming, and it is hard for you to organize your thoughts or make decisions and get things accomplished.

9. Often odd and unpredictable things will intrude into your thinking that are uncomfortable and even terrifying.

10. Your relationships with loved ones are probably very confusing to you because of your mixed feelings about them. You feel angry and hateful towards them and loving and warm at the same time.

11. This also may lead you to feeling guilty and even worse about yourself.

12. Because of your confusing thoughts and dark, uncomfortable feelings, there is little in life that pleases you right now.

13. Consequently, life must feel terribly grey, empty, and even meaningless.

14. You may feel very lonely but at the same time you desperately avoid getting close to people and allowing them to get to know you.

15. Being around people makes you feel even more uncomfortable than when you are alone.

16. Your profile also shows that you are extremely sensitive to the anger of others.

17. If anyone is hostile or angry toward you, it completely disorganizes you making it hard for you to think clearly and respond.

Issues—T-score: MMPI-1, 70-79; MMPI-2, 66-75

1. Right now the world is a rather confusing and frightening place for you.

2. It is hard for you to understand other people's reactions to you.

3. There are times when you may say something you think is appropriate, funny, or sympathetic to someone and they will respond in an angry or indifferent way.

4. It seems that right now you are feeling bad about yourself. You think that you are not worthwhile or worth liking.

5. Perhaps you are afraid that if you let others get too close they will undermine you, take advantage of you, or make fun of you.

6. You may find yourself overcome by dark moods from time to time which seem to well up from nowhere.

7. It is at these times when you feel most alone, disconnected, and bleak.

8. You may also be bothered by odd and peculiar thoughts intruding into your thoughts.

9. Some of these thoughts may be violent and sexual, and others may startle and frighten you with their unpleasantness.

10. You may find that your relationships with loved ones are sometimes confused by your mixed feelings towards them.

11. You may find yourself feeling anger and even hatred towards those you usually love.

12. At times you may push people away and even be cruel to them but not fully understand what you are doing.

13. You may be going through a period where not much in life gives you satisfaction or joy.

14. *Your confusing thoughts and strong mixed feelings towards the people you love may leave you feeling empty
and bleak and unable to enjoy things that usually give
you pleasure.*

15. *At these times you may push people away and withdraw
to attend to your black mood.*

16. *You are a person who is very sensitive to hostility, and
when someone is angry with you it tends to muddle your
thinking.*

17. *With your mind teeming with confusing thoughts, making
decisions is very difficult for you. You don't feel able to
think things through clearly.*

Issues—T-score: MMPI-1, 55-69; MMPI-2, 56-65

1. *You are a bright and creative person who enjoys your own
fantasies and idiosyncracies.*

2. *You enjoy your fantasy world and may retreat to it as a
safe and happy place when the outside world feels like
nothing but trouble.*

3. *There are other times, however, when disturbing thoughts
can interrupt your concentration.*

4. *You may feel that these thoughts come from nowhere, but
you are usually able to deal with them without too much
difficulty.*

5. *You may experience bad moods when you feel empty,
alone and disconnected from others.*

6. *At these times you may wish to be alone and not bothered
by others. Intrusions may make you tense.*

7. *Your profile also suggests that your relationships can often
be complex and puzzling.*

8. You don't like to be open or vulnerable with others until you are certain that they won't be angry or hostile.

9. When you sense that someone is angry with you, your thinking gets muddled and you wonder what's wrong with you.

10. At other times you may have positive and negative feelings toward the same person and wonder where they came from and why you are feeling them.

11. In this way, you may angrily push people away whom you actually love and not understand why you are doing this.

12. However, you are generally a healthy, creative, and sensitive person.

Issues—T-score: MMPI-1, 40-49; MMPI-2, 41-55

1. You tend to have a good self-image, expecting to like most people and that others will like you.

2. Speculative fantasizing is not as appealing to you as is having concrete and attainable goals.

3. You are healthful, concerned about success, and enjoy having status, influence, and power.

4. Generally you are good natured, adaptable, and well-balanced.

Issues—T-score: MMPI-1, < 40; MMPI-2, < 41

1. You generally are so "grounded in reality" that others may see you as blunt, unimaginative and coldly objective.

2. You tend to accept and may even prefer a great deal of structure and routine.

3. Your acceptance of authority may at times lead others to seeing you as submissive and compliant.

4. Generally you expect people to accept you and you almost never doubt yourself about your abilities.

5. In fact, your self-reliance may appear to others as avoidance of deep emotional commitments and ties.

Background and Early Learning Experiences

People with your profile often grew up in homes where they were subjected to a great deal of anger and hostility from the important adults in their lives. You may have been treated with contempt, ignored, or as though you didn't exist. You probably were a sensitive child and their treatment of you was very painful and frightening. When you needed support it was difficult to go to them because they seemed so distant and indifferent. You may have tried to protect yourself by daydreaming and trying to escape into fantasies. You may be going through a similar time right now with someone being cruel and hostile to you.

Self-help Suggestions

1. Because the world seems so frightening to you right now it is probably hard to think that there is anything you can do to feel better. If this is so, sometimes medication can relieve you of feeling so afraid and you should discuss this with your therapist.

2. When you feel a bad mood coming on, avoid scolding yourself and feeling that you are a terrible person. Although it may seem quite difficult, focus on thoughts that make you feel good, even if you must force yourself to do so.

3. When you notice that someone is trying to get close to you, try not to push them away. If you feel like withdrawing,

simply tell people around you to leave you alone for a while but don't push them away by saying something that might unintentionally offend them.

4. When you find yourself daydreaming about unpleasant or uncomfortable things, see if you are in fact worrying about a possible confrontation or unpleasant encounter. Perhaps you are angry with someone and do not want to have to deal with them. Or perhaps you suspect that someone is angry with you. In either case, force yourself to face the situation and deal with it.

5. If you find yourself in a sad or bad mood and feel alienated from others, rather than withdrawing into the mood, force yourself to find something to do that could make you feel better. Talk yourself out of withdrawing as a solution.

6. When you find yourself daydreaming, especially if the fantasy seems peculiar or disturbing, see whether you are feeling vulnerable to someone's anger and unwilling to face it. Force yourself to deal with the anger.

7. When you feel hurt by something someone has said or done, try to tell them about it rather than let them know in an indirect or roundabout way.

CODETYPE 8-9/9-8

Descriptors

Concerns/Complaints: Pressures, trust, unhappiness, failures, fantasies, family problems, fear or emotional ties and involvement, possible delusions, hallucinations, drug abuse.

Thoughts: Ruminative, unusual, perplexed, vague, confused, distractible, circumstantial, suspicious, negativistic, grandiose, daydreaming, flight of ideas; possibly disoriented, delusional, hallucinatory, bizarre associations, neologisms, echolalia.

Emotions: Feeling tense, anxious, fearful, irritable, depressed, hyperactive, labile, excitable.

Traits/Behaviors: Self-centered, infantile, demanding, distrustful, evasive, boastful, fickle, unpredictable, unrealistic, confused, odd, lacking in skills with the opposite sex.

Therapist's Notes

Clients with this profile will appear tense, restless, demanding and high strung. Clients with T-scores over 70 are usually in a severe phase of an identity crises. They tend to be self-critical perfectionists who consider any failure as catastrophic to their self-esteem. They can be agitated and confused and at times will manifest paranoid, persecutory, and expansive thoughts such as receiving special messages. They may display an intense "burning" gaze, and at other times exhibit inappropriate surges of exuberance and anger.

Initially difficulty will be encountered in eliciting the precipitating circumstances because they will contradict themselves, positivizing their painful experiences which they perceive either as sexual rejection or some other kind of performance failure. They typically ignore their own achievements, focusing instead on the things they feel they should have accomplished.

The hypothesis is that as children these clients were motivated to succeed by their desire to avoid humiliation. The assumption is that their parents were very demanding and perfectionistic and that one of them, usually the parent of the opposite sex, was constantly critical and judgmental. Frequently this parent's own negative self-image translated into an unconscious dislike of the child but they wanted the child to achieve as proof of their worth as a parent. Presumably this provided the mixed message: "Perform well to get my approval, but you will never succeed because you are damaged and unworthy."

Therapy should focus on helping them learn new ways of relaxing, ways to stop negative thinking, to solve specific and immediate problems, to develop a better self-image, and to identify more appropriate and self-enhancing life goals. Group therapy is usually contra-indicated in the initial phase because of their profound fear of being rejected.

Medication Notes

Patients with this profile tend to be highly responsive to medication, but will frequently require high dosage levels for an optimal response. Haloperidol and the sedating phenothiazines are usually effective for patients with elevated **8-9** profiles and lithium is the drug of choice for those with **9-8** elevations. However, the best procedure is to treat these initially with an anti-psychotic as well as lithium because lithium does not control the manic symptoms as quickly as desired. Long-term treatment with lithium is often necessary to prevent reoccurrence but the anti-psychotics may be tapered and discontinued as the patient's symptoms subside.

FEEDBACK STATEMENTS

Issues—T-score: MMPI-1, $\geq$ 80; MMPI-2, NA (Not Applicable)

1. *Your profile shows that you have a number of significant strengths. You have a great deal of energy, drive, and ambition.*

2. Your mind works extremely quickly so that you can often see the connections between things in advance.

3. You are a person with high standards and you try hard to live up to them.

4. You may also be a creative person with an unusual way of looking at things.

5. You probably have a rich imagination so it is easy for you to turn inward and fantasize or daydream about creative and innovative ways to solve problems.

6. However, currently some of your strengths may be working against you. You are going through a period of intense soul-searching and self-examination.

7. Your natural ability to turn inward and analyze yourself is merging with your great desire to achieve and succeed. And what this combination adds up to are feelings of inadequacy—feelings that you are not quite good enough or that you are not worth liking.

8. It seems that you are extremely self-critical right now, chastising yourself and at the same time demanding a great deal from yourself in order to prove that you are really worthwhile.

9. Periodically you may go through moments of panic, terrified that no matter what you do you will always be a failure.

10. Your high energy and drive also may be working against you. Perhaps you are getting involved in projects or activities which you feel will be the answer to your problems, or even to all of the problems of all humankind.

11. Your desire to do something very special and wonderfully worthwhile may mean that you put tremendous energy into these projects, even at the expense of your sleep and rest.

12. You may experience periodic surges of exuberance, of optimism and charged energy which are interspersed with periods of feeling intensely negative—with a deep sense of self-dislike.

13. Your impossibly high standards which you set for yourself may mean that approaching persons of the opposite sex is extremely difficult for you.

14. In fact some people with your profile, when they are rebuffed by a person of the opposite sex will immediately feel that there may be something wrong with them, even to the point of feeling that perhaps they are really homosexual.

15. All of these feelings must be very confusing to you right now.

16. You probably have so many thoughts racing through your head that you feel exhausted and unable to think clearly.

17. On the one hand, making decisions may be difficult at times, but on the other hand there are times when you move forward with a deep conviction that you have all the answers.

18. You may have periods when you have deep, religious ideas and insights and even thoughts about what your personal mission in life may be.

19. People with your profile often become very self-critical and self-doubting if they feel that they have been rejected or if they feel they have failed somehow in a mission they set out to accomplish.

20. Sometimes you may not get enough sleep or rest because you feel driven to stay up late into the night to work on an important project.

21. Sometimes, when you search for the right resolution to your difficulties, you are led to unusual and sometimes even dangerous solutions.

22. *If you use drugs or alcohol, your feelings of confusion, self-dislike, and surges of positive and negative energy could all be significantly exaggerated.*

Issues—T-score: MMPI-1, 70-79; MMPI-2, NA

1. *Your profile indicates that you have a number of strengths. You are an energetic, ambitious, and creative person.*

2. *You probably have a rich imagination. You can turn your thoughts inward and daydream some creative and unusual fantasies.*

3. *You set high standards for yourself and demand the best from yourself.*

4. *You have a very lively mind and can anticipate the connection between many different ideas and values.*

5. *You also may have a good deal of ambition and a strong desire to do something unusual and important.*

6. *Right now some of these strengths may be working against you. Perhaps something happened recently which has given your sense of self a serious jolt.*

7. *It seems that right now you don't like yourself very well, and you are afraid that you may never be good enough to like yourself again.*

8. *While you may be an active and energetic person, right now you may be driving yourself too hard, over-committing yourself and getting involved in projects that take up a great deal of time and energy.*

9. *You may go through periods where you feel great surges of optimism, exuberance, and happiness. But then these are followed by periods of feeling hopeless and unhappy.*

10. *You may go through a period where many thoughts race around in your head which makes you feel confused.*

11. You may quickly see a complex pattern of connections between ideas but before you can get those thoughts to the surface, other thoughts begin to break in.

12. You may be confused about your goals and about just who you are and what your identity is.

13. Sometimes you feel you have important work to do in this life, a mission, and an important purpose, then other times you feel you are not good enough and you will never do anything of importance or real value with your life.

14. At these times you may feel hopeless about ever feeling good about yourself.

15. Perhaps these feelings come of expecting so much from yourself.

16. You probably demand perfection from yourself in everything you undertake and these days nothing seems quite good enough to you.

17. Perhaps you are driving yourself too hard, staying up very late at night or even staying up all night, as though you were driven to prove yourself.

18. People with your profile are extremely sensitive to any kind of perceived rejection or failure.

19. You are so hard on yourself and so demanding that you see rejection or failure as confirming that you are not good enough or worthwhile.

20. Perhaps you feel that recently you failed at something important, or someone you care about has disappointed you and let you down.

21. You may be having difficulty reaching out to persons of the opposite sex.

22. Because of the high expectations you have of yourself, rejection from such persons leave you feeling terrible about yourself.

23. Sometimes people with your profile have used chemicals such as drugs or alcohol as a way of relieving tension only to find it makes them feel even more confused and impulsive.

Issues—T-score: MMPI-1, 55-69; MMPI-2, NA

1. Your profile is well within the normal range and shows that you have a number of strengths. You are an energetic and probably rather creative person.

2. You have a rich fantasy life and a creative and unusual way of looking at problems and how to resolve them.

3. Very likely you have a lively mind which often sees the creative connections between things.

4. You also may have high standards and you probably try hard to live by them.

5. It appears that currently you may be going through an identity search, examining your goals, thinking about who you are and what you want to accomplish in life.

6. You also may be feeling some confusion, wondering if you have all the necessary talents and abilities to accomplish what you want.

7. At these times when you doubt yourself, you may feel dark moods come over you.

8. At other times you may experience surges of enthusiasm and optimism about your goals and plans.

9. Your profile also suggests that while your energy and drive can be productive, you have a tendency to over-commit yourself to too many tasks and activities.

10. While having such high standards for yourself may be a positive thing, it also may mean that your demands are

too high. Then when things don't come out as you planned, you are overly harsh and disappointed with yourself.

11. *Periodically you may give up on projects and goals when you feel things aren't going perfectly.*

12. *Sometimes you also may drive yourself too hard—perhaps staying up all night to work at a problem or project.*

13. *People with your profile are often sensitive to any kind of rejection, especially from persons of the opposite sex.*

14. *Sometimes feeling a slight emotional withdrawal by them is seen as a serious emotional rejection.*

Background and Early Learning Experiences

Your profile suggests that you were reared in a family where great things were expected of you. Your parents may have set high standards for you but you may have felt that no matter what you did or how hard you tried, you were never quite good enough to deserve their approval. Perhaps they were afraid of praising you too much or they found it difficult to express their approval. You may have developed the notion that you had to do something very special to prove yourself or satisfy them, but no matter how hard you worked at it, you felt you were somehow bad or defective. Recently someone may have rejected you or something may have happened which makes you feel that nothing you can ever do will be acceptable to anyone.

Self-help Suggestions When Applicable

1. *If you are feeling confused and if you are unable to sleep because of strong surges of energy, then usually some medication can help you feel better. At first you may not want medication because you enjoy your surges of energy. However, you need rest so that you can think clearly and be productive.*

2. You may be angry with yourself—or driving yourself to do some extraordinary fete to prove your worth and be deserving of approval and affection. As a simple exercise, write all the things that you have done in your life that you feel good about. Then on a daily basis try to focus on the things you are doing well and try not to be harsh with yourself about the things that have gone wrong.

3. Do not anticipate that you are going to be rejected by a member of the opposite sex before you have given that person a chance to get to know you. Try not to be different and special, because then you are not yourself. You probably are a creative person with a lot of strengths. These strengths will become evident when someone gets to know you.

4. If people respond to you negatively, do not assume that they are rejecting you. Sometimes people respond negatively to others without realizing that they are doing so. You have a tendency to assume that if something goes wrong between you and another person it is because you are the defective one. Try to remember that other people also have bad moods as well as personal peculiarities and eccentricities which may cause them to push you away or treat you badly, but this may have little to do with you.

5. With the help of your therapist, write a list of affirmations which you can say to yourself every day in order to help you develop a more realistic self-image.

6. Because you are so quick to chastise yourself if you fail at something, it is wise to have a number of projects going that you enjoy, then if one thing doesn't work out you won't feel that your whole world has crumbled. Most people try to have a number of interests so as not to invest their whole energy into a single project.

7. People with your profile often do not get enough sleep because they drive themselves to accomplish so many goals and projects. It is important that you look to your sleeping and eating habits and protect your health.

8. *The most important goal for you to learn is "Praise and approve of yourself for all the things you have done well and for all the successes you have achieved." Do this rather than driving yourself and constantly trying to prove yourself.*

SCALE 9

Descriptors: High T-scores

Concerns/Complaints: Self-worth, importance, expectations, commitments; fear of boredom, limitations, failures; difficulties at work, possible feelings toward domineering parents, confusion, drugs.

Thoughts: Enterprising, creative, overactive, exaggerated, expansive, grandiose, flighty, purposeless, competitive, manipulative, enthusiastic, superficial; possible confusion, religiosity, delusions, hallucinations, mania.

Emotions: Feels tense, worried, anxious, nervous; is enthusiastic, energetic, easily upset, impulsive, excitable, uninhibited, euphoric, labile, episodically irritable, hostile, aggressive, depressed; fantasizing, denying, overcompensating, acting-out.

Traits/Behaviors: Friendly, outgoing, gregarious, pleasant, versatile, talkative, energetic, enthusiastic, eager, exuberant, wholehearted, zestful; also restless, impatient, hyperactive, unreliable, deceptive, narcissistic, easily bored, agitated, ineffectual, disorganized.

Descriptors: Low T-scores

Concerns/Complaints: Energy, self-confidence, motivation; possible fatigue, exhaustion, depression.

Thoughts: Slow, listless.

Emotions: Feeling empty, lethargic, apathetic, depressed.

Traits/Behaviors: Quiet, modest, humble, sincere, conscientious, overcontrolled, unpopular, dependent, seeks reassurance.

Therapist's Notes

The hypothesis is that clients with **Scale 9** elevations are protecting themselves against the frustration and unhappiness associated with failure. The assumption is that these clients were reared by parents who had high expectations of them. The parents were seen as pushing the child to achieve constantly, but at the same time they tried to control the resulting surges of energy and impulsivity. These parents rewarded the successes of the child by partial or inconsistent rewards. They also tended to withhold regular or predictable rewards in their efforts to control the child. This only increased the drive state and, in effect, increased the elevation of **Scale 9.**

The purpose of therapy is to help the client stop the cycles of anxious striving and fully enjoy the present moment. These clients are oriented to the future and are afraid that if they slow down they will have to deal with painful feelings of frustration or loss. They also are afraid that if they stop driving themselves they might achieve less. They need help to distinguish between their own needs and their desire to please others in order to elicit approval. Gestalt techniques are usually effective for helping the client to focus on the present, rather than trying to deal with past events or anticipated events in the future.

FEEDBACK STATEMENTS

Issues—T-score: MMPI-1, $\geq$ 80; MMPI-2, > 75

1. *You are a person with a very high level of energy and you are unusually optimistic, even in situations where other people might feel defeated or disgruntled.*

2. *You probably feel very optimistic, even euphoric, with periods when you feel that everything is going better than it has ever gone in your whole life before.*

3. *You may find yourself so optimistic that you make promises that are hard to keep.*

4. *Working on one task is difficult for you. You see, very quickly, how things connect and you are probably easily side-tracked into unrelated or tangential matters.*

5. You get very excited by the prospect of something new and then it is hard for you to rest or to focus on the task at hand.

6. You need novelty, excitement and challenge.

7. Doing the same thing twice is very boring to you and you avoid any routine that requires attention to detail.

8. In fact, it is hard for you to realize that others cannot keep up with your pace or accomplish as much as you do in the same period of time.

9. Consequently you may find yourself impatient with others, hurrying them and demanding they keep up with your pace.

10. The world appears to be moving too slowly for you. At times you will finish people's sentences for them or walk away from them before they have finished speaking.

11. In fact, you may find yourself having such great spurts of energy and optimism that you feel you can conquer the world.

12. At these times you are likely to make more promises than you have time to fulfill. This may get you into trouble with your family and co-workers.

13. People with your profile constantly shift from one goal to another and will often change even their entire life goals.

14. You may have changed your own career once, twice, or even more during the course of your life.

15. People with your profile are usually attracted to making plans for the future.

16. You probably spend most of the time thinking about what you will be doing in the future and how much fun you will be having.

17. Almost none of your time is spent thinking or feeling about the present.

Issues—T-score: MMPI-1, 70-79; MMPI-2, 66-75

1. You have a high level of energy.

2. You are generally a very optimistic person, even in situations where other people might feel disappointed.

3. It is important for you to stay positive and cheerful but you are likely to get irritated if people suggest that your goals may be unrealistic.

4. Occasionally you will suffer periods of disappointment but they are usually tied to some specific achievement failures.

5. Working on a single task may be difficult for you.

6. You feel you can see the connections between things and are easily distracted and side-tracked into tangential and unrelated matters.

7. The prospect of something new may get you so excited that it is hard for you to rest and turn your attention to the task at hand.

8. You need novelty, excitement, and challenge.

9. Repetition, routine, and attending to details bores you.

10. It is hard for you to realize that others may not be able to keep the pace you do.

11. Occasionally you may find yourself impatient with people, hurrying them along and expecting them to keep up with you.

12. People with your profile often finish other people's sentences for them because they already know what they will be saying.

13. They may walk away from people before they finish speaking for the same reason.

Issues—T-score: MMPI-1, 55-69; MMPI-2, 56-65

1. You have a moderately high level of energy.

2. You are generally optimistic, even in times of difficulty, and people probably see you as cheerful and happy.

3. You may occasionally have periods of disappointment which are usually tied to a specific achievement failure.

4. People with your profile tend to be somewhat distractible.

5. You may get involved in something and then you see all the implications which can distract you from the objective.

6. You may get so excited about an issue and its implications that when you are talking to someone about it, you end up losing your train of thought.

7. Generally you are excitable and you are inspired by new ideas and opportunities.

8. Because your pace and energy is greater than average, you may expect that others keep up with you.

9. You may be impatient with them, pushing them to keep up and conform to your schedule and pace.

10. You like to handle a number of projects at the same time and sometimes you will take on more than you can possibly finish on time.

11. At times you probably feel that the world moves too slowly for you and you get impatient with how long it takes others to do things.

12. For example, you may find yourself finishing people's sentences for them or walking away before they have

finished speaking because you already know what they are going to say.

13. *You also tend to work in spurts, letting things pile up before you finish them.*

14. *Your profile suggests that you are interested primarily in the future.*

15. *Talking about your present activities may not be as interesting to you as talking about future challenges and potentially more exciting events.*

16. *You prefer a life that is filled with new events and excitement. You find attention to detail and routine to be boring and dull.*

Issues—T-score: MMPI-1, < 45; MMPI-2, < 50

1. *Your level of energy right now is very low.*

2. *Whatever you take on, you like to finish without pressuring yourself.*

3. *You are not a person who works in spurts, and you tend to be cautious about taking on more than you can handle.*

4. *Your mood also tends to be fairly even without great fluctuations.*

5. *Your frustration tolerance tends to be high so you can work on boring and even irritating tasks without getting upset.*

6. *People with your profile tend to persevere towards their goals without great changes in ambitions or careers.*

Background and Early Learning Experiences

People with your profile have always had a lot of energy and ambition. At times your parents may have held you back when you really wanted to do something and then at other times pressured you to do something that you didn't want to do. Rewards from your parents were not always predictable or forthcoming. At times they might have withheld rewards so that no matter how hard you tried, they never totally approved of you nor were they completely pleased by your accomplishments.

Self-help Suggestions

1. Make a list of things you wish to do in the immediate future and start to do them, one by one, without being distracted. Try to finish one thing before beginning another.

2. Because of your high energy and frenetic pace, you may need medication to slow down, especially if your sleep is disrupted. You should discuss this with your therapist.

3. Your response to stress may be inappropriately positive and cheerful. If so, you should discuss this with your therapist. If you find yourself talking only about positive things, perhaps you are avoiding some negative issues.

4. When talking to someone try not to become distracted. Focus on what you are talking about without trying to include all aspects or tangential issues.

5. Reward yourself frequently and regularly for completing tasks.

6. Do not make any changes in your career or life goals until you have discussed these and thought them through with someone else.

7. *Try not to commit yourself to too many tasks and activities. You may be unrealistic about what you can actually accomplish.*

8. *Set a realistic goal and try to achieve it before you turn your attention to a new task. When you are frustrated or bored, it is easy for you to change direction and try another new or more exciting project.*

9. *You like to do things that are unusual and noteworthy. This may relate to your childhood when you felt that you had to prove to others that you were worthy of their approval.*

SCALE 0

Descriptors: High T-scores

Concerns/Complaints: Security, self-confidence, trust, social discomfort, lacking in social skills, physical appearance, possible somatic discomfort, religious, marital difficulties.

Thoughts: Worrisome, ruminating, indecisive, self-effacing, self-depreciating, suspicious, rigid, inflexible.

Emotions: Feeling anxious, moody, easily embarrassed, irritable, guilty, inferior, overcontrolled, withdrawing, insulating, isolating, fantacizing.

Traits/Behaviors: Shy, timid, reserved, retiring, aloof, reclusive, asocial, alienated, distant, introverted, submissive; also compliant, conventional, dependable, reliable, serious, resourceful, self-directed, self-reliant, independent, prefers being alone.

Descriptors: Low T-scores

Concerns/Complaints: Security, self-confidence, approval, support; possible achievement, superficiality in relationships.

Thoughts: Verbally fluent, flighty, competitive; power, status, recognition.

Emotions: Feels confident, competent, socially poised; impulsive, expressive, undercontrolled, arouses resentment in others.

Traits/Behaviors: Friendly, outgoing, gregarious, sociable, talkative, extroverted, other directed, active, vigorous, energetic, assertive, aggressive, persuasive, opportunistic, manipulative, socially adept, self-indulgent, dependent, immature, prefers being with others.

Therapist's Notes

Studies of introversion have revealed that elevations on **Scale 0** tend to be stable over time. People who were shy and socially uncomfortable as children often remain so as adults. The socially extroverted child or the adolescent who has trouble studying because of constant socializing often becomes the adult who is constantly engaged in social events. The hypothesis is that T-scores between 40 and 60 are determined genetically. T-scores above 70 may reflect a childhood characterized by an absence of warmth and physical contact from others. Elevated scores suggest that these people have extinguished their feeling response to physical touch and affection. They suffer from a form of "affect hunger" and yet they feel conflicted about close, intimate relationships.

Depressed T-scores below 40, suggests a strong need for social stimulation which may be driven by insecurity rather than a proclivity for intense social experiences.

Clients who have elevated scores should focus, in therapy, on finding ways to accept and enjoy their shyness rather than trying to change or to blame themselves for it. Clients who have depressed T-scores should be helped to enhance their self-confidence and structure their socializing so that it doesn't interfere with responsibilities.

FEEDBACK STATEMENTS

Issues—T-score: MMPI-1, $\geq$ 80; MMPI-2, $>$ 75

1. *You are an extremely shy and sensitive person, uncomfortable around strangers and in large groups of people.*

2. *Right now you may be feeling so vulnerable that it is hard to know who to trust with your feelings. Your feelings are so easily hurt.*

3. *It is difficult for you to meet new people and make easy conversation.*

4. You probably feel very self-conscious and you find yourself at a loss for words, especially with people you do not know.

5. In stressful situations you probably withdraw and prefer to be by yourself.

6. People with your profile rarely need much social stimulation and spend most of their time on their own.

7. When they are with people, they usually are thinking of routes of escape so they can leave if they need to.

8. You probably also tend to feel very uncomfortable in confrontations with others and you will try hard to avoid them.

9. Even with people that you know and care about, it may be difficult for you to express your caring in an open and physical manner.

10. Even with people you love, physical intimacy can be an uncomfortable and, at times, a disturbing experience.

11. Generally you tend to be a very independent and self-reliant person who turns inward to find direction rather than seeking other people's approval or guidance.

12. Others may misperceive you as aloof and indifferent because you guard your privacy rather jealously.

Issues—T-score: MMPI-1, 70-79; MMPI-2, 66-75

1. You are shy, somewhat sensitive, and extremely uncomfortable with strangers and in large groups of people.

2. Around new people you probably feel self-conscious and insecure.

3. In new situations you may find yourself unable to converse comfortably.

4. Right now it may be hard for you to know whom to trust or with whom to share your very sensitive feelings. You are often so easily hurt.

5. You are a person who rarely needs social stimulation and would rather spend time by yourself.

6. When you are with new people you probably think of routes of escape so that you can get away the moment you need to.

7. Even with people that you know and care about it may be difficult for you to express your caring and love in an open and physical way.

8. Even when you love someone, being physically intimate can make you uneasy.

9. Very likely you also will feel uncomfortable in confrontations with others and will do whatever you can to avoid it.

10. People with your profile tend to be independent and self-reliant.

11. They prefer to turn to themselves for direction rather than seeking the approval or guidance of others.

12. As a result, others might see you as reserved and somewhat reclusive.

Issues—T-score: MMPI-1, 60-69; MMPI-2, 56-65

1. You are a shy person who is especially uncomfortable in large groups of new people.

2. You also are sensitive and tend to be a little on guard in relations to strangers.

3. When you are in new social situations, you probably find yourself planning ways to escape the moment you feel trapped.

4. Dealing with people in an assertive or aggressive way is quite difficult for you.

5. People with your profile are usually most comfortable with just a few friends.

6. While you do not need many new or exciting friends, you enjoy small groups of people you know well.

7. When you are around people you don't know, you probably feel self-conscious and are at times lost for words.

8. Although you may feel warmly and caring towards someone, you may find it uncomfortable to express those feelings physically by touching or hugging.

9. If you are in a job or other situation which demands confronting someone this can pose a particular problem.

Issues—T-score: MMPI-1, 55-59; MMPI-2, NA (Not Applicable)

1. You are a little shy, reserved and become somewhat uncomfortable with large groups of new people.

2. With strangers you may feel self-conscious and periodically at a loss for words.

3. If you have to relate to new people in a structured situation, such as in delivering a prepared speech, then you may be quite comfortable.

4. It is in unstructured situations with strangers that you are likely to be uncomfortable.

5. You do not need many new or exciting friends, but you do enjoy small groups of people you know well.

6. People with your profile like to avoid aggressive confrontations with others.

Issues—T-score: MMPI-1, 46-54; MMPI-2, 45-55

1. You enjoy social and personal relationships and feel comfortable with others and enjoy making new friends.

2. You prefer a balance of social and personal activity and may easily become bored if you are not around people.

3. You do not mind confronting someone when you feel they deserve it.

Issues—T-score: MMPI-1, 35-45; MMPI-2 < 45

1. People with your profile are outgoing and gregarious and enjoy being around others.

2. In fact, if they are not around people, they are easily bored.

3. You probably have many friends and are happiest when you are with them.

4. You may even enjoy being around others so much that it interferes with other aspects of your life.

5. There may be times when you are so busy socializing that it is hard to get your work done.

6. You have a need for people's attention, and you also may need and seek out their approval and support.

7. You may be the kind of person who is quite comfortable being touched and hugged, and who enjoys outward displays of affection and warmth.

8. You should have no difficulty confronting someone if you feel that it is justified or deserved.

Issues—T-score: MMPI-1, < 35; MMPI-2, NA

1. *You are a person who is extremely extroverted, and you like to be around people most of the time.*

2. *You are probably so involved with others that you spend little if any time by yourself.*

3. *It is quite possible that your socializing interferes with other aspects of your life.*

4. *People with your profile need and seek out the approval of others, especially their friends, as an indication of their worth.*

Background and Early Learning Experiences for Elevated T-scores

You probably have always been somewhat shy, reticent, and reserved. Your adolescence very likely was difficult for you because of your shyness which made it hard for you to socialize, especially with members of the opposite sex. Throughout life your shyness may have hampered you in making friends and in feeling comfortable in social situations. Your parents may have been warm and caring, but may not have emphasized or demonstrated much outward physical affection by touching, kissing, holding, or embracing you, each other, or others.

CHAPTER 5

PROVIDING AND PROCESSING FEEDBACK

Providing a client feedback requires practice, sensitivity, and tact. Clients can be fearful that the professional might humiliate, disapprove or disparage them for their vulnerabilities and weaknesses. This is not necessarily "paranoid" on the part of the client. The fear often evolves from a belief that emotional pain is somehow self-induced. Also a tendency exists for some health professionals to become discouraged with clients who present potential frustration and failure for the professional. This may lead to subtle judgment disguised in psychological language. The professional's feelings of frustration are frequently sensed by the client. Experienced therapists have long recognized these feelings in themselves and try not to allow them to interfere with an effective treatment relationship. Therefore, important steps for the therapist include not only selection and preparation of the most appropriate interpretations for feedback, but also conduction and verification of the feedback must be in such a manner that both client and therapist feel at ease and most comfortable. For these reasons we propose two means of giving feedback—The Take-home Report and The In-session Report—each based on a different purpose for testing and each serving a different testing goal. Both ways begin with a written report, composed by the therapist after scoring and prior to the feedback. The report consists of the client's approach to the test, follows with the issues and background experiences, and, at the discretion of the therapist, concludes with the suggestions for self-help. (See Chapter 3 for an illustrative report.) The report to the client does not include notes to the therapist which are specifically addressed to the professional.

THE IN-SESSION REPORT

The preferred procedure requires the client to become as informed and active in discussing and validating the feedback as in the treatment process itself. Not all clients can collaborate in equally reflective and verbal ways, but our experience has been that most can follow the "road map" example by exploring the issues on which to work and the directions toward which they would like to progress.

Following this method the client and therapist each has a copy of the report and the client is asked to read aloud, discuss, and validate each statement as it applies to self. The approach does not preclude disagreements between the client and therapist; to the contrary, it tries to facilitate an open exchange in which each will participate in discussing and validating each aspect of the report. The in-session format also permits the more experienced MMPI user latitude to integrate the feedback into a narrative form or, as an alternative, to present the report directly to the client as illustrated in the case examples in this chapter.

We typically encourage our clients to tape-record the feedback session(s) so that they can listen to the tapes during their leisure in more relaxed surroundings. Many clients appreciate this suggestion and report that they frequently will listen to the tape more than once, often asking their spouse to listen as well. As with a Take-home Report, a desirable procedure is that at some point prior to the feedback the professional needs to have read the **Notes to the Therapist** associated with the client's particular codetype or, in a single scale analysis, with the two-highest scales of the client's coded test results.

Procedure

We have found the following procedure useful for the In-session Report:

1. Seat the client comfortably with a copy of his or her feedback results.

2. Describe the test briefly as follows:

> "The MMPI is by now the most widely used objective personality test in the world. It was developed by comparing answers of persons sharing certain psychological characteristics with persons in general not showing those characteristics and identifying items that statistically distinguished the two groups (For less sophisticated clients simplify as appropriate). These items were then added to form scales measuring different personality dimensions and the scales were standardized with an average or mean score of 50 and a standard deviation of 10. There are fourteen such scales of interest to us here. The first four scales are called validity scales and the next ten are clinical scales."

> The four validity scales tell us the manner in which you approached the test. "Did you answer all or most of the items?" "Were you self-critical and eager to tell us how you are feeling or were you playing your cards close to the chest?" "The ten clinical scales reveal different aspects of your personality. Remember, 50 is an average score and most people score somewhere between 30 and 70 (MMPI-1) or between 35-65 (MMPI-2) on each of the scales. Scores that are below or above these scores tell us that the person is experiencing some difficulties and the purpose of feedback is to discover and discuss just what these difficulties may be.

Often at this point clients will comment about their scores being "high" or "low" or will ask "Does it matter that the score is so up or down?" When this occurs reassure them that you are going to explain everything to them, that nothing will be held back, and that they need not be worried. Encourage the client to comment or ask questions about what you have said up to this point.

3. Hand the client a copy of the feedback report with a copy for your use. The feedback itself can be given by one of the following procedures:

   a. Ask the client to read the report aloud, discuss and validate each segment of it. You then would follow with your copy, participate in the discussion, and note any differences in your perception of the client as compared to the client's validations of self.

   b. Read the report aloud and ask the client to follow, discuss, and validate each section, statement by statement. You then would participate in the discussion and note as above any differences in your perception of the client as based upon his or her own validation of statements.

   c. Integrate issues into themes and summarize them aloud in a narrative form which you and the client could discuss theme by theme jointly in-session. In some cases the client could take home the written report to read, comment on, validate, and return during the next session if you felt that doing so will not be emotionally disturbing to the client. You then evaluate your copy of the report based upon your own perception of the client.

4. Begin feedback with the appropriate (**L, F,** and/or **K**) statement(s) about the person's approach to the test. Remember that the client may be cautious and defensive, anticipating being criticized and judged. If the client argues with you, then chances are you have made the client defensive and are defeating your purpose. If at any stage the client disagrees with you, see this as an opportunity to gain his or her perspective by asking questions like, "Well, tell me how you see it?" or "How am I missing the mark?"

5. Continue with the rest of the feedback. Remember that you are trying to be empathic, sensitive, and understanding. Watch for when the client "shuts down" (often due to

anxiety) and stops listening, or when the client "interrupts" and diverts his or her attention to another topic. When this happens, allow the client to take "a breather" and discuss only as much of the feedback as he or she is able to process at one time.

6. Strive towards organizing the feedback into a few themes that you can explore which lead to other issues if it progresses well. For example, a theme for **Scale 4** centers around self-survival such as in the issue "Your profile suggests that you are a survivor and that right now you are being cautious about letting yourself get emotionally involved in case you are let down and disappointed." Here the therapist could ask "Why are you being cautious, what is going on?" "Have you been let down recently?" Frequently the client will immediately respond and other issues can then be explored.

7. Reassure the client that he/she can interrupt anytime, does not have to agree with any of the statements, should tell you when an issue does not apply, and should mark the issue with a rating that most closely corresponds to his/her feelings at the time. Remind the client also that the purpose of feedback is primarily for his/her own benefit and that the report belongs to him/her. What you wish to learn is how the client experiences each issue. Some clients will want to hear all of the feedback before responding, perhaps to see how accurate the interpretations will be.

8. At the end of a feedback session, ask the client to summarize what has been heard about himself/herself. This should be done during the last ten minutes or so, so that any misunderstandings can be clarified before leaving the session.

A number of ways can be utilized to modify feedback based upon the stage of testing and the particular treatment approach. For example, a second MMPI administered during the course of therapy may reveal that a client is feeling more despondent and self-disliking than was reported at the time of original testing. This, shared with the client, could then open up questions such as "Is the client responding to re-awakened old memories brought alive in therapy by blaming self for what happened in the past?" In this instance the feedback dialogue can be used to facilitate treatment. Moreover, in brief treatment approaches, clients could be given feedback so that behavioral corrective measures could be suggested to alleviate their present distress. For example, a client with a **2-7/7-2 codetype** or with elevations on **Scales 2** and **7** could be given specific behavioral techniques (such as in the suggestions for self-help) for lowering anxiety without further intervention, if the latter is not desirable or possible at the time.

THE TAKE-HOME REPORT

The Take-home Report provides the client with a written interpretation of his or her MMPI results from an experiential perspective. The approach intentionally limits the therapist's involvement in feedback and may be especially useful for professionals working as personality assessors (i.e., in a more traditional "diagnostic" capacity), in screening activities, or in personnel or career development work. The purpose of the Take-home Report is to provide clients with a written report of their test results with instructions to confirm or disconfirm each aspect of the findings. The latter is a critical aspect of the process and should be monitored by the therapist until it is done. (See the Appendix for a form designed for summarizing and recording the client's as well as the therapist's evaluations of the feedback report.)

In using this method the therapist should explain how the test was developed and scored and its limitations, and then hand the client a copy of the report and request that it be read, validated, and returned within a prescribed period of time. In any case at some earlier point a desirable procedure is for the professional to have read the section on **Notes to the Therapist** associated with the client's particular codetype or, in the case of a single scale analysis, with the two-highest scales of the client's coded test results. If this method is used, the therapist should be available to discuss any possible misunderstandings and deal with feelings generated by the feedback.

The therapist needs to re-emphasize that unlike the more traditional clinical report, the feedback report is designed and worded expressly for the client. Thus, regardless of the procedure for providing feedback, the client "owns" the feedback and at some point should be given a copy of the validated report.

EVALUATING FEEDBACK

As stated throughout this *Guide*, the feedback process is envisioned as a collaborative exploration between client and therapist of the client's thoughts, feelings, and concerns at the time of completing the test. The authors consider as an essential procedure that the client validate each section of the report and that the therapist evaluate his or her own views of the same client's experiences, as well as the accuracy and utility of the feedback report. This can be accomplished either in-session with the client or out-of-session with the take-home version of the feedback report if the therapist believes the client is able to do so. In either instance the therapist should summarize the information using copies of the form provided in the Appendix, and is requested to send the authors copies of these evaluations.

ILLUSTRATIVE CASE—SINGLE

Clinical Summary

In June of 1985, Patricia was a 40 year old white medical researcher, happily married to a fellow professional and the mother of two children, a boy age 8 and a girl age 6. She and her husband brought their son to the clinic for an evaluation because he was having minor behavioral problems at school and with his peers. The MMPI is routinely given to parents of all children seen in this clinic as part of the diagnostic process. The mother's results, as can be seen below, were normal in all respects.

PATRICIA'S MMPI-1 RESULTS

T Sc	<50 43 46 51 41 55 54 42 39 55 55 49 55 53	
Scale	? L F K 1 2 3 4 5 6 7 8 9 0	
Code	2679308415	Test Date: 6-10-85

In giving her feedback on her first MMPI results, she admitted to feeling depressed, unable to relax unless "everyone else is happy," having mood swings, pushing herself hard to "get everything done" to have time for herself but "never gets there." She reported that she had suffered significant losses about two years prior to being seen, having lost her beloved father and unexpectedly a valued and much loved older brother. She was advised that individual therapy could be helpful and that she should arrange to be in a regular exercise program.

Patricia was seen together with one or both children and at times with her husband on a monthly basis with the primary focus on the children's problems. Although the children responded well to the suggested changes in parenting practices, a review of the progress notes suggested that the therapist should have explored her mild depression identified by the initial MMPI and the initial feedback session.

Six months after the last family session Patricia had surgery for a malignant tumor, followed by a successful course of chemotherapy. She reported that just prior to her surgery she recalled that "I was doing everything. I was working long hours. I was very emotional and I recall feeling on the edge. If things didn't go right, I'd start to hyperventilate. Minutes were critical." She reported having a great sense of relief following the surgery because she could retire from the extraordinary demands of her full-time research work and focus on her role as a mother and wife. A second exploratory surgery after the chemotherapy revealed no evidence of recurrence of the malignancy but this was followed by a complication which almost cost her her life and which required a third major surgical procedure.

Approximately two years after her initial cancer surgery Patricia returned to the clinic complaining of ". . . waking up feeling gloomy and tired, on the verge of tears all the time. I fear I'm going to lose it. I constantly feel a need to control myself. I can't match what I feel with what is going on around me. I can't feel joy when I should." (Her tests were negative for recurrent cancer at that time and continue so to the present.)

A mental status examination revealed a significantly depressed woman who made valiant efforts to present herself as a capable, mature adult. She appeared anxious and close to tears at all times. No other abnormality was noted. A second MMPI was administered at that time and when scored found to be significantly higher than her previous test result.

PATRICIA'S SECOND MMPI-1 RESULTS

T Sc   <50 44 44 53 46 71 57 53 39 62 68 57 60 66

Scale   ? L F K 1 2 3 4 5 6 7 8 9 0

Code   2706938415   Test Date: 2-16-88

Feedback On Second MMPI Results

Therapist: Pat, you answered all the questions. (Hands a copy of the results to Pat.) The MMPI is the most widely used personality test in the world. It was developed by comparing answers of persons with certain psychological features with persons in general not having those features. They then identified items that statistically separated the two groups. These items were added to scales measuring different personality dimensions and the scales were standardized so that an average score would be 50 and the standard deviation would be 10. There are 14 of these scales. The first four here are validity scales and the next 10 here are clinical scales.

The four validity scales tell us how you approached the test and the 10 clinical scales tell us about different aspects of your personality. Remember, 50 is an average score and most people score somewhere between 30 and 70 on each of the scales (of MMPI-1). Scores below or above these scores tell us that the person is experiencing some difficulties and the purpose of feedback is to discover and discuss what these difficulties might be. Usually the higher the score the more pain, anguish, conflict, and discomfort the person is experiencing. "Ok? Do you have any questions?"

Client: So these scales come from all of the questions I answered?

Therapist: Yes

Client: And this score T-score 50 is average?

Therapist: Yes.

Client: I see.

Therapist: Okay. Let me tell you what your results suggest and you let me know how accurate they are. It seems that something has really got to you. You appear to be feeling tense and anxious, spending a lot of energy analyzing and thinking, perhaps not feeling like you are getting anywhere, feeling hopeless, less optimistic, less happy than before. Something may have taken the wind out of your sails and left you somewhat withdrawn. It is as if you have been let down somehow. Right now you may be feeling sad much of the time and you can't make decisions easily. Perhaps you've been unpredictably let-down and now you have withdrawn, you are not as light-hearted and cheery as before and you can't think as well. You are not as optimistic as you would like to be and you are withdrawing from people. It is like "once bitten, twice shy" . . . . .as though you are hiding, protecting yourself from further loss. What has happened recently?

> **Commentary:** The **2-7** codetype is broadly explained; feelings of anxiety and depression are typical of this codetype as well as fear of further unpredictable loss in the future.

Client: (slight giggle) Er, well—a lot of things have happened over the last two years but the two major things are that I had an ovarian cancer.

Therapist: Oh!

Client: I had just finished a course of chemotherapy last August after surgery for cancer and then my father passed away in October. Those are the two main things; and then before I was ill my stepdaughter was very ill and my father-in-law has been ill.

> **Commentary:** This patient did not develop elevation on **Scale 1** (hypochondriasis). Instead, she became anxious and depressed due to unpredictable

losses. Her fears were focused outward rather than directed toward her own body.

Therapist: So, you are doing very well. What the profile suggests is that you are cautious about being optimistic. You probably find yourself fretting being tense and anxious and then withdrawing a little from people.

> **Commentary:** The issues form a starting point for discussion.

Client: Why would I withdraw from people?

Therapist: Are you?

Client: Well, yes.

Therapist: Why do you think? Is something making you feel guilty? Are you blaming yourself for what's happened?

> **Commentary:** The therapist is eliciting responses of guilt and self-blame, typical of elevations on **Scale 2.**

Client: I don't think I blame myself. Perhaps I do. Well, the only way I can blame myself for my own illness is—you know, I've wondered about it—whether stress is related to cancer. Because I led an extremely stressful life prior to becoming ill.

Therapist: Did you?

Client: Yeah, you know (slight giggle)

Therapist: What happened?

Client: I just kept working and trying to be a "super-mom." You know, I was real active in the kids' lives. Work is real stressful, trying to keep up—stay on top of things, you're responsible for everything. So I felt very stressed out. Before I got ill I was actually cutting down all my responsibilities. I had sort of recognized that I was stressed and I have to cut down. I was virtually on the edge and I couldn't stand it. I had a lot of professional responsibilities, lecturing and teaching.

Therapist: What did you teach?

Client: Nutritional Research.

Therapist: I see. So, you are in nutritional research and some people say that cancer and other illnesses may be related to nutrition or to stress.

> **Commentary:** The therapist is trying to determine if the client is blaming herself for her cancer and is looking for the emotional-behavioral characteristics of **2-7.**

Client: Well, I'm not in the field of cancer, but I've always been slightly aware of that.

Therapist: Are you blaming yourself somehow for your cancer?

Client: Well, not really. I've thought about that, wondering if it could be stress related. I've certainly had my stress levels pushed up. There's a lot of cancer in the family too so I'm not, not that I'm saying, you know that it may be my fault but it's more, I guess part of it is saying there's this fear that I'll do it again. When I got sick, it was almost a feeling of relief because it was such a good excuse to slow down. That was in my mind at the time. Oh boy, nobody can get upset and mad with me for not doing everything, you know, giving all these lectures and having a heavy teaching schedule was obviously—when you're sick you can't do these things. I can't do it, I had to slow down. There was a relief almost. There has been, those feelings were so terrible, I do have a fear that they will creep back up on me because I tend to keep my life jam packed full. I have a busy schedule and I tend to over-commit myself and so I do have that fear and so I. . . .

> **Commentary:** Notice the subtle self-blame.

Therapist: You are so responsible. You probably worry about getting everything done and making sure that all your responsibilities are taken care of. Do you feel constantly on edge, as if some detail you have overlooked is going to come back and haunt you?

Client: That would be there always. I would say that was just a characteristic, that I go around thinking "I'm not doing enough." If I end up with free time in my day, I go into a mood of "I've forgotten something." There shouldn't be any free time, what have I forgotten to do? My inclination would be to sit down and make a list of all the things, the fringe things that I would do if there was time. I would make another schedule for myself so I can go about being busy.

> **Commentary:** This is a classic **2-7** symptom, guilt when relaxing—a constant fear of some unpredictable loss.

Therapist: Do you get worried often? I think in your earlier test you were also responsible. You tended to sacrifice yourself for others, but not to the extent that you are today.

Client: Is that worse now?

Therapist: Do you think it's worse?

Client: Yes, I think so.

Therapist: I think so too. It's as if you feel now, even more pressure to make sure you "cross your t's and dot your i's." It's as if you feel more pressure than ever. It is as if you are feeling a little pessimistic about being able to catch up with yourself. A few years ago you had a tendency to give up your wants for others and be "Mrs. Nice Gal" and feel fretful if anyone's angry with you. Now it seems that you're feeling that life is a big responsibility and there isn't much point in looking forward to anything because it might get taken away. It's as if you've become more cautious about being optimistic and more cautious about anticipating good consequences. Perhaps you've become more aware of possible negative consequences, more tense, more guilty, more self-blaming, more on edge about making a mistake, and cautious about reaching out to people. Before, you liked to be with small groups of people you knew.

Client: Uh uh (meaning yes).

Therapist: How much of this is true? You know better than I. The interpretation may miss the mark in places.

Client: I think a lot of it is true. In some ways, I don't think that reaching out to other people has changed that much. I've always been a—not a real sociable person. Very content to be by myself and many times preferring to have a quiet evening at home to going out to a party, although I enjoy parties, so it's a mixture. I guess I feel—I really don't have it characterized, maybe a little bit less like making social pretenses now or talking about insignificant things or—you know, I'd rather spend my time doing something else, feeling sort of like I can't perhaps maybe pull up to the effort, to be cheerful and focused on things which don't feel real important. It's more of an effort to be socially outgoing. A lot of it is tedious I mean like going to a cocktail party and talking with people I didn't really know. I enjoy them on one level but find it sort of. . .

Commentary: Notice the high *Scale 0* statements.

Therapist: Tedious?

Client: Yes. I'd much rather have three or four people that I talk to in a small group. I prefer to have dinner with a small group. I'd rather have that, more one on one.

Therapist: Uh-huh.

Client: I don't know. I guess I do have a feeling like I can't, that I'm not, that I can't deal as well with complex issues or just being tenacious. I get discouraged easily. I get tired of socializing.

Commentary: Notice her being fatigued and her labored thinking which are characteristic of depression.

Therapist: Right, you're exhausted by it. What brought you here to see Dr. _____ initially?

Client: I was feeling real emotional of late. I was getting in real dark, black moods where I couldn't get out of them and I was just feeling really discouraged. You know, part of it to me seems like it was a continuation from before because it just seems like it (the depression) was occurring before I got sick. You know my cancer was eventually cured, I think. At least I'm way up in good statistics and from that point I should be feeling on top of the world that I've beat this thing. But I wasn't feeling happy. I was discouraged and I'd get in these awful moods. That's what my husband actually said. I told him I felt bad and he's the one who really pushed me to see Dr. _____ .

> **Commentary:** Notice the subjective depression part of the **Scale 2** elevations, the complaint of "black moods."

Therapist: Yes, I think you've developed an anxious depression in response to those many serious losses you have experienced. It is likely to be amenable to treatment. I think the cancer "took the wind out of your sails." Clearly all the losses and the cancer "stopped you in your tracks" and you've "got your tail between your legs" psychologically. You are feeling guilty and self-blaming. Your response to these losses has been to feel a little defeated, a little down and sad, and perhaps pessimistic about things getting better.

Pause. . . .

Therapist: There are two possible ways to go: one would be to give you an anti-depressant medication which could lift the depression fairly quickly, the other would be to do it through psychotherapy, which I think would not be too difficult with you. I think you have to "think through and feel through" what has happened to you. It must have been a frightening time and I am sure you are feeling some of the things that any of us would feel, which is "Why me?" and "What did I do wrong?" and "What does this mean?" and "Can I enjoy life again or is it going to come back?" That is what the test is suggesting. You are on edge anticipating some unexpected painful loss. Do you think this is accurate?

Client: This is making sense—it explains a lot. I had a funny reaction to being ill. The actual psychological part was obviously unpleasant and I didn't want to go through any of that but I don't remember ever feeling like I was going to die. I don't remember coping with those kinds of fears and I wonder if it was because when they went in for my first surgery they thought I was going to have a cyst—an ovarian cyst—and when they told me afterwards that it was malignant I was still pretty high on pain medications and they coupled that with telling me over and over again that the treatment was very good. So by the time I was really fully conscious, I had it drilled into me over and over again that the treatment was very good, it was successful. I don't remember ever feeling quite as though I was going to die. I don't worry about it returning.

Therapist: Really? Tell me, right now, "I am not afraid that it is going to come back".

> **Commentary:** The therapist is asking her to emphatically state that she has no fear of her cancer recurring to see if she will engage the opposite, a fear of the cancer returning.

Client: It's not a conscious worry to me: it's not something that . . . .

Therapist: Good, so just repeat it. Try it on for size.

Client: (Nervous laughter) I'm not afraid that it is going to come back.

Therapist: Good. Now what do you feel? Did that feel accurate?

Client: I'm recognizing that you're trying to see if it's hard to say that (nervous laughter). It was a little hard to say, so maybe there is a fear.

Therapist: It would be natural that there would be fear. The stakes are so high. If there's one chance in a million that it could come back, you or anybody would be anxious—the stakes are so high.

Client: Yes, I see it intellectually but I don't feel it emotionally.

> **Commentary:** Distancing from affect is a **2-7** attribute.

Therapist: Perhaps you don't feel it emotionally because it is scary to feel it. What you are doing instead is staying vigilant and tense, anxious, on guard. As if, if you relax something is going to happen. That may be a manifestation of that fear. If you can bring some of these fears to consciousness and live with them, you may not be so tense and anxious when you have time to relax.

> **Commentary:** Perhaps if this client can recognize and engage her fear of her cancer returning, she will not discharge it with compulsive responsibility and periods of anxiety.

Client: The only time I remember being scared was when I had one of my tests. I used to go in monthly for check ups and once some cells were questionable, so for about a week and a half while we were waiting for the report I was scared and I really felt it. That was the only time when it seemed possible that I could have a recurrence and during that time I felt like I should have felt the other times. I must be a real effective. . ., I understand what you are saying, but I must be a real effective blocker.

> **Commentary:** She is engaging some of her fear now and gaining insight.

Client: What you say feels somewhat close. I guess I feel a little bit like maybe there's a missing element of how I should be living my life. Maybe that's part of it. Here I've got my second chance, life should be wonderful. I shouldn't waste it. But I don't know what to do.

Therapist: Talk about that. There's something to that.

Client: That's one of the things I guess that I was feeling. When I was first talking to my husband about it, I felt I should be overwhelmingly happy that I kicked it and I want life to be wonderful and it is real discouraging when it is not. It's more discouraging and that's when I get more depressed. I want things to fall in line and when they don't it bothers me more. I feel a real frustration of why can't I feel joy every day? Why can't I wake up and feel wonderfully excited? Why do I feel this dullness, sort of plodding and dragging? Why can't I pull myself together and get real excited about things? So there is that element.

Commentary: The client has never engaged the feelings of what happened to her and so she has never had the opportunity to process them. Her depression is making her feel even more guilty.

Client: That was sort of all the way through it—as the good news came—as I went through the second surgery and I was clean. Everybody else was whooping it up around my bed and I was sort of like, well, I sort of expected it would be, why are you guys—I would sort of look at them suspiciously like— why are you so happy? Did you expect it to be worse?

Therapist: It wouldn't be surprising if they had prepared for the worst but hoped for the best.

Client: I expected it (the cancer test) to be clean so telling it to me was not a big deal because I expected it to be clean. I almost said to them, I very definitely had feelings of "are you keeping something from me because I seem to be much more optimistic than anyone else" and they would be so happy about things and I would be going. "Why are you so excited about that? I expected it to be that way, weren't you? You guys had told me all along that the treatment was working and that every sign that we could look at along the way was positive, so why are you, why is it like such a surprise?" Great! So there was that feeling of "are you guys not telling me everything? Should I be more worried that I am?" That was emotional. My feelings about it. "Is there something you guys aren't telling me? Have I really got the whole story?"

Therapist: It sound like you never allowed yourself to engage the enormity of what was happening to you and so you can't enjoy the relief that it isn't. That you stayed in the same neutral spot that you were in when they told you so you can't celebrate that you are fine.

Commentary: Perhaps the patient's rejoicing process was blocked because she had never allowed herself to engage the enormity of what had happened to her.

Client: Yes, that sounds true.

Therapist: It would be understandable that you were psychologically and emotionally stunned when you were told about the cancer and the way you dealt with the shock was to refuse to believe it was real or a danger so that when the danger passed there was no relief because you had not engaged it in the first place.

Client: Yes, that *sounds* right but I don't really *feel* what you are saying.

Therapist: It's like you've been through this whole thing in a bubble. People around you got really down about it and really up that it was fine and you stayed the same. You may need to go through a process where you engage the enormity of what has happened to you, fear and trembling about the close call and then rejoicing that you are fine and then you will be able to start planning your life again. You seem to be on hold. You're sort of stuck where you were when you were told you had cancer. You're still sort of holding your breath. Do you feel any relief as we talk? Take a couple of deep breaths. I can see that you don't breathe deeply. Take a nice deep breath, a nice deep one—all the way to your stomach. Now repeat after me, "Aah, it's so good it didn't happen. I can't believe it didn't happen. I can't believe it's all over with. Just say that a couple of times—role play it as if you mean it. Just say the words."

Client: That I'm glad I'm alright?

Therapist: Just say the words, I can't believe what a close call I had.

Client: I can't believe what a close call I had. It feels so good to be alright.

Therapist: Now where did your thoughts want to go? Or did you "role-play" that?

Client: Away (nervous laughter). You know when I say I'm so. . ., you know, that it was a close call and that I'm glad that it turned out all right my brain was flickering onto. . . during it there were times that I felt I'm glad it didn't happen to anybody else, I'm glad it happened to me because It's going to turn out alright and I can handle it.

> **Commentary:** Could this be reaction formation that blocked the anger which would be associated with such an experience?

Therapist: And yet, you could be saying, Damn it all, why did it happen to me?

Client: Yes, I had a brother that died about. . .Gee, you know I say all these things without really linking them together. I had a brother who died of leukemia about five years ago and it was extremely devastating to the family. There is an element, I'm sure I haven't fully engaged yet. I'm feeling guilty that mine turned out alright. I felt a little guilty about my sister-in-law and I've wondered whether she would have angry feelings about me being cured, carrying on, and a lot. . .I haven't brought this to my conscious but a lot of the reasons that his course was very rapid was that he didn't get medical care, he wasn't a medical family. My husband being a doctor, I really got top notch care and rapid and you know, there could be an element in there of fear. I know the thought occurred to me when I was sick that I was glad that it didn't happen to my brothers and sisters, there just seems to be a lot of cancer in the family. There is a fear now with me that I'm just one more statistic, that there will be more cancer in the family. I've thought about that.

Therapist: It's probably hard to celebrate isn't it? It may be hard to celebrate your victory. Not only because you never engaged the possibility of dying to begin with but because you feel guilty that you survived and your brother didn't, and you are frightened that you may be mourning soon for other members of your family.

> **Commentary:** The patient is feeling guilty that she recovered and her brother did not.

Client: Hm-Hm.

Therapist: So say that aloud. "I am so scared to be happy." Just say it aloud.

Client: I am so scared to be happy. Perhaps, maybe that's one of the reasons I blocked, my brother's death was so devastating to everyone, it was like reliving it.

Therapist: Uh-huh.

Client: The last few months I've also been going around (nervous laughter), it's been funny, I've been asking everybody what they were doing and how they were feeling. I asked my mother several times, I've wanted to know—when she was told that I had cancer was she told right away that the treatment options were so good, and it's been real important for me to know how scared she was, and how rapidly she was reassured and how long she was left thinking that I had a malignancy and underlying, I'm sure, was that fear, you know, teary-eyes, and how long did they go thinking that I was going to die too, you know, and how scary was that for me, and it has just been in the last month or two that I've been wanting to go around and say. . .like because I asked my sister that too, you know, "when my husband told you, did he tell you about the treatment options at the same time, did you know it was going to come out good?" I was really asking "how long were you scared?"

Therapist: So you identified with them because you knew what it was like when your brother was going through it. Did you feel guilty because of the pain you caused them? It's like you can't enjoy this victory over cancer because you've first got to do all your emotional chores and make sure everybody has somehow forgiven you for the suffering you may have caused them or you've made it up to them somehow. Perhaps you're blocked on so many levels from enjoying this victory, aren't you? Is that what's happening?

Client: Yes. You know what I feel guilty about? I've never really liked people sacrificing for me and when all this happened I felt very, you know, I thought a lot about the . . . ummm, you know, that my sister left her family and came out and took care of mine while I was in the hospital. I don't know how I felt. . .I guess I felt guilty about it. At least on some levels. On other levels, I can understand it because I would do the same thing, but I. . .there was a level of 'My gosh, she did this for me' and I was feeling guilty that it was necessary.

Therapist: Interesting isn't it, how it all conspires to keep you stuck in your feelings.

Client: Why would I do that?

Therapist: Well, I don't think you did anything, but a number of events occurred together so that the end product is that you went into a 'freeze' response. You just couldn't get over this cancer because first of all you were stunned by the enormity of your situation and you refused to accept that you had it, and you refused to accept that you were worried and scared about it. At the same time it reawakened all the feelings you had when your brother was sick. You identified with everyone around you taking care of you, so you felt guilty. When it was all over, you couldn't enjoy it because you still hadn't accepted that it was dangerous and you still hadn't accepted your own fear and at the same time you were so guilty about having caused other people concern and pain. And you were guilty that you survived.

Client: Mmmm, it seems really. . .it's just amazing to me that I can do it so completely without any conscious awareness that that's what's going on.

Therapist: Does it make any sense?

Client: It makes sense—it seems like, you know all through the year I've wondered why my feelings were so out of line with what everybody else was doing. You know, frequently I thought "Why is it that I'm not worried, why is it that I feel so comfortable" and then you know after it happened, you know, my response was like you were saying before-it's no big deal! So it's beginning to make sense, but you know, at the time it was just so complete and the other things were not creeping in around the edges where I was having to shove them back.

Therapist: Our psychological system can protect us from pain for a period of time but then long term it leaks out somehow. But you have lots of food for thought today. Maybe if you can give yourself permission to engage your brother's loss and how sad you are that he's died, allow yourself to mourn him again and then maybe you can engage how frightening it was to have this cancer, and then you may be able to rejoice that it is over. If you can find some little ritual that you can do once you have allowed yourself to psychologically engage these scary, sad issues—once you have done that, to come up with a ritual to rejoice that it's over. Consciously come up with some celebrations—it's a momentous occasion. That's what we would do in therapy—just tease it out, process it, tease out all your feelings.

Client: I can see the little snippets of it as I talk about it right now. I feel relief.

Therapist: Okay?

Client: It's sure to be an interesting process. My ability to push things down and away is so amazing.

Therapist: But look how much came up today, so it's not that far below the surface.

At the beginning of the session Patricia had been given a copy of the feedback report and was asked to take it home, read it over, validate and return it by the time of her next session. The following is a copy of her validated feedback report.

MMPI-1 Adult Feedback Report

Client's Name: Patricia   Gender: F

Test Date: 8-20-88   Report Date: 8-28-88

Patricia, your MMPI results indicate that you've completed the test in the following manner and that the following issues and experiences are important to you. Please read each and then *circle* on the scale following the number corresponding to your feelings about it right now.

5	4	3	2	1	0
Very True	Mostly True	Partially True	Mostly False	Very False	Uncertain

Approach to the Test

You answered the questions openly without trying to be too self-critical. You tried to be honest and accurate about how you feel and what troubles you at this time.
(5) 4 3 2 1 0

Issues (Primary thoughts, feelings and concerns)

1. You are a person who is prone towards worry, especially about responsibilities and making decisions.
   (5) 4 3 2 1 0

2. You tend to be on guard for unexpected problems and so focus on the things that could go wrong.
   5 (4) 3 2 1 0

3. Making important decisions can be difficult for you and when stresses accumulate your concentration may suffer.
   (5) 4 3 2 1 0

4. You have a tendency to analyze your decisions to see where you could have avoided mistakes.
   (5) 4 3 2 1 0

5. People with your profile experience guilt as a familiar companion.
   5 (4) 3 2 1 0

6. More than likely you have a tendency to feel guilty whenever you relax, going over and over in your mind all of the things you feel you should be doing and worrying about.
   (5) 4 3 2 1 0

7. *Periodically when stress accumulates, you may experience some sleepless nights or you may awaken very early in the morning flooded with worries.*
   ⑤ 4 3 2 1 0

8. *At times your sex drive and appetite may be adversely affected, and your general level of energy and efficiency may diminish.*
   5 ④ 3 2 1 0

9. *When stresses build, you may develop symptoms such as constipation, headaches, neckaches, or backache.*
   5 ④ 3 2 1 0

10. *You can worry about everything—including concerns that your health and stamina are not what they should be.*
    ⑤ 4 3 2 1 0

11. *You also may be somewhat the perfectionist, wanting everything to be just so to minimize the possibility that something unexpected could go wrong.*
    ⑤ 4 3 2 1 0

12 *People with your profile tend to be very responsible, especially about family financial and security matters.*
    ⑤ 4 3 2 1 0

13. *Financial matters may worry you more than most people and you are not likely to take many serious risks.*
    5 ④ 3 2 1 0

14. *When stresses at work accumulate you probably become tense, irritable, and concerned about disasters such as losing your job or disappointing your superiors.*
    ⑤ 4 3 2 1 0

15. *You are a person who finds conflicts and asserting yourself generally unpleasant.*
    ⑤ 4 3 2 1 0

16. *People with your profile respect authority and tend to follow the rules.*
    ⑤ 4 3 2 1 0

17. Consequently you may have difficulty confronting a person with authority even if you know the person has done something unreasonable or unfair.
⑤ 4 3 2 1 0

18. Perhaps because of your caution about unexpected loss, you may be seen by others as less than optimistic.
5 4 3 2 1 ⓪

0/19. You are a shy person who is especially uncomfortable with large groups of new people.
5 ④ 3 2 1 0

0/20. You also are sensitive and tend to be a little on guard in relating to strangers.
⑤ 4 3 2 1 0

0/21. When you are in new social situations you probably find yourself planning ways "to escape" the moment you feel trapped.
5 4 ③ 2 1 0

0/22. Dealing with people in an assertive or aggressive way is quite difficult for you.
⑤ 4 3 2 1 0

0/23. People with your profile are usually most comfortable with just a few friends.
⑤ 4 3 2 1 0

5/24. Women with your profile tend to be both idealistic and practical.
⑤ 4 3 2 1 0

5/25. They enjoy beauty and attractiveness, but also can have some interest in how things work.
⑤ 4 3 2 1 0

5/26. You are a person who likes gentle and sensitive companions who can relate to the complexity of your feelings and ideas. ⑤ 4 3 2 1 0

5/27. In fact talking about feelings, accomplishments and relationships with family and friends is important to you and may occupy a significant part of your time.
5 ④ 3 2 1 0

5/28. Generally you enjoy a balance between romantic ideas and practical things.
5 4 ③ 2 1 0

Background Experiences

People with your profile often had unexpected losses as children. Perhaps one of your parents died when you were young or perhaps your parents were divorced leaving you with an unreasonable amount of responsibility as a child. Childhood is meant to have periods of carefree play; perhaps you were deprived of such pleasant times. When children are burdened with too much responsibility, they worry or escape into daydreams. They often anticipate problems to avoid making mistakes. You probably have continued to do this throughout your life, but right now you spend most of your time anticipating all the things that can go wrong. This makes you feel overburdened and unable to concentrate, think clearly, and make important decisions.
⑤ 4 3 2 1 0

Self-help
(Suggestions of things you can do)

1. Whenever you start to think about all of the things that may have gone wrong in the past, try to "shut off the noise in your head and refuse to think about them. Going over and over past mistakes over-loads you and does more harm than good.

2. Try not to think through all the things that you ought to do. Just start by taking on one job that needs doing and finish it. It will be easier to think clearly if you can accomplish one thing at a time rather than getting caught up in a great whirl-wind of duties where you try and remember everything and try to sort out their relative importance.

3. Whenever you finish or accomplish something, give yourself a reward. The reward may be just to sit down and read something pleasant or to do something pleasant just for yourself. Don't allow yourself to be driven directly to the next chore.

4. If something does go wrong, try not to blame yourself for the mistake. Rather, tell yourself that everyone makes mistakes and that it is alright for you to make a few yourself.

5. If you do have periodic stressful, anxious, and worried times, make sure you are getting plenty of exercise which will relieve some of the tension.

ILLUSTRATIVE CASE—COUPLE

Clinical Summary

Twenty-seven year old Joan was referred to the clinic by her pediatrician who felt that she was depressed and perhaps overwhelmed by the needs of her three children, two boys ages four and two and a three month old baby girl. Joan complained of feeling sad, lonely, and isolated but was particularly distressed by conflicting needs to stay at home with her three small children and her need to continue her very successful business career. Joan had no complaints about her twenty-seven year old husband, Jack who functioned well as a father, husband, and provider.

Joan responded well to six months of therapy for depression after the birth of her second son. She has an intense conflicted relationship with her wealthy mother and stepfather. Her natural father, who never married her mother, committed suicide when Joan was sixteen. Joan's daughter was born exactly one year after she suffered a miscarriage which was followed by several weeks of intense sadness and depression.

The following are MMPI results for Joan and Jack, the narrative report of their in-session feedback, and the written reports validated by them shortly after their MMPI feedback.

JOAN'S MMPI-1 RESULTS

T Sc	<50 53 73 46 52 75 63 71 41 70 66 77 58 55
Scale	? L F K 1 2 3 4 5 6 7 8 9 0
Code	8246739015

Age: 27   Gender: F   Marital Status: M   Date: 7-15-88

JACK'S MMPI-1 RESULTS

T Sc	<50 50 50 64 57 68 65 64 67 59 64 63 60 49
Scale	? L F K 1 2 3 4 5 6 7 8 9 0
Code	2534789610

Age: 27   Gender: M   Marital Status: M   Date: 7-15-88

MMPI Feedback Session

Therapist: The purpose of the session today is to give you feedback on your MMPI results and for you to give me feedback about whether my feedback is accurate or not. I would like us to discuss what you think the problems are, so we can move forward with a plan about what to do next. Okay? (Hands a copy of the results to Jack and Joan.)

Clients: Nod . . . Okay.

Therapist: The MMPI is the most widely used personality test in the world. It was developed by comparing the answers to all those questions of people with certain psychological characteristics with others not having the characteristics. Like, for example, comparing people who were known to be depressed with people who were not depressed. Items were then identified that statistically distinguished the two groups. These items were added to scales measuring different personality dimensions and the scales were standardized with an average score of 50 and a standard deviation of 10. There are 14 of these scales (pointing to the T-scores of the client's results). The first four scales here (pointing to ?, L, F, and K) are validity scales and the next 10 scales (pointing to scales 1 through 0) are clinical scales.

The validity scales tell us how each of you approached the test, and the clinical scales tell us about different aspects of your personality. Fifty is an average score and most people score somewhere between 30 and 70 on each of the scales. Scores that are high and low tell us that a person is experiencing some difficulties and the purpose of feedback is to locate and discuss what these difficulties might be. Usually, the higher the score the more pain, discomfort and conflict the person is experiencing. Do you have any questions?

Joan: You don't mind if I tape this, do you?

Therapist: No, of course not. Um, I've forgotten your first name!

Jack and Joan: Jack.

Therapist: Well, let me start off with you Joan. Your test taking attitude, the way you approached the test, which tells me a lot about the way you deal with your current difficulties, shows you may be experiencing a lot of emotional pain. You are in a lot of pain and you are not feeling good about yourself. Perhaps you are feeling somehow self-blaming. It is as if you feel that your problems are at times overwhelming, that somehow you feel like the pain you are in is extreme. It is an uncomfortable time for you and you are telling us, "Yes I feel uncomfortable and I need help." The good news is that people with this kind of approach are very amenable to getting help. You are asking for help. You are saying "somebody help me. I feel terrible." When you have this attitude you are much more easily helped.

Now let us look at what kind of problems you are experiencing. The primary problem is a moderate depression. The depression may be experienced by you as sadness, difficulty concentrating, difficulty thinking clearly and making decisions, periods of hopelessness and anger, and a sort of general feeling that life is not going well. You feel unhappy and you may be angry about it. There may be times when you find yourself in these dark moods, when you feel empty and alone but feel that there is nothing that you or anyone else can do to make yourself feel better. It may feel like "leave me alone" but don't leave me alone!"

> **Commentary:** This introduces first the **Scale 2** correlates, then the feelings of **Scales 8** and **4,** alienation and anger.

Joan: He hears that all the time.

Therapist: Do you say that a lot? I need to be alone? When he does leave you alone do you find yourself angry with him?

Jack: Yeah, that I left her alone. That I don't care

Therapist: Right, a very uncomfortable spot for you both to be in. Neither of you feels good in that situation.

Joan: It's hard. I mean I do want to be alone, but then I want him to be there, I mean it's hard.

> **Commentary:** Is this the ambivalence commonly associated with **Scale 8?**

Therapist: Suppose you don't want to feel abandoned even when you want to be alone?

Joan: Uh huh

Therapist: Is making decisions hard for you right now? Can you tell me about that?

> **Commentary:** **2-8/8-2** elevations are often associated with difficulties in concentrating and in decision making.

Joan: I don't know, there's. . . .(laughter). I don't know that's a good one though, not making decisions. It's just hard. You know like little trivial things I kinda. . . . like really think about. Like I never have before. It's like there's been such a change in my whole personality or my whole being of being able to make decisions. It's just, I think about things and that's what. . . (baby crying) interrupts. . . that's what's difficult. I'm always thinking, but not really. . . .

Therapist: Getting clear?

Joan: Yes.

Therapist: Mmm, and I bet you are also feeling some anger and at times feeling negative?

Joan: Yeah.

Therapist: Tell me a little bit about the anger. How do you experience the anger?

Joan: When I get really angry, I just try and leave. I just try and walk away because I don't want to take out any anger on the kids. . . .(baby squealing). We have a four year old and a three year old. They tend to be real frustrating and if I get real angry I just try and leave because we try not to hit them and . . . (inaudible). We have our two year old who is very destructive, very obstinate, very difficult, and he says things to me that I realize he is not meaning at the time and yet they make me very upset.

Jack: They hurt your feelings.

Joan: Yeah. He's at the age where he's just getting in touch with his feelings and I teach him to be verbal and he says things like I hate you and you're a mean mom and it hurts me because I try and be a good mom.

Therapist: Uh huh.

Joan: And I get really angry so I leave because I don't want to hit him. I just find myself just wanting to explode so I just leave, walk outside.

Therapist: Have you been finding it hard to sleep, so you don't feel rested and ready for the frustrations of the day?

Commentary: Exploring for the vegetative signs of depression, problems sleeping.

Jack: She does have difficulty sleeping.

Joan: But is that just because of the baby or. . . .

Therapist: Do you find yourself waking up early in the morning, fretting and worrying? Do you have nightmares?

Joan: I wake up in the middle of the night when I nurse her and I can't go back to sleep.

Therapist: What do you think about at those times?

Joan: Ummm, I don't know, sometimes I think it's just really. . . I don't know, things that are. . .I worry a lot about just normal things like the kids, and going to school, and her, and I worry about Jack.

Jack: Finances.

Joan: And finances, and then I worry about whether or not I'm being a good mom and then I worry about why I'm always so sad and I always cry. If it's related to her and nursing or if it's not, is it just me and. . .

Therapist: Have you been blaming yourself a lot, feeling there is something wrong with you, putting yourself down, feeling like you're just not good enough?

Commentary: Exploring the guilt, self-blame, and negative self-image of *2-8/8-2.*

Joan: Yes, I feel that. . . I don't know, I just feel that I have lost control. I got really nervous about coming here today. Like, I cleaned out all the closets in the house yesterday.

Therapist: Were you scared about the feedback, that I might say negative things about you?

Joan: Not negative, it's just. . .I realize that I need help and I realize that. . .(big sigh). I'm going to cry. . .(embarrassed laugh). . .that ummm I was hurting and it's hard for me. . . (client cries).

Therapist: (Gives tissue). It's hard to talk about, especially to a stranger.

Joan: Yes, but it feels a relief that you know.

Joan: You know, I don't yell a lot and it seems like. . . .

Therapist: You get quiet and find time to be by yourself I bet, when you are angry?

Joan: Yeah, when something has really hurt me, I become very quiet about it and I almost. . .you know, the kids know that they have really gotten mom mad if I just look at them and say "Okay." They realize and. . . I sometimes think I don't show how I feel really. I just feel down and sort of empty.

Therapist: When do these dark moods sweep over you? Is there any particular time when you feel this kind of emptiness?

> **Commentary:** Clients with codetypes **2-8/8-2** and **4-8/8-4** feel a kind of anhedonia they describe as a feeling of emptiness.

Joan: The first one was around Mother's Day this year and I can remember another one this week. The first one was on Mother's Day and I was really sad and I couldn't figure out why I was really sad and I figured out, or I think I figured out, that I was mourning. We lost a baby between her and our second one that nobody knew about and nobody experienced the loss except me because it was really early in the pregnancy. I was about ten weeks pregnant and I lost it by myself and it was like really I was pregnant and nobody knew I had a loss.

Therapist: Did Jack?

Joan: Jack knew but he never saw anything. You know when you are that little pregnant. . . .

Jack: I didn't feel the loss.

Therapist: You didn't experience it right?

Joan: He didn't.

Jack: It wasn't part of me yet.

Therapist: Of course.

Joan: And so it was just really hard and I just got real down.

Therapist: Do you sometimes get too concerned that your body is letting you down somehow?

> **Commentary:** Exploring the "broken" self-image of *Scale 8.*

Joan: No.

Therapist: Good. How about feeling rested? Do you find yourself feeling tired in the mornings? Is it hard to get going in the morning?

Joan: As a matter of fact, if I can sleep, I sleep best from about five o'clock in the morning until about eleven o'clock, that's when I really sleep. That's when I'm at peace. Until about five o'clock I don't really sleep.

Therapist: Is it hard to get your mind to calm down at the end of the day?

Joan: Yes, and I mean I'm real aware of diet-type things, I don't drink caffeine at night or anything like that so that I can relax, but a lot of the times Jack works until like eleven o'clock so I put the children down to bed at nine and then I do a lot of my work that I enjoy doing from like nine to eleven and then at eleven when Jack gets home then I stay up with him and talk to him and then we go to bed and then I still am awake.

Therapist: What do you do Jack.

Jack: I work at a department store.

Therapist: Generally, has it been really hard for you to assert yourself, allow yourself to get angry and ask for what you want from others?

Joan: It's not normally.

Therapist: That's great.

Jack: It's hard for you to show anger.

Joan: It's hard for me to show. . .yeah I'd say anger.

Jack: Yeah, she doesn't show anger.

Therapist: But you feel it inside, uh?

> **Commentary:** Clients with a *2-8/8-2* profile often withdraw when angry. They express anger symbolically.

Joan: Yeah. It's um, I don't know, I think I've been a better communicator with anger but now it's like I don't fight anymore about things and I don't really get angry, I just get sad.

Jack: But even when. . .even a couple of years ago, I never knew when she was angry. I never could tell when she was serious. . .(inaudible). . .I didn't know until she had to yell at me.

Joan: See it's like. . .I'll tell people things and I almost feel like nobody listens until something becomes really desperate and then it's like "Oh, okay, oh you needed help, or you want this done or. . .and it's like well "Why do I have to do that." It's like telling a child. It's like "please don't touch that: or "please do this" and they don't do it and they don't do it and finally I have to yell at them and they do it. I ask them, "Why do I need to yell at you, just do what I ask you to do because I don't want to yell."

Therapist: Uh huh, so much of everyday life feels like a fight, a struggle right now.

Joan: Yeah and I don't like to fight, I just like to get along.

Therapist: Are you generally a pretty independent person. Do you like adventure and excitement when you feel less down?

Commentary: Exploring the *Scale 4* issues

Joan: Not adventure and excitement, it's just that I have very strong beliefs about the children and how they should be raised, and our home and what a family is. I suppose that is independent.

Jack: She is very liberal.

Joan: I'm Catholic, I'm a very liberal Catholic. There's a lot of things that I disagree on with the Church and he really believes (inaudible—baby crying) in them. I do go my own way.

Therapist: What set this recent depression, this recent sense of being bogged down and exhausted and feeling overwhelmed by life and not being able to think clearly and make decisions? What set it off?

Joan: What really made it come to a climax?

Jack: Having a third child, we think.

Joan: We had a . . .I worked, ummm

Jack: Oh that, yeah.

Joan: We made this decision for me to stay at home with this third baby, even though it would mean finances would be tight and I stayed at home and I worked for one week in May at a department store because we needed the money.

Jack: And it was a holiday and it was your birthday.

Joan: And I worked for one week and it was my birthday and nobody had remembered by birthday and the children didn't know it was my birthday because Jack didn't share that with them and holidays are always kind of hard because I'm always responsible for them and . . .(inaudible—baby squealing). . .and Jack had wished me happy birthday but hadn't done anything special and we were in the same store and worked together and somehow it all felt useless.

Therapist: Did you feel that he *really* didn't care?

Joan: Yeah, well it's just, I do a lot for everybody's birthday and make them feel special and I do a lot at Christmas and I do a lot every other day.

Therapist: What was it like for you growing up. Did you have to do a lot of the work at home in terms of taking care of others?

> **Commentary:** Exploring for early conditioning experiences.

Joan: I grew up with a single mother and she is a very cold...

Jack: Domineering.

Joan: A dominant person and very manipulative.

Therapist: Your mother was a cold, dominant, manipulative woman?

Joan: (Laughter, conversation inaudible) She really is. It's not ummm, I mean it's not nice but it's true. She is that way.

Jack: She's not a happy person.

Joan: She's not happy at all.

Therapist: Mom and dad divorced?

Joan: No, I was born illegitimate and my mom had an affair with a married man for twenty years and she just married him now. She and he fight terrible. He was around a lot during my growing up.

Jack: He was her father figure.

Joan: And when I was sixteen, I asked him to adopt me and he said no.

Therapist: So for you, you've worked hard to make sure that you really gave to your kids, their birthdays, a family life, and then when Jack forgot your birthday, it must have brought back memories of not being given to as a child.

Joan: See my mom would leave on trips with George and they'd ring me up and stuff on my birthday or Christmas and holidays and I'd be lonely. So I strive with my kids to give them a holiday and Jack works so much of the holidays or he just comes home for that short time that it's very burdensome and you know it's not the way I wanted it.

Jack: It's not complete, it's not a family unit.

Joan: Because I know what it's like to miss a Dad and I didn't want our kids to . . .(crying). . .feel the same.

Therapist: I think that perhaps what is happening to you is that some old painful memories of your past have resurfaced recently. You did not have a chance to put aside, put away all the pain you experienced as a child. You are a sensitive woman and you experienced a great deal of pain and anguish. Growing up there was no one there for you to help you through that. Your mother was angry and distant and there was no one there to help you with your feelings. Now you have a family of your own. The last straw recently was your birthday. When Jack forgot to celebrate your birthday it might have left you feeling uncertain about ever creating a family life that would work differently than your own childhood.

Joan: Yeah, because there is just umm, I mean the type of work that Jack has chosen it's like on Sundays we. . .(baby squealing) because he works and he knows all of this, I've spoken to him about it and he's happy at what he does so I can't ask him to change. I don't like him being gone all the time.

Therapist: Well Jack let's look at your test results and let's see if there's something that we can help you with.

Joan: You know what I think too, is that when we got married and had children I always wanted boys, I didn't want girls because my relationship with my mother is so strange.

Therapist: So painful?

Joan: Yeah, and too, like the day that Rachel cried her first tear. I felt enormously sad for her because it was like real symbolic (crying and embarrassed laughter). I don't know if that makes sense.

Therapist: That makes perfect sense. It was sort of like your own tears.

Joan: Yeah, since her being a girl I think it's brought back all the stuff and I'm scared of her.

Therapist: You're scared of her. In what way?

Joan: (inaudible—crying).

Therapist: Is it like you're scared to do something wrong. To do what was done to you? You are so responsible as a mother. With all that anguish and pain that you grew up with you want to make sure you do it right.

Joan: I do, I want. . ., when we got married, I'd say now this is for keeps, this is so important to me, this isn't like let's get married and let's have babies and if it doesn't work out, we can leave. That's not how I am. It's like. . ., it's important to me and it is important that they have a father and that they have siblings and that they love each other and (inaudible). . .

Therapist: That's wonderful.

Joan: I mean she's real happy now and I know everything's fine with her now.

Jack: She's a good baby and she's a good mother.

Therapist: Well Jack let me take a look at your test results and maybe then I can tell you a little bit about the two of you and the way you interact. You also have the results of a sensitive person. Your scores are that of "Mr Nice Guy." Are you the kind of guy who avoids conflicts and wants to make sure that you keep the peace?

Jack: I avoid conflicts.

Therapist: You tend to approach life with a kind of "stiff upper lip" don't you? You don't wear your feelings on your sleeve.

Jack: I don't know what that means, what does that mean?

Therapist: You're not someone who expresses your emotions as you feel them.

Commentary: Exploring the moderate **K** evaluation.

Jack: That's true, I internalize a lot.

Therapist: And you can look quite calm even if you are tense inside. So that makes you kind of hard to read.

Therapist: Joan, is it hard to read Jack sometimes?

Joan: Yes, I would say things to him like "I feel that something is wrong Jacky" and he would say "Nothing is, nothing is" and then three days down the road he will come back and he'll say "Yes something's wrong and. . ." but he takes care of his own problems, he doesn't share. Like with me, I want to tell him what is concerning me with the children, where he just thinks about it and figures it out first and then he says "Okay this is how I feel and this is what was wrong."

Therapist: He is not as spontaneous with his feelings. Jack have you been feeling a little down too? A little less up, a little less bubbly, a little more burdened, tense?

Jack: I know I'm more burdened with finances and I'm really worried about my wife, so I have a little bit, yeah.

Therapist: Tense and kind of down and just not feeling quite as up. A little off balance.

Jack: Actually, no I'm a little on the up side. I usually go up and down with how our finances are so actually I'm a little up now, I'm a little nervous too. (nervous laughter).

Therapist: A little nervous about the feedback?

Jack: Yeah, yeah.

Therapist: Uh ha, what's the fear, what's the concern, what would be the worst thing that could happen today?

Jack: I don't know. That it would be my fault that everything's wrong. That I'm not as thoughtful, that I'm not a good husband.

Therapist: Well I think that you are a sensitive, caring man. Your relationships are important to you. I think that you probably approach your problems with "I've got to take care of others, I can't show my emotions." You are cautious about getting too emotional. You also come across as trying to avoid conflict and trying to please and trying to make sure that you don't hurt people's feelings. Sometimes you carry your burdens inside. Do you think that's true?

Jack: Yeah, pretty much.

> **Commentary:** Notice the cautious endorsement which is characteristic of his **K Scale** elevation.

Therapist: Joan, do you feel that from him? Can you tell when something is bugging him? You are very sensitive to anger.

Joan: He withdraws.

Therapist: He withdraws?

Joan: I can feel him withdraw and I can tell, he gets very distant. You know, I mean I don't think anybody else could ever know but I can feel his distance and I mean he's still the same way. You know, he'll hug and kiss me and he'll be as supportive as ever, but I just feel that. . .

Therapist: Like he's withdrawn some?

Joan: Yeah, like he's not really there.

Therapist: Jack do you think you're being cautious about being optimistic, cautious about being too hopeful? Did you feel scared about the recent problems and so now you're sort of putting yourself on hold emotionally, waiting to see what happens, getting things done, trying to earn money, but you don't want to be too spontaneous, too happy, because things might go wrong?

Jack: No, I don't think so. I think that . . . I'm pretty optimistic. I like to do things and if the problem is okay, I think tomorrow it'll be fine that I can just work it out fine. I don't think I'm putting anything on hold.

Joan: I think you are. You're putting your education on hold. You don't know what you really want to do because you're waiting. You're waiting in a lot of areas, you're waiting to see how long we can financially sustain without either opening a business, your sustaining not going back to school because you're waiting to see what you want to do.

Jack: But I think he's talking about emotionally, or do you mean other facets.

Therapist: I don't really know. I'm exploring how you feel right now and your input helps me decide what you both need and what you need Jack. Your results suggest you are a normal, healthy person. They also suggest that maybe you are going through life right now trying to look on the positive side of things, trying to not let things get to you, but that underneath you are a little more tense than you would like to be.

Jack: I'm getting a little more testy at times I think.

Therapist: More testy?

Jack: I guess I had a pretty normal upbringing. I was pretty much of a loner then too. I was pretty much an inner-person.

Therapist: Was your father explosive?

Jack: Not explosive, but he was pretty strict. He was not an explosive person, he was pretty regulated like me. Pretty much so.

Therapist: Regulated? Tell me more about that.

Jack: Well, I just get quiet when I have problems.

Therapist: Joan, when he withdraws do you feel bad?

Joan: Yeah, because it's like, I mean I know that we can overcome it. I mean I know we can if he would share it with me and to me it does not seem as dreadful when he tells me a little about it. When you don't tell somebody about it, you worry about it all by yourself. When I don't know what he is thinking I think the worst.

Therapist: Do you become concerned that he is fed up with you at these times.

Joan: Or there's too many demands on him at home. I mean I never had a father and I've never had a husband before so I would never, I mean I know my expectations are very high on what I expect him to do at night. I feel I've overwhelmed him.

Jack: Which is sometimes difficult because she expects me to be a "Leave it to Beaver" father figure because that's probably all she associated with.

Joan: No, that's not what I associate it with.

Jack: That's what the ideal is for you.

Joan: I just want, I mean I married Jack for the characteristics that you said. I mean he's sensitive and he's caring and he has such a draw with other people and people trust him and he's very stable and that's why I married him and that's what I want to give to our children.

Therapist: Jack I think that maybe what you need to work on is learning to recognize when you are getting tense and angry and talk about it rather than think you have to carry all the weight yourself. Rather than to feel like you have to be perfect and that you have to be brave and that you cannot be negative. Your results suggest that you get tense and bottled up and you don't let yourself explore your negative feelings. While you probably do that because you do not want to make things worse for Joan. In fact, Joan reads your preoccupation as being fed up with her.

Therapist: Joan, when he forgot your birthday, did you feel that he was angry with you?

Joan: Yeah, I felt that I wasn't important. I felt that I must have done something that had hurt him, that had made him upset or something. I felt I had asked too much from him.

Jack: I'm not the most thoughtful person and I realize that and she is much more thoughtful in that area but it wasn't forgotten. I had planned to get some stuff on the way home, which I did and it was not totally neglected, I was busy.

Joan: (Talking over Jack—inaudible) . . . It had gotten past that point. I don't like to, I guess, and I know this is a problem with me, I don't like to tell people all my needs all the time. I think, it's like I know when the children need something, like I can give them what they need. I know when Jack needs something and I help him and I know when people need things and I give it to them. When I need something, I have to almost say "This is what I want for my birthday, this is what I want to do" and I don't want to have to do that. I want somebody to just say "gosh I know what you like." I'm not talking about insurmountable, wonderful things like balloon rides or something, I'm just talking about sweet things. Like when I left, I left for five days to the desert, I drew big hearts on the mirror so that he would know that I was thinking of him everyday because I knew he would be there everyday, and just stuff like that, not. . .

Therapist: I think Jack you are probably a warm considerate person but I think you've been tense and kind of bottled up and maybe kind of angry and feeling a little burdened yourself. When you get that way, you probably shut down some, you probably just sort of go on automatic pilot and lose your sense of awareness of Joan's needs.

Jack: I just go through the motions I guess.

Joan: He does that a lot. I go, "Jack I'm talking to you and I know you're not here with me, what's wrong?" I don't like people who say what are you thinking right now? I mean like, thoughts should be private if they want them to be, so I try not to do that to him, but it's like I just feel that he's not here, he's not home?

Therapist: What do you do to make yourself feel better Jack when you are tense?

Jack: I eat more. That's another problem, I'm always concerned about my weight. I used to be overweight when I was young; Really overweight.

Joan: Very overweight.

Jack: And so whenever I gain weight, I get very concerned about it. I've gone on lots of diets and stuff.

Joan: He hasn't gained weight lately. And see then I get real sensitive to that because I know that that's a real, I know just when he starts eating and gaining weight, and then I know something is wrong.

Jack: That's my way of showing tension.

Joan: And see, now I love to cook and I love to cook and I love to make things and I mean to me, eating is such a primary need. . .

Therapist: It's such a family thing.

Joan: And it's such a way to show that you love somebody. I mean I know the special things that he loves and I make them for him and it's just a way for me to say I love you, I'm making this for you because I love you and I want to feed you and make you healthy but then I don't want to do that because I know he is having problems with that right now and so then I feel bad. I love to cook for all the kids and for Jack.

Therapist: When did things just start to go really wrong?

Joan and Jack (in unison): June 4th.

Therapist: And that's when you really started to feel worse.

Joan: I tried to run away from home—I did. It sounds very funny but. . .

Jack: She packed.

Therapist: No, it's not funny.

Joan: It sounds very funny to me now. I packed and I had everything hidden and I had the children taken care of and I was going to take Rachel because she nurses and for some weird reason, Jack went in the room where my baggage was and he found all of it.

Therapist: You just felt so abandoned—you wanted to run away and abandon him.

Joan: I had to leave, yeah. I didn't know. . .I know I needed help and my mom didn't even call me on my birthday (nervous laughter) and I needed to get away. I needed to figure out what was going on.

Therapist: Jack, recently then you have been under a lot of pressures and you have been trying to stay brave and yet inside you have been tense, bottled up, and angry—not letting yourself explore your feelings but eating to try and feel better.

Jack: I think I've explored them, I just haven't shared them.

Therapist: You haven't allowed yourself to talk about them, so perhaps Joan's been feeling badly because she is blaming herself for all the difficulties?

Jack: Well I take a lot of the blame for this also. Like if I was making more money, she wouldn't be having as much problems as she has as far as the financial end anyway. She feels guilty about being at home too.

Joan: . . .Not working. Because see I mean, I'm the kind of person that when I married Jack I said now I want to be responsible for this family. I don't want to just, you know you have all the financial responsibilities and I liked working. I was very good at what I did and it was very nice to have those two salaries and now it's like we don't. I feel bad because I'd like, I ummm, I do a lot of things around the house that Jack loves because Jack is a very environmental person. I mean he's very happy when his environment is very peaceful and very beautiful but I still feel guilty.

Therapist: He is very environmentally oriented?

Commentary: Men with elevated *Scale 5* are usually concerned about the environment.

Joan: Yes, he is very, like even visually, how people look.

Jack: Yes, I notice the cobwebs in your corner.

Therapist: My cleaners are short and they don't get them down.

Joan: And you know I don't even notice that. I mean things like that don't. . .

Jack: See I see things like that. If the bathroom is dirty, I'll see it.

Joan: And so I do things around the house. . .

Jack: I'm not compulsive and I don't expect her to . . .

Therapist: No, but you're oriented to how your environment looks?

Joan: And I know that and so I do things around the house that. . ., like everything is perfect because that's the way he likes it and I mean I like it and I know that that hasn't helped situations yet I want to do it because I love him and I want the house to be beautiful for him.

Therapist: And you've been eating, Jack, as a way of dealing with your tension? It's easier for you Joan to encourage that because you like to please him—you love to cook.

Joan: Like if he said "Gosh I'd love some custard or some whatever," it's like I cook. I know what he wants to eat and I cook it.

Therapist: Well you know I think what we'll need to do is let me sit down and talk to Dr. _____ . I think we need to help you with your current depression Joan. I don't think it's going to be too difficult to help you with that, and then if we can help you both strengthen your partnership because you are under a lot of stress too. Joan is so sensitive she can pick up the fact that you are stressed Jack and it makes her feel worse when you don't talk about it. She blames herself for making demands on you. She will feel a lot better if the two of you can talk about your stress without blaming. But you need to express your tension and your frustration and your fears.

Therapist: So let me talk to Dr. _____. Our receptionist will help you with the insurance.

Joan: It's very important to us though too. We have good insurance right now through Jack's work, but they will not cover marriage and family counseling. I'm afraid we won't be able to afford it.

Therapist: Well, let me discuss that with Dr. _____ . Our receptionist will help you with the insurance.

MMPI-1 Feedback Report For Joan

Client's Name: Joan   Gender: F

Test Date: 7-10-88   Report Date: 7-18-88

Joan, your MMPI results indicate that you've completed the test in the following manner and that the following issues and experiences are important to you. Please read each and then **circle** *on the scale following the number corresponding to your feelings about it right now.*

5	4	3	2	1	0
Very True	*Mostly True*	*Partially True*	*Mostly False*	*Very False*	*Uncertain*

Approach to the Test

Joan, the way you approached the test suggests that you try to avoid criticism for saying the "wrong" things.
⑤ 4 3 2 1 0

Your profile suggests that you may be experiencing a good deal of stress right now that is troubling you and you feel may be hard to manage.
⑤ 4 3 2 1 0

You answered the questions in a very frank and open way admitting to how you feel and what troubles you without trying to put up a positive front.
⑤ 4 3 2 1 0

Issues
(Primary thoughts, feelings and concerns)

1. *Right now you are going through a period of sadness, confusion and a feeling of aloneness.*
   ⑤ 4 3 2 1 0

2. You tend to get down on yourself; You think you aren't worthy of the love and acceptance you get from people you care about.
   (5) 4 3 2 1 0

3. You also may have dark moods when you feel negative, angry, and sad, but are not quite sure where these moods come from.
   (5) 4 3 2 1 0

4. At these times you may feel hopeless about ever really being happy.
   (5) 4 3 2 1 0

5. At other times you can bounce back and feel hopeful and even reasonably content.
   (5) 4 3 2 1 0

6. You may periodically worry about your body and whether it is going to fall apart.
   5 4 3 2 (1) 0

7. Some of the time you may find it hard to think clearly and make decisions because it feels like your head is filled with "cotton" or "wool."
   (5) 4 3 2 1 0

8. At other times you may find your mind wandering or filled with "intrusive" or uncomfortable thoughts that are not related to what you are trying to concentrate on.
   (5) 4 3 2 1 0

9. Your concentration has probably been affected by your recent sadness and you may worry about your efficiency or fear you are losing your memory.
   5 4 3 2 (1) 0

10. You may have occasional sleep problems; either difficulty getting to sleep or perhaps waking early in the morning, long before you want to get up.
    5 4 3 2 (1) 0

11. *Upon awakening in the morning you may find yourself still tired and having to push yourself to get going.*
   ⑤ 4 3 2 1 0

12. *Getting close to people is also somewhat frightening to you.*
   ⑤ 4 3 2 1 0

13. *You experience concerns about feeling "good enough" to be liked, so you tend to be cautious about revealing yourself to people in case they reject or humiliate you.*
   ⑤ 4 3 2 1 0

14. *You are a very sensitive person; anger or hostility from others causes considerable distress.*
   ⑤ 4 3 2 1 0

15. *If someone is angry with you, it tends to disorganize your thinking and it becomes difficult to mobilize your thoughts to protect yourself.*
   ⑤ 4 3 2 1 0

16. *Generally, asserting yourself is quite difficult, and express-ing anger when you feel it is also very difficult.*
   ⑤ 4 3 2 1 0

17. *Letting go of control and expressing warm and positive feelings may frighten you.*
   ⑤ 4 3 2 1 0

18. *There are times when you cannot trust your feelings or responses to others. This frightens you and makes you unsure of how you should act in a given situation.*
   ⑤ 4 3 2 1 0

19. *It is as if you cannot quite understand why people respond to you in the way they do which leads you to mistrust your ability to comprehend social situations correctly.*
   5 ④ 3 2 1 0

20. *Generally you try hard to be responsible and sensitive to others and you avoid conflict and hurting others.*
   ⑤ 4 3 2 1 0

4/21. You are a person who loves adventure, excitement, and new challenges.
⑤ 4 3 2 1 0

4/22. You are somewhat of a rebel, uncomfortable with rules and regulations, and you want to do things your own way.
⑤ 4 3 2 1 0

4/23. People with your profile are often interesting conversationalists and storytellers.
⑤ 4 3 2 1 0

4/24. They will frequently exaggerate and embellish their stories for the sake of entertaining others.
⑤ 4 3 2 1 0

4/25. Your profile shows that you are easily bored and so you look for excitement.
⑤ 4 3 2 1 0

0/26. You are a little shy, reserved and become somewhat uncomfortable with large groups of new people.
5 ④ 3 2 1 0

0/27. With strangers you may feel self-conscious and periodically at a "loss" for words.
⑤ 4 3 2 1 0

0/28. If you have to relate to new people in a structured situation, such as in giving a prepared speech, then you may be quite comfortable.
⑤ 4 3 2 1 0

0/29. You do not need many new and exciting friends, but you do enjoy small groups of people you know well.
⑤ 4 3 2 1 0

0/30. It is in unstructured situations with people you do not know that is likely to bother you.
⑤ 4 3 2 1 0

5/31. Women with your profile tend to be both practical and idealistic.
ⓢ 4 3 2 1 0

5/32. They enjoy beauty and attractiveness, but can also have some interest in how things work.
ⓢ 4 3 2 1 0

5/33. You are a woman who likes gentle and sensitive companions who can understand your feelings and ideas.
5 ④ 3 2 1 0

5/34. In fact talking about feelings, accomplishments and relationships with family and friends is important to you and may occupy a significant part of your time.
ⓢ 4 3 2 1 0

5/35. Generally you enjoy a balance between romantic and practical things.
ⓢ 4 3 2 1 0

Background Experiences

Early in life, people with your profile were often not provided the warmth and security they needed. Right now you may feel that someone previously supportive has withdrawn from you and is treating you in an angry, cold, and rejecting way. This may reawaken some old feelings from your childhood—times when you felt alone and disliked and had no one to turn to for understanding. When you were growing up, perhaps one of your parents treated you with angry silence or indifference. If that was so, you may be feeling that same anger and hostility from someone else right now. This is upsetting. It may make you feel hopeless about ever being acceptable or loved by someone again. Furthermore you blame yourself when people close to you withdraw.
5 ④ 3 2 1 0

Self-help Suggestions

1. *Whenever you feel a dark mood sweep over you, see if you have been unfairly treated or treated in a mean or angry way. Try to confront the person who has treated you so badly. Tell them how you feel and what happened to make you feel that way.*

2. *Often medication can be useful in reducing the sudden surges of these moods and the periods of confusion and anxiety which follow. Discuss this with your therapist.*

3. *Whenever you feel depressed and alone, try not to push your friends and family away. Tell them that you feel bad and that it is not your intention to withdraw or abandon them.*

4. *Try to stop your negative thoughts, especially thoughts when you tell yourself that you are defective and undeserving of love and respect.*

MMPI-1 Feedback Report for Jack

Client's Name: Jack   Gender: M

Test Date: 7-10-88   Report Date: 7-18-88

Jack, your MMPI results indicate that you've completed the test in the following manner and that the following issues and experiences are important to you. Please read each and then **circle** *on the scale following the number corresponding to your feelings about it right now.*

5	4	3	2	1	0
Very True	Mostly True	Partially True	Mostly False	Very False	Uncertain

Approach to the Test

Jack, the way you approached the test suggests that you try to avoid criticism for saying the "wrong" things.
5 ④ 3 2 1 0

You answered the questions in a way suggesting you deal with your thoughts and feelings well enough that you rarely are unbalanced by them.
⑤ 4 3 2 1 0

This might mean that sometimes you are not as spontaneous as you might like to be, but generally you have the ability to control yourself and be socially and emotionally appropriate.
5 ④ 3 2 1 0

Issues
(Primary thoughts, feelings and concerns)

2/1. Right now you are feeling more sad and dejected than you normally feel.
5 4 ③ 2 1 0

2/2. Perhaps you are feeling uncertain and less optimistic now because of a recent setback or perceived loss. Or perhaps you are somewhat cautious and circumspect by nature.
5 4 3 ② 1 0

2/3. You're feeling less optimistic and hopeful about the future than usual. You experience periods of guilt and anxiety about mistakes you've made in the past.
5 4 ③ 2 1 0

2/4. Perhaps a recent loss or a perceived loss has make you reluctant to invest hope or optimism in the future for fear you might suffer another loss or disappointment.
5 4 3 2 ① 0

2/5. You also may be experiencing a little more guilt and anxiety than you normally do.
5 ④ 3 2 1 0

2/6. You're probably being a little more circumspect than usual and a little less likely to take risks.
5 ④ 3 2 1 0

2/7. Perhaps you are analyzing the mistakes that you made and blaming yourself for making them.
5 ④ 3 2 1 0

2/8. You may experience less energy and interest in life than you would like right now.
5 4 3 ② 1 0

2/9. Daily activities may seem burdensome and tiring and so you guard against getting involved in new ones.
5 4 3 ② 1 0

2/10. When your worries accumulate, your sleep suffers as does your interest in sex.
5 4 3 2 ① 0

5/11. Men with your profile usually have a good balance between their "masculine" and "feminine" interests.
5 ④ 3 2 1 0

5/12. You have some cultural, verbal and aesthetic interests but you also enjoy some traditionally masculine interests.
5 4 3 ② 1 0

5/13. You can be as comfortable in your relationships with men as in your relationships with women.
5 ④ 3 2 1 0

5/14. Men with your profile typically enjoy indoor as well as outdoor activities both as a participant and an observer.
5 4 ③ 2 1 0

5/15. You probably like sports and the challenges of physical and competitive activities.
5 ④ 3 2 1 0

5/16. Matters of practicality do not weigh more heavily than those of appearances for you.
⑤ 4 3 2 1 0

5/17. You usually will try to balance how something looks and feels with what it costs and how useful it will be.
⑤ 4 3 2 1 0

3/18. You have a number of strengths. You enjoy people, are kind and sensitive to people's feelings, and you like to make others feel comfortable and happy.
⑤ 4 3 2 1 0

3/19. You are an agreeable, perhaps even sentimental and romantic, person who wants people to get along and not cause others pain.
⑤ 4 3 2 1 0

3/20. People with your profile typically deal with unpleasant and painful events by trying to stay positive and cheerful. You hope that the negative will just go away.
⑤ 4 3 2 1 0

3/21. This tendency may lead those closest to you to see you as Pollyanish at times.
5 ④ 3 2 1 0

3/22. Because of your tendency to look at the bright side of things and see the best in people, others may also see you as childlike and naive.
5 ④ 3 2 1 0

0/23. You enjoy social and personal relationships and feel comfortable with others and making new friends.
5 4 ③ 2 1 0

0/24. You prefer a balance of social and personal activity and may easily become bored if you are not around people.
5 ④ 3 2 1 0

0/25. You do not mind confronting someone when you feel they deserve it.
5 4 ③ 2 1 0

Background Experiences

People with your profile often had childhoods with little opportunity for play or carefree periods of pleasure. Perhaps a parental illness, divorce, or the early death of a parent or brother or sister left you with more responsibility that a child can reasonably be expected to handle. Or perhaps some more recent loss has left you feeling that happiness is hopelessly unattainable to you, and that life will only become more difficult and painful in the future. In any instance, you probably feel bad about yourself and blame yourself for the losses in your past. Your self-image is poor and it's hard right now to see how everything you do could make things better.

Self-help Suggestions

1. *Try to find small rewards and pleasures that you can give yourself on a daily basis and keep a record of these.*

2. *When you are feeling pessimistic about the future, force yourself (if necessary) to write some of the things that have gone well for you recently so you can keep them in perspective.*

3. *Try to stop from constantly blaming yourself for things you think have gone wrong.*

4. *Begin an exercise program. Exercise will actually change your body chemistry that underlies your depression.*

5. *Keep a record of your accomplishments and things you have done well.*

6. *When you experience physical symptoms such as headaches, backaches, stomachaches, etc., see if, in fact, you are struggling with some angry feelings which are difficult to express. See if you are worried about confronting someone, someone you don't want to confront.*

7. *Whenever you find yourself even mildly resentful or angry toward someone, try to express your feelings to them immediately even in small matters.*

8. Rather than trying to make others feel better when you see them in distress, stop and ask yourself whether you really want to offer help or if you could even do so beneficially.

9. Try to see what is negative as well as positive in a given situation and attempt to balance the two extremes.

APPENDIX

MMPI ADULT FEEDBACK REPORT
SUMMARY FORM

MMPI Code: Client's Name (Case Code):
Client's Gender: F   M   Age: Race: Marital Status:
Education (years):   Occupation:
Therapist's knowledge of client: ____ Extensive   ____ Moderate   ____ Slight
Treatment setting: ____ Office   ____ Clinic   ____ Hospital   Other: ____
Reason for taking the MMPI:

INSTRUCTIONS: This form is designed to summarize ratings of the feedback report and should be completed as follows:
1. Enter the information indicated above.
2. Transfer the client's validation of approach, issues and background experiences from the original report to Part A by *circling* the corresponding rating on each of the scales below.
3. Indicate, also, for each of the scales below any discrepancy in your own perception of the client by *checking* an alternate rating.

The authors would appreciate a "Case Coded" copy of this report together with your evaluation of its accuracy and utility. Please also complete Part B, write in any comments, and address your "feedback on feedback" to: MMPI Feedback, P.O. Box 2555, Del Mar, CA 92014.

PART A

Section	Code type or Scales	Nos.	Very True	True	Partially True	False	Very False	Uncertain
Ap-	L		5	4	3	2	1	0
proach	F		5	4	3	2	1	0
	K		5	4	3	2	1	0
	(Enter)							
Issues		1.	5	4	3	2	1	0
		2.	5	4	3	2	1	0
		3.	5	4	3	2	1	0
		4.	5	4	3	2	1	0
		5.	5	4	3	2	1	0
		6.	5	4	3	2	1	0
		7.	5	4	3	2	1	0
		8.	5	4	3	2	1	0
		9.	5	4	3	2	1	0
		10.	5	4	3	2	1	0
		11.	5	4	3	2	1	0
		12.	5	4	3	2	1	0
		13.	5	4	3	2	1	0
		14.	5	4	3	2	1	0

Section	Code type or Scales	Nos.	Very True	True	Partially True	False	Very False	Uncertain
		15.	5	4	3	2	1	0
		16.	5	4	3	2	1	0
		17.	5	4	3	2	1	0
		18.	5	4	3	2	1	0
		19.	5	4	3	2	1	0
		20.	5	4	3	2	1	0
		21.	5	4	3	2	1	0
		22.	5	4	3	2	1	0
		23.	5	4	3	2	1	0
		24.	5	4	3	2	1	0
		25.	5	4	3	2	1	0
		26.	5	4	3	2	1	0
		27.	5	4	3	2	1	0
		28.	5	4	3	2	1	0
		29.	5	4	3	2	1	0
		30.	5	4	3	2	1	0
		31.	5	4	3	2	1	0
		32.	5	4	3	2	1	0
		33.	5	4	3	2	1	0
		34.	5	4	3	2	1	0
		35.	5	4	3	2	1	0
		36.	5	4	3	2	1	0
		37.	5	4	3	2	1	0
		38.	5	4	3	2	1	0
		39.	5	4	3	2	1	0
		40.	5	4	3	2	1	0
Back-		1.	5	4	3	2	1	0
ground		2.	5	4	3	2	1	0

PART B

Overall Accuracy	Excel- lent	Good	Satis- factory	Poor	Very Poor	Uncer- tain
Therapists Notes	5	4	3	2	1	0
Medication Notes	5	4	3	2	1	0
Test Approach	5	4	3	2	1	0
Issues	5	4	3	2	1	0
Background Exper.	5	4	3	2	1	0
Self-help	5	4	3	2	1	0

Overall Utility	Excel- lent	Good	Satis- factory	Poor	Very Poor	Uncer- tain
Therapist Notes	5	4	3	2	1	0
Medication Notes	5	4	3	2	1	0
Test Approach	5	4	3	2	1	0
Issues	5	4	3	2	1	0
Background Exper.	5	4	3	2	1	0
Self-help	5	4	3	2	1	0

Comments:

Address copies to: MMPI Feedback, P.O. Box 2555, Del Mar, Ca 92014

REFERENCES

Advanced Psychological Studies Institute (1987). Basic and advanced programs on the MMPI. Del Mar, CA: P.A. Marks.

American Psychological Association (1981). *Ethical standards for psychologists* (rev. ed.). Washington, D.C., Author.

American Psychological Association (1985). *Standards for educational and psychological testing.* Washington, D.C., Author.

American Psychological Association (1987). General guidelines for providers of psychological services. *American Psychologist, 42,* 712-723.

Aronson, E. (1980). *The social animal.* San Francisco: W.H. Freeman.

Berg, M. (1985). The feedback process in diagnostic psychological testing. *Bulletin of the Menninger Clinic, 49*(1), 52 69.

Bernard, H.W., & Huckins, W.C. (1975). *Dynamics of personal adjustment.* Boston: Holbrook Press.

Blatt, S.J. (1975). The validity of projective techniques and their research and clinical contribution. *Journal of Personality Assessment. 39,* 327-343.

Boerger, A.R., Graham, J.R., & Lilly, R.S. (1974). Behavioral correlates of single scale MMPI code types. *Journal of Consulting and Clinical Psychology, 42,* 398-402.

Buechley, R., & Ball, H. (1952). A new test of the "validity" for the group MMPI. *Journal of Consulting Psychology. 16,* 299-301.

Butcher, J.N. (Ed.). (1987). *Computerized psychological assessment: A practitioner's guide.* New York: Basic Books.

Caldwell, A.B. (1972). Families of MMPI patterns types. Paper presented at the Seventh Annual Symposium on the MMPI, Mexico City, Mexico.

Caldwell, A.B. (1976, January). MMPI profile types. Paper presented at the 11th Annual MMPI Workshop and Symposium. Minneapolis, MN.

Caldwell, A.B. (1977, February). *Treatment recommendations for patients with different MMPI types.* Paper presented at the 12th Annual MMPI Workshop Sponsored by the University of Minnesota, St. Petersburg Beach, FL.

Caldwell, A.B. (1978, March). *Assessing potential for treatment with the MMPI.* Paper presented at the 13th Annual MMPI Workshop sponsored by the University of Minnesota and the Universidad de las Americas, Cholula, Mexico.

Caldwell, A.B. (1984, April). *Clinical decision making with the MMPI.* Workshop sponsored by the Advanced Psychological Studies Institute and Northwestern University, Chicago, IL.

Caldwell, A.B. (1985, August). Advanced clinical interpretation of the MMPI. Workshop sponsored by the Advanced Psychological Studies Institute, Los Angeles, CA.

Carson, R.C. (1969). Interpretive manual to the MMPI. In J.N. Butcher (Ed.), *MMPI research developments and clinical applications,* (pp. 279-296). New York: McGraw-Hill.

Carson, R.C. (1986, August). *Use of the MMPI in psychotherapy.* Workshop sponsored by the Advanced Psychological Studies Institute, Washington, DC.

Carson, R.C., Butcher, J.N., & Coleman, J.C. (1988). *Abnormal psychology and modern life, 8th ed.* Glenview, IL: Scott, Foresman and Co.

Craddick, R.A. (1975). Sharing oneself in the assessment procedure. *Professional Psychology, 6,* 279-282.

Dahlstrom, W.G., Welsh, G.S., & Dahlstrom, L.E. (1972). *An MMPI handbook Volume 1: Clinical interpretation.* Minneapolis: University of Minnesota Press.

Dahlstrom, W.G., Welsh, G.S., & Dahlstrom, L.E. (1975). *An MMPI handbook: Volume II.* Minneapolis, MN: University of Minnesota Press.

Dana, R.H. (1982). *A human science model for personality assessment with projective techniques.* Springfield, IL. C.C. Thomas.

Dana, R.H. (1985). A service-delivery paradigm for personality assessment. *Journal of Personality Assessment, 49,* 598-604.

Dana, R.H. & Graham, E.D. (1976). Feedback of client-relevant information and clinical practice. *Journal of Personality Assessment, 40,* 464-469.

Diamond, S. (1957). *Personality and temperament.* New York: Harper.

Drake, L.E. & Oetting, E.R. (1959). *An MMPI codebook to counselors.* Minneapolis: University of Minnesota Press.

Duckworth, J.C., & Anderson, W.P. (1986). *MMPI Interpretation manual for counselors and clinicians, third ed.* Muncie, IN: Accelerated Development.

Erdberg, P. (1979). A systematic approach to providing feedback from the MMPI. In C.S. Newmark (Ed.) *MMPI clinical and research trends.* New York: Praeger Publishers.

Erdberg, P. (1985, August). *The MMPI in individual psychotherapy.* Workshop sponsored by the Advanced Psychological Studies Institute, Los Angeles, CA.

Evans, R.G. (1984). The test-retest index and high F MMPI profiles. *Journal of Clinical Psychology, 40,* 516-518.

Fischer, C.T. (1972). Paradigm changes which allow sharing of results. *Professional Psychology, 3,* 364-369.

Fischer, C.T. (1979). Individualized assessment and phenomenological psychology. *Journal of Personality Assessment, 43,* 115-122.

Fischer, C.T. (1985). *Individualizing psychological assessment.* Monterey, CA: Brooks/Cole.

Fischer, C.T., & Brodsky, S.L. (Eds.) (1978). *Client participation in human services: The prometheus principle.* New Brunswick, NJ: Transaction.

Franks, C.M., Wilson, G.T., Kendall, P.C., & Brownell, K.D. (1982). *Annual review of behavior therapy* (Vol. 8). New York: The Guilford Press.

Franks, C.M., Wilson, G.T., Kendall, P.C., & Brownell, K.D. (1984). *Annual review of behavior therapy* (Vol. 10). New York: The Guilford Press.

Friedman, A.F., Webb, J.T., & Lewak, R.W. (1989). *Psychological Assessment with the MMPI.* Hillsdale, NJ: Lawrence Erlbaum.

Gallucci, N.T. (1984). Prediction of dissimulation on the MMPI in a clinical field setting. *Journal of Consulting and Clinical Psychology. 52,* 917-918.

Gilberstadt, H., & Duker, J. (1965). *A handbook for clinical and actuarial MMPI interpretation.* Philadelphia: W.B. Saunders.

Goldberg, L.R. (1982). From ace to zombie: Some explorations in the language of personality. In C.D. Spielberger and J.N. Butcher (Eds.) *Advances in personality assessment, Vol. 1.* Hillsdale, NJ: Lawrence Erlbaum.

Goldstein, G., & Hersen, M. (Eds.). (1984). *Handbook of psychological assessment.* Elmsford, NY: Pergamon.

Gough, H.G. (1950). The F minus K dissimulation index for the MMPI. *Journal of Consulting Psychology, 14,* 408-413.

Graham, J.R. (1987). *The MMPI: A practical guide, second edition.* New York: Oxford University Press.

Graham, J.R., & McCord, G. (1985). Interpretation of moderately elevated MMPI scores for normal subjects. *Journal of Personality Assessment, 49,* 477-484.

Greene, R.L. (1978). An empirically derived MMPI carelessness scale. *Journal of Clinical Psychology, 34,* 407-410.

Greene, R.L. (1979). Response consistency on the MMPI: The TR index. *Journal of Personality Assessment, 43,* 69-71.

Greene, R.L. (1980). *The MMPI: An Interpretive Manual.* New York: Grune & Stratton.

Grow, R., McVaugh, W., & Emo, T.D. (1980). Faking and the MMPI. *Journal of Clinical Psychology, 36,* 910-917.

Gynther, M.D., Altman, H., & Sletten, I.W. (1973). Replicated correlates of MMPI two-point code types: The Missouri Actuarial System. *Journal of Clinical Psychology, 29,* 263-289.

Halperin, K.M., & Snyder, C.R. (1979). Effects of enhanced psychological test feedback on treatment outcome: Therapeutic implications of the Barnum effect. *Journal of Consulting and Clinical Psychology, 47,* 140-146.

Harris, M.E., & Greene, R.L. (1984). Students' perception of actual, trivial, and inaccurate personality feedback. *Journal of Personality Assessment, 48,* 179-184.

Hathaway, S.R. (1947). A coding system for MMPI profiles. *Journal of Consulting Psychology, 11,* 334-337.

Hathaway, S.R., & McKinley, J.C. (1983). *The Minnesota Multiphasic Personality Inventory Manual.* Minneapolis: National Computer Systems.

Hathaway, S.R., & McKinley, J.C. (1989). *MMPI-2: Minnesota Multiphasic Personality Inventory-2. Manual for Administration and Scoring.* Minneapolis: University of Minnesota Press.

Hathaway, S.R., & Meehl, P.E. (1951). *An atlas for the clinical use of the MMPI.* Minneapolis: University of Minneapolis Press.

Hayes, S.C., Nelson, R.O., & Jarrett, R.B. (1987). The treatment utility of assessment. *American Psychologist, 42,* 11, 963-974.

Hedlund, J.L. (1977). MMPI clinical scale correlates. *Journal of Consulting and Clinical Psychology, 45,* 739-750.

Heller, K. (1972). *The clinical psychology handbook.* New York: Pergamon.

Kunce, J.T. (1979). MMPI scores and adaptive behaviors. In C.S. Newmark (Ed.), *MMPI: Clinical and research trends.* New York: Praeger Publishers.

Kunce, J.T., & Anderson, W.P. (1976). Normalizing the MMPI. *Journal of Clinical Psychology, 32,* 776-780.

Lachar, D. (1968). MMPI two point code-type correlates in a state hospital population. *Journal of Clinical Psychology, 24,* 424-427.

Lachar, D. (1974). *The MMPI: Clinical assessment and automated interpretation.* Los Angeles: Western Psychological Services.

Layne, C. (1979). The Barnum effect. Rationality versus gullibility? *Journal of Consulting and Clinical Psychology, 47,* 219-221.

Layne, C., & Ally, G. (1980). How and why people accept personality feedback. *Journal of Personality Assessment,* 44, 541-546.

Lewak, R. (1985, April). A framework for interpreting MMPI results to clients. Workshop presented at the Advanced Psychological Studies Institute, Chicago, IL.

Lewak, R. (1987, April). Providing MMPI feedback for normal range profiles. Workshop presented at the Advanced Psychological Studies Institute, Chicago, IL.

Lewak, R., & Duckworth, J.C. (1986, April). Use of the MMPI in marital and family therapy. Workshop presented at the Advanced Psychological Studies Institute. Chicago, IL.

Lewak, R., & Marks, P.A. (1987, January). Use of the MMPI: Providing feedback with adults. Workshop presented at The Professional School of Psychology, Sacramento, CA.

Lewak, R., & Marks, P.A., & Nelson, G. (1988). *The Lewak-Marks MMPI feedback report and manual.* Wakefield, RI: Applied Innovations.

Lewandowski, D., & Graham, J.R. (1972). Empirical correlates of frequently occurring two-point MMPI code types: A replicated study. *Journal of Consulting and Clinical Psychology, 39,* 467-472.

London, P. (1985). *The modes and morals of psychotherapy.* New York: Hemisphere. (2nd ed.).

Lubin, B., Larsen, R.M., & Matarazzo, J. (1984). Patterns of psychological test usage in the United States, 1935-1982. *American Psychologist, 39,* 451-454.

McReynolds, P. (1985). Psychological assessment and clinical practice: Problems and prospects. In J.N. Butcher and C.D. Spielberger (Eds.), *Advances in personality assessment* (Vol. 4, pp. 1-30). Hillsdale, NJ: Lawrence Erlbaum.

Mahalik, J.R., & Kivlighan, D.M. (1988). Self-help for depression: Who succeeds? *Journal of Counseling Psychology, 35,* 237-242.

Mahoney, M.J. & Thoresen, C.E. (1974). *Self-control: Power to the person.* Monterey, CA: Brooks-Cole.

Marks, P.A. (1961). An assessment of the diagnostic process in a child guidance setting. *Psychological Monographs, 74,* (Whole No. 507), 1-41.

Marks, P.A. (1982, March). Personality correlates of "normophrenia." In J.N. Butcher (Chair), *Recent Developments in the Use of the MMPI.* Paper presented at meetings of the 17th annual MMPI symposium, Tampa, FL.

Marks, P.A. (1984). MMPI two point code distributions of five different samples. Columbus, OH: Author.

Marks, P.A. (1987). *The Marks MMPI adolescent report and manual.* Wakefield, RI: Applied Innovations.

Marks, P.A., & Seeman, W. (1963). *The actuarial description of abnormal personality: An atlas for use with the MMPI.* Baltimore: Williams and Wilkins.

Marks, P.A., Seeman, W., & Haller, D.L. (1974). *The actuarial use of the MMPI with adolescents and adults.* New York: Oxford University Press.

Marks, P.A., & Sines, J.O. (1969). Methodological problems of cookbook construction. In J.N. Butcher (Ed.). *MMPI: Research Developments and Clinical Applications* (pp. 71-95). New York: McGraw-Hill.

Meehl, P.E. (1945) An investigation of a general normality or control factor in personality testing. *Psychological Monographs, 59,* 4 (Whole No. 274).

Meehl, P.E. (1956). Wanted—a good cookbook. *American Psychologist 11,* 263-272.

Meehl, P.E. (1959). Some ruminations on the validation of clinical procedures. *Canadian Journal of Psychology, 18,* 102-128.

Meehl, P.E., & Hathaway, S.R. (1946). The K factor as a suppressor variable in the MMPI. *Journal of Applied Psychology, 30,* 525-564.

National Computer Systems. (1985, 1988, 1989). *Professional Assessment Sciences catalogue of tests and scoring services.* (Test Users Qualification Policy, p. 60). Minneapolis, MN: National Computer Systems.

Nelson, L., & Marks, P.A. (1986). Empirical correlates of infrequently occurring MMPI personality types. *Journal of Clinical Psychology, 41,* 477-482.

Nichols, D.S. (1986). The use of the MMPI in predicting response to Psychiatric drugs. Unpublished manuscript.

Nichols, D.S., Greene, R.L., & Schmolck, P. (1989). Criteria for assessing inconsistant patterns of item endorsement on the MMPI: Rationale development empirical trials. *Journal of Clinical Psychology,* Vol. 45, 339-350.

Norman, W.T. (1967). *2800 personality trait descriptors: Normative operating characteristics for a university population.* Ann Arbor, MI: Author.

Pope, K.S. (1988). Avoid malpractice in the area of diagnosis, assessment, and testing. *The Independent Practitioners, 8.* No. 3, 18-25.

Pope, K.S., Tabachnick, B.G., & Keith-Speigel, P. (1987). Ethics of Practice. *American Psychologist, 42,* 11, 993-1006.

Ritz, G.H. (1965). *The use of the MMPI in the recommendation of the psychoactive drugs.* Cleveland, OH: Private Practice Press.

Siddall, J.W., & Keogh, N.J. (1980). Psychotherapeutic drug recommendations based on the mini-mult. *Psychological Reports, 47,* 1283-1288.

Silberschatz, G., Fretter, P.B., & Curtis, J.T. (1986). How do interpretations influence the process of psychotherapy? *Journal of Consulting and Clinical Psychology, 54,* 646-652.

Singer, J.L. (1984). *The human personality: An introductory text.* San Diego, CA: Harcourt, Brace, Javanovich.

Sines, L.K., Baucom, D.H., & Gruba, G.H. (1979). A validity scale sign calling for caution in the interpretation of MMPI's among psychiatric inpatients. *Journal of Personality Assessment, 43,* 604-607

Snyder, C.R., Ingram, R.E., Handelman, M.M., Wells, D.S., & Heiwieler, R. (1982). Desire for personal feedback: Who wants it and what does it mean for psychotherapy. *Journal of Personality, 50,* 316-330.

Snyder, C.R., Ingram, R.E., & Newburg, C.L. (1982). The roles of feedback in helping relationships. In T.A. Wills (Ed.). *Basic processes in helping relationships.* New York: Academic Press.

Strassberg, D.S., Cooper, L.M., & Marks, P.A. (1987). *The Marks adult MMPI report and manual.* Wakefield, RI: Applied Innovations, Inc.

Sugarman, A. (1978). Is psychodiagnostic assessment humanistic? *Journal of Personality Assessment, 42,* 11-21.

Sundberg, N.D. (1977). *Assessment of persons.* Englewood Cliffs, NJ: Prentice-Hall.

Swann, W.B., & Read, S.J. (1981). Acquiring self-knowledge. The search for feedback that fits. *Journal of Personality and Social Psychology, 41,* 119-128.

Swenson, W.M., Pearson, J.S., & Osborne, D. (1973). *An MMPI source book: Basic item, scale and pattern data on 50,000 medical patients.* Minneapolis: University of Minnesota Press.

Thoresen, C.E., & Mahoney, M.J. (1974). *Behavioral self-control.* New York: Holt, Rinehart & Winston.

Trimboli, R., & Killgore, R. (1983). A psychodynamic approach to MMPI interpretation. *Journal of Personality Assessment, 47,* 614-626.

University of Minnesota. (1987). MMPI workshops and symposia. Department of Professional Development and Conference Services, Minneapolis: G.J. Amundson.

Urban, H.B. (1983). Phenomenological-humanistic approaches. In M. Hersen, A.E. Kasdin, and A.S. Bellack (Eds.). *The clinical psychology handbook.* New York: Pergamon Press.

Urban, H.B., & Ford, D.H. (1971). Some historical and conceptual perspectives on psychotherapy and behavior change. In A.E. Bergin & S.L. Garfield (Eds.), *Handbook of psychotherapy and behavior change: An empirical analysis.* New York: Wiley.

Webb, J.T. (1970, April). The relation of MMPI two-point codes to age, sex and educational level in a representative Nationwide sample of psychiatric outpatients. Paper presented at the Southeastern Psychological Association, Louisville, KY.

Webb. J.T., McNamara, K.M., & Rodgers, D.A. (1986). *Configural interpretation of the MMPI and CPI.* Columbus, OH: Ohio Psychology Publishing.

Welsh, G.S. (1948). An extension of Hathaway's MMPI profile coding system. *Journal of Consulting Psychology, 15,* 82-84.

INDEX

INDEX

A

ABOUT

THE

AUTHORS

RICHARD W. LEWAK, Ph.D.

Richard W. Lewak is a Licensed Clinical Psychologist working at the Del Mar Psychiatric Clinic in San Diego, California.

Born and reared in England, he attended the University of Keele before coming to San Diego to do a Ph.D. in Clinical Psychology. After attending the University of California in San Diego, he obtained his Ph.D. from the California School of Professional Psychology where he now teaches MMPI courses. He has presented numerous workshops on the MMPI nationally and is known as a lively and creative MMPI thinker. His primary interest is in using the MMPI as an aid in marital, family, and individual psychotherapy. The providing of accurate and empathic feedback is an integral part of this work. Helping couples understand each other rather than blame each other forms the basis of his marital work. He is co-author of *Psychological Assessment with the MMPI* and the co-author with Gerald E. Nelson, M.D. of a popular parenting book—*Who's the Boss.*

PHILIP A. MARKS, Ph.D.

Philip A. Marks is now practicing at the Del Mar Psychiatric Clinic in Del Mar, California. He is professor emeritus of the Ohio State University where he served as Director of Clinical Psychology in the College of Medicine. He is an international authority on the MMPI and has authored over fifty MMPI papers, articles, and books including *The Actuarial Use of the MMPI With Adolescents and Adults* of which he is senior author.

GERALD E. NELSON, M.D.

Gerald E. Nelson, M.D., is a Child Psychiatrist practicing at the Del Mar Psychiatric Clinic in San Diego, California. He is on the clinical faculty of the Department of Psychiatry at the University of California in San Diego. Dr. Nelson has written and lectured extensively on child and family issues and is the co-author of the popular parenting book—*Who's the Boss*.

Since obtaining his M.D. from the University of Minnesota he has used the MMPI, first as a family practitioner and then as a psychiatrist, since 1969. He is particularly interested in how the MMPI can offer light on family dynamics as they relate to children.